Collocations and Action Research

Also available from Bloomsbury

English Collocation Studies, Ramesh Krishnamurthy, Robert Daley,
Susan Jones, and John Sinclair
The Developmental Dimension in Instructed Second Language Learning,
Paul A. Malovrh and James F. Lee
The Grammar Dimension in Instructed Second Language Learning,
edited by Alessandro Benati, Cécile Laval, and María J. Arche

Collocations and Action Research

Learning Vocabulary through Collocations

Joshua Brook Antle

BLOOMSBURY ACADEMIC
LONDON • NEW YORK • OXFORD • NEW DELHI • SYDNEY

BLOOMSBURY ACADEMIC
Bloomsbury Publishing Plc
50 Bedford Square, London, WC1B 3DP, UK
1385 Broadway, New York, NY 10018, USA

BLOOMSBURY, BLOOMSBURY ACADEMIC and the Diana logo are
trademarks of Bloomsbury Publishing Plc

First published 2018
Paperback edition first published 2019

A catalogue record for this book is available from the British Library.

Library of Congress Cataloging-in-Publication Data
Names: Antle, Joshua Brook, author.
Title: Collocations and action research : learning vocabulary through collocations /
Joshua Brook Antle. Description: New York : Bloomsbury Academic, an imprint of
Bloomsbury Publishing Plc, [2018] | Includes bibliographical references and index.
Identifiers: LCCN 2017049025 (print) | LCCN 2017053792 (ebook) |
ISBN 9781350049888 (PDF eBook) | ISBN 9781350049871 (EPUB eBook) |ISBN
9781350049864 (hardback)
Subjects: LCSH: Collocation (Linguistics)–Research. |
Second language acquisition–Research–Methodology. |
Language and languages–Word frequency–Research. |
Lexicology. Classification: LCC P325.5.C56 (ebook) |
LCC P325.5.C56 A68 2018 (print) | DDC 401/.93–dc23
LC record available at https://lccn.loc.gov/2017049025

ISBN: HB: 978-1-3500-4986-4
       PB: 978-1-3501-2666-4
       ePDF: 978-1-3500-4988-8
       ePub: 978-1-3500-4987-1

Typeset by Newgen KnowledgeWorks Pvt. Ltd., Chennai, India

To find out more about our authors and books visit
www.bloomsbury.com and sign up for our newsletters.

I would especially like to thank Professor Anne Burns, Dr Sue Garton and Dr Muna Morris-Adams for all the support and advice they provide. Additionally, I would like to thank my wife Tomoko for her support and my daughter Sara for being my "little buddy."

Contents

Figure and Tables

Figure

Tables

1

Introduction

The inspiration for this study came after two semesters of teaching words from West's (1953) General Service List (GSL) to low-proficiency university students in Japan. I had first been exposed to the GSL during my masters course and had thought at the time that it would be an invaluable tool for English language instruction. It seemed manageable in terms of quantity, yet it represented a considerable portion of the individual words that are commonly used in English. However, despite devoting a considerable amount of class and homework time to a vocabulary component of a communicative English class, the students' productive abilities in the taught words did not seem to improve as much as expected. The students themselves confirmed this impression in informal follow-up discussions. They felt they understood the words that were covered but were unable to use them.

The lack of productive ability in the target vocabulary presented a problem: it was hard to justify the inclusion of this component of the classes if the students did not improve their active vocabularies, and extending it was not possible because there was not enough class time available. Therefore, adding more productive activities involving the target words was not an option. The option of abandoning this section of the class was also quickly dismissed because it was clear the students' limited vocabulary was hindering their ability to communicate. A new approach was needed that would improve the students' spoken fluency while not placing unreasonable demands on class time. Because I was a classroom teacher searching for new ways to improve, it seemed valuable to engage in a form of practitioner action research (AR) that would allow me to address this shortcoming in my teaching within the constraints of my classes. According to the literature reviewed, a focus on teaching collocations as opposed to individual words seemed to be a way to address the shortcomings referred to above. However, the literature presents a series of proposals for practice rather than evidence-based claims supported by current research. In fact, there is a surprisingly small number of studies that has addressed ways of teaching collocations in the classroom.

Collocation research has been the domain of corpus linguists with results being of a statistical nature.

Before deciding to target collocations, I also considered several alternatives for the vocabulary component of my classes. The most promising of these alternatives was a theme-based approach in which the students would engage in speaking tasks designed around a specific topic or situation. Prior to the speaking tasks, the students would study a collection of individual words useful when discussing the given theme. For example, I would have given a word list consisting of words such as "matinee," "aisle," and "concession" for a theme about movie theaters. I thought the positive attributes of this approach would be my ability to target themes of high interest for the students and my ability to design speaking exercises to elicit these words. I also believed this approach would have been easily incorporated into my classes despite the time constraints I previously described. However, targeting collocations had two advantages. First, a collocation represents a larger portion of an utterance than an individual word. I felt that if the students were to learn a verb + noun chunk of language, they would be more capable of productively using this structure than by only learning an individual word. Second, I felt that if I compiled word lists around a particular theme, I would not be able to account for frequency to the same degree as I had in my GSL instruction. Based on the literature I reviewed at this time and my own impressions of vocabulary acquisition, I felt a collocation focus was the best option for improving the students' spoken abilities with targeted vocabulary.

If collocation teaching is to play a greater role in language classrooms, the pedagogical exploration of classroom approaches needs to be a focus of research (or highlighted in research studies). This current research is intended to be a step in that direction.

AR was chosen as a methodology for this study partly because of its close relationship to the classroom and its goals of investigating areas of practical and immediate practitioner concern. The justification for using AR is explained in greater detail in the methodology chapter (Chapter 4), but the main reason it was chosen as a methodological approach is the desire to produce practical knowledge that will be of pedagogical value. I aim to build on the work done in previous studies and investigate gaps in current knowledge. Previous collocation studies have focused on advanced-level students (Eyckmans, 2009; Jiang, 2009, Komuro, 2009; Nesselhauf, 2003; Revier, 2009), whereas the student population being investigated for this study is low-proficiency university students.

In one of the few studies researching low-proficiency students, Webb and Kagimoto (2009) found that for low-level learners, receptive tasks were more

beneficial than productive tasks in regard to studying collocations. The researchers gave several possible reasons why the students in the receptive group outperformed the productive group (such as the added learning burden of the
productive tasks decreasing the amount of time the students could focus on the
collocations), but more research could provide further insight. Researching productive and receptive tasks for language acquisition has clear pedagogical implications. This study builds on these findings by including both productive and
receptive approaches.

A great deal of the literature about collocations suggests that by focusing on
collocation, instruction teachers can help the students' spoken and written fluency (Hill, 2000; Hill, Michael Lewis, & Morgan Lewis, 2000; M. Lewis, 1994;
Michael Lewis, 2000; Morgan Lewis, 2000). It is easy to see the rationale behind
this belief. When helped to recognize and use larger chunks of language, students may be able to produce spoken language more effectively. Native speakers string together chunks of language that are stored as individual items in
the mental lexicon (Hill, 2000; Michael Lewis, 2000). This allows speakers to
produce language quickly. It also allows the listener to understand spoken language quickly because they are more able to accurately predict what the speaker
will say. By using the data collected from initial and post-intervention speaking
assessments, this study, to the best of my knowledge, is the first to investigate
explicit collocation instruction in regard to spoken fluency for low-proficiency
language learners.

This study also explores student perceptions of studying collocations. Given
the nature of AR, where the variables in student progress are not controlled and
could be the result of other influences, it is difficult to accurately measure vocabulary acquisition. For this reason, data regarding student perceptions was also
collected. This data was both quantitative and qualitative. The study builds on
the research done by others and adopts some of the approaches they recommend, such as the use of questionnaire to collect data about productive use of
collocations and the employment of AR methodology. Nesi (2009) also states the
importance of including questionnaire data for AR studies.

1.1 The structure of the book

Chapter 2 is a literature review of collocations from a cognitive perspective.
Initially, various definitions for the term "collocation" are given along with a
description of how these representations have influenced research to date.

Collocations' role in the cognitive process of producing fluent speech are then detailed for both children learning their first language and adults learning a second language for whom collocations are problematic. This chapter concludes with a description of corpora programs and their pedagogical value.

The second half of the literature review, which is presented in Chapter 3, introduces the research to date focusing on the classroom implications of collocations. The debate on English as a lingua franca is discussed from the viewpoint of low-proficiency language learners and use of collocations. The discussion then shifts toward fluency and the productive use of collocations. Chapter 3 closes with an examination of the research to date in regard to the teaching of collocations.

Chapter 4 is the methodology section of the study. In this chapter, I describe AR by explaining the qualities of this methodology that make it particularly suitable for this investigation. I also introduce the participants and the research context in this chapter. The English as a foreign language (EFL) research context was used largely because this is the context in which I teach. However, I feel it is appropriate given the fact that the original weakness in my approach to vocabulary instruction originated from this teaching context, and by conducting the study within an EFL setting, the findings likely have practical value. The data collection tools used throughout the study are also described and justified for their appropriateness in eliciting data that address the research questions. In addition, the process used for analyzing the qualitative data is exemplified.

Chapters 5 and 6 present the findings from the four reflective cycles. In Chapter 5 the first reflective cycle is presented, which focuses on the learners' responses to the change in instructional focus from individual lexical items to collocations. The second reflective cycle is also described in this chapter, and this cycle focuses on the merits of productive and receptive tasks for the instruction of collocations.

Chapter 6 presents the findings from reflective cycles 3 and 4. The third reflective cycle further investigates productive tasks for collocation instruction, while reflective cycle 4 adds robustness to the study by looking at a different type of collocation. The four cycles are presented in chronological order and represent two years of data collection.

The final chapter analyzes the findings from the perspective of current views on collocation within the field of second language instruction. The findings are compared with established theory in vocabulary acquisition. Furthermore, the implications of this study for vocabulary instruction and second language teacher education are explored. This chapter also includes a personal description of the process of conducting an AR study, in addition to describing some limitations of the findings and a possible future research agenda.

1.2 Research context

The participants in this study are introduced in more detail in Chapter 4. However, it is helpful to initially consider the research context in order to grasp the decisions that were made in regard to the research design and goals.

This AR study was undertaken over the course of three years. The first two years of the study took place at a private university in Japan, while the third year took place at a public university in Japan. The data collection and intervention was administered during the participants' English communication classes that meet for one 90-minute class per week for 15 weeks. Despite the differences between the two universities, the research conditions were similar in regard to the learners' English proficiency level, the students' motivation, and the number of students per class. Furthermore, I used the same curriculum for the communication classes at both universities, so I believed there would be little disruption in terms of data collection and analysis.

The intervention in my teaching practice (a change from individual GSL items to collocations) took place during the last 15 minutes of each lesson. The prior 75 minutes of class time were largely spent on speaking tasks and listening activities. The main goal of the class was to improve the students' oral communication skills and confidence in using English by engaging them in speaking activities. I structured these classes based on Nation's (2001) "The Four Strands" in which class time is equally divided between meaning-focused input, meaning-focused output, language-focused learning, and fluency practice. The intervention treatment for this study mostly represents the language-focused learning strand, but as with the first 75 minutes of these classes, some activities can also involve aspects associated with the other strands. For example, vocabulary instruction was not limited to the teaching of collocations during the final 15 minutes of my communication classes. While the framework for my lessons stated that the first 75 minutes of the classes were dedicated to communicative activities, vocabulary, including individual words, was also taught when it naturally occurred during a lesson or if I felt it would aid the student in completing an activity normally associated with one of the other three strands.

The materials used during the first 75 minutes of the class did not expose the students to the targeted collocations. Each lesson was designed around a general theme or a grammatical structure such as "jobs," "present perfect," or "comparatives." However, within each lesson, the students had many opportunities to use English freely in conversations with a partner or a small group. For example, the lessons often started with a five-minute small talk activity in which the students were free to discuss several given topics such as "weather," "sports," "music," and "restaurants." It is possible the students used the targeted collocations during these communicative activities.

Similar to the GSL vocabulary tasks described previously, the collocation exercises were presented to the students as part of their normal course work. Given the curriculum and class time constraints, it was not possible to dedicate more time to this component of my lessons. However, by conducting the research within the limitations of an actual communicative English course, I believe the findings are of practical value to language instructors.

1.3 Preview of the four reflective cycles

As described in the previous section, this investigation took place over the course of three years, and four reflective cycles were necessary to address the research questions. The justification for each reflective cycle was based on the previous cycle's findings as opposed to a needs analysis. This preview is included to give the reader an initial idea of the research goals and a better understanding of the direction of the research.

Preview of reflective cycle 1

The first reflective cycle is smaller in scale than subsequent cycles. The research goals, which are outlined in Chapter 5, focus on the students' perceptions of a switch from a classroom focus on individual lexical items to collocations. The research questions for this cycle were as follows:

1. What are low-proficiency Japanese university students' responses to studying collocations?
2. Will the students feel capable of using the collocations in conversation?
3. In the students' opinion, is the productive task of writing sentences helpful?
4. From the students' perspective, how many collocations should be targeted each week?

The rationale behind this initial research design was to collect data that would justify the change in my classroom practice and to trial a procedure for introducing and teaching collocations to the students. All of the targeted collocations were composed of frequent words from the GSL, at least one of which was a verb. This type of collocation was chosen because I felt the students would be more able to produce utterances using these structures as opposed to a different type of collocation, such as adjective + noun collocations. This cycle was exploratory and its main purpose was to provide direction for the overall investigation.

Preview of reflective cycle 2

The second reflective cycle, including research questions, is also described in Chapter 5. The knowledge gained from the first reflective cycle influenced the research design for this cycle in three ways. First of all, based on the difficulties my students had in using the delexicalized verb collocations from the initial collocation list, I decided to narrow my teaching focus to these structures. A review of literature showed that collocations containing delexicalized verbs are common sources of error for students (Chan & Liou, 2005; Nation, 2001; Nesselhauf, 2005). For these collocations, the meaning is usually carried in the noun component (e.g., have a shower), so language learners often use the incorrect verb (e.g., get a shower). The Chan and Liou study (2005) found that Chinese language learners made greater improvements for these types of collocations than for synonymous verbs, hypernym verbs (Y is a hypernym of X if every X is a [kind of] Y; for example, "create" and "compose"), and troponym verbs (the verb Y is a troponym of the verb X if the activity Y is doing X in some manner; for example, "break" and "damage"). For these reasons, I have chosen to target collocations containing delexicalized verbs for the participants in this reflective cycle.

The second change in design was an investigation into both receptive and productive tasks for teaching collocations. In reflective cycle 1, the students wrote sentences containing the targeted collocations. However, this approach was not plausible given the greater number of students in this cycle. The students were divided into two groups (receptive and productive) and given tasks that could be completed in the final 15 minutes of class. The intervention for this cycle did not include the communicative activities present in subsequent reflective cycles.

The final change is the inclusion of a spoken assessment. In reflective cycle 1, the students had a positive impression of the collocation activities and believed their productive abilities had improved. However, I believed it is important to ascertain if the students' perceived improvement was an actuality. The spoken assessment provided a quantitative measurement for spoken fluency.

Preview of reflective cycle 3

The third reflective cycle is described in Chapter 6. Based on the findings from reflective cycle 2, I altered the procedure for both introducing and further exposing the students to the targeted collocations. Similar to reflective cycle 2, delexicalized verb collocations were targeted and a spoken assessment was administered. However, because of the findings from the previous cycles, I used tasks that were highly productively challenging. I believed these tasks could be administered within the allotted class time and would result in a greater improvement in spoken fluency.

Preview of reflective cycle 4

The final reflective cycle is also described in Chapter 6. This cycle was included in the investigation to add robustness to the findings by investigating a different type of structure: frequent adjective + noun collocations. The procedure that was used is similar to the third cycle with the exception of the different language target; however, a spoken assessment was not administered since the main focus of this cycle was to determine the students' impressions of the change from targeting delexicalized verb collocations to frequent adjective + noun collocations.

Collocations, Units of Meaning, and Formulaic Language

2.1 Introduction

The definition for "collocation" is important because it influences what language structures are considered to be collocations in different studies. Collocations have been widely researched, and as a result researchers have attributed different characteristics to the term collocation depending on their specific field of research. However, it is possible to categorize the various definitions into two general groups: statistical and phraseological. Researchers using a statistical definition tend to be corpus linguists who emphasize frequency as a trait of collocations. Other researchers use a phraseological definition that, while still acknowledging the importance of frequency, also accentuates other characteristics such as semantics, syntax, and the mental lexicon.

Language acquisition involves the storage of collocations in the mental lexicon, and producing fluent speech requires the quick retrieval of collocations from the mental lexicon. The differences and similarities between how children acquire their L1 and adults acquire an L2 are discussed in regard to language acquisition and collocation usage. The discussion then focuses on the problems L2 adults face when acquiring collocational competence and the relevant studies in this area.

Various corpora programs are compared and contrasted in consideration of their usefulness for collocation research and teaching. The research done using corpora programs has also been used to distinguish between the two main groups of definitions for the term collocation, which is described in Section 2.2: statistical and phraseological. In addition, studies using a corpus and proposals for how a corpus can be of pedagogical value are presented along with the common criticisms of corpus research.

2.2 What is a collocation?

Collocation is one of many terms in the field of Applied Linguistics that lacks a clear and precise definition. It is useful to consider a number of different definitions presented from different theoretical viewpoints.

A common approach is to research the phenomenon of collocation from a statistical perspective, which is by using a large corpus, such as the British National Corpus (BNC), and searching for word combinations that occur frequently together. Following this approach, Durrant states that "collocations are sets of two or more words which appear together more frequently than their individual frequencies would lead us to expect" (2009, p. 158). Corpus linguists, such as Hoey (2005), Sinclair (1991), and Stubbs (1995) view collocations in a similar way. This view is also consistent with how Carter (1987), Krishnamurthy (2006), Lewis (1994), Shin and Nation (2008), and Webb and Kagimoto (2009) perceive the phenomenon of collocation.

Other definitions of collocation, which are discussed in the following paragraphs, have deemphasized grammatical collocations and collocations where the meaning is easily understood from the individual lexical components. While both the Durrant (2009) and Shin and Nation (2008) studies (described in the following section) were valuable from a frequency perspective, they have been criticized from the standpoint of their pragmatic limitations. As Hill points out that "frequency alone should not be the over-riding parameter . . . Another item may be highly frequent in native speaker English but may be unsuitable for learners" (2000, p. 65). Shin and Nation (2008) themselves state that:

> Although frequency in the language is an important criterion for selecting what to focus on, it is only one of several important criteria like learner need, range of use (for example in both spoken and written use), difficulty, teachability, and suitability for the age and background of the learners. (pp. 345–6)

Another set of definitions of collocation is not characterized by statistical frequency, but illustrates how collocations are stored in the mental lexicon. Sinclair defines collocations as "semi-preconstructed phrases that constitute single choices for the speaker" (1987, p. 320). Wray (2000) includes the point that collocations are single choices in her definition. She defines a formulaic sequence as follows:

> A sequence, continuous or discontinuous, of words or other meaning elements, which is, or appears to be, prefabricated: that is, stored and retrieved whole from

memory at the time of use, rather than being subject to generation or analysis by the language grammar. (p. 465)

Wray chooses to use the term "formulaic sequence," which includes a variety of multiword units including terms such as idioms, chunks of language, and collocations.

Acceptability of word combinations is also addressed in the definitions of collocation. Celce-Murcia (1991) defines collocations as lexical items that co-occur, and can differ in frequency or acceptability. An additional definition, relevant to acceptability, is provided by Dzierzanowska (as cited in Martyńska, 2004): "Words that make up a collocation do not combine with each other at random. Collocation cannot be invented by a second language user. Native speakers use them instinctively" (p. 4).

The final group of terms that are introduced here adds the requirement that semantics and word type should be considered when determining what qualifies as a collocation. Nesselhauf recommends to "use a phraseological rather than a frequency-based definition. This definition denotes a type of word combination rather than a co-occurrence of words in a certain span" (2003, p. 224). Teubert adds the following to previous definitions, "[Collocations] have to have a meaning of their own, a meaning that is not obvious from the meaning of the parts they are composed of" (2004, p. 173).

To summarize, previous definitions have emphasized the following characteristics of a collocation:

- words that frequently co-occur
- semi-preconstructed phrases representing single choices for a speaker
- word combinations differing in acceptability
- a certain type of word combination (verb + noun)
- semantics (having a meaning of their own)

The pedagogical importance of each of these characteristics is discussed in greater detail throughout this paper.

The wide range of definitions in linguistic research illustrates how many approaches to analysis are available under the umbrella of collocations. Having a common definition of a linguistic term might not be realistic or necessary. However, researchers need to clearly state the definition of collocation that is used for their research.

In relation to this point it is possible to present the initial definition of a phraseological collocation used in this study:

a set of two or more words that frequently occur together, that represent a single choice in a native speaker's mental lexicon, and whose meaning cannot be easily determined by the individual words themselves.

As the research proceeded, the final collocation list used for this study included several other parameters that are discussed later in this chapter.

Previous collocation lists

Durrant (2009) and Shin and Nation (2008) have used the type of definition presented above as the basis for creating collocation lists. While creating a list of target collocations was not the primary purpose of this investigation, it was necessary to compile a collection of useful collocations at an appropriate level for the learners in this study, so that they could be used during class instruction. The two studies described below were influential in establishing criteria for inclusion of a collocation in the lists I used. Durrant (2009) created a list for English for Academic Purposes (EAP), while Shin and Nation (2008) focused on the highest frequency collocations in spoken English.

Durrant's EAP collocation list

Durrant's study (2009) produced a list of 1,000 two-word collocations. Durrant's aim was to produce a list of highly frequent EAP collocations that could be used as a pedagogical tool. It is intended to be a pedagogically manageable body of learning to which learners should pay special attention.

The corpus used to compile this list was created by collecting five million words from five different faculties (Life Sciences, Science and Engineering, Social-Psychological, Social-Administrative, and Arts and Humanities). Durrant used a four-word span, which means that there had to be a co-occurrence of the individual lexical items within four words to qualify. He characterized academic collocations as those pairs that appear significantly more frequently in academic than in non-academic texts. This disparity was calculated by comparing the total frequency of collocations in the academic corpus with their frequency in an 85-million-word subsection of the BNC, comprising only non-academic texts. Each collocation had to appear at least once per million words in each of the five parts of the corpus. Collocations were removed if: (1) they included an acronym or abbreviation, a proper name, an article, or a number or ordinal other than one and first; (2) the collocation corresponded to a single Latin word (e.g., ad hoc, per cent); (3) the majority of their occurrences appeared to be in writing outside the main text of the articles, for example, in bibliographies, copyright information, or acknowledgements.

The resulting list had 763 collocations that were "grammatical": meaning that one of the words was non-lexical (prepositions, determiners, modal verbs, etc.). Durrant justified including these collocations by stating that "one benefit to learners of a listing of high-frequency grammatical collocations is that the most typical versions of the patterns they need, and the most typical patterns of the words they need, can be brought to their attention" (2009, p. 163). However, in this respect, Wollard (2000) believes it is better to restrict the use of the term collocation to relationships between nouns, verbs, adjectives and adverbs.

One interesting finding was a lack of overlap between this collocation list and the items on the Academic Word List (AWL), developed by Coxhead (2000). Of the 1,000 collocations on Durrant's collocation list, only 425 include an item from the AWL. Durrant argues that this lack of overlap indicates a shortcoming of traditional approaches to identifying academic vocabulary, rather than a weakness of his list. To explain Durrant's point further, the AWL excludes items that are on West's (1953) General Service List on the grounds that students of EAP are likely already to have mastered these items. Durrant believes the strategy of eliminating all high-frequency words from AWLs, therefore, seems suspect: many items that are excluded by this strategy may be of considerable importance for learners of EAP.

Durrant concedes two weaknesses of his collocation list. First, he acknowledges that by limiting his search to two-word collocations, he is likely missing many valuable collocations of three or more words. Second, this analysis looked only at the forms, as opposed to the functions of the collocations. Therefore, while the collocations appeared at least five times in each part of the corpus, it is not clear that all disciplines use them in the same way. However, analysis of the use of collocations would need to be undertaken manually and would be a labor-intensive task.

Shin and Nation's collocation list for spoken English

The Shin and Nation (2008) study determined the most frequent collocations in spoken English based on the spoken section of the BNC. For Shin and Nation's study, collocation refers to a group of two or more words occurring together with each collocation having two parts: a pivot word and its collocate(s). The pivot word is the focal point of the collocation. For example, in the collocations "high school," "high court," and "too high," "high" is the pivot word and "school," "court," and "too" are the collocates. Shin and Nation investigated the 1,000 most frequent word types from the spoken section of the BNC as pivot words. They used six criteria to find collocations in the corpus:

- Each pivot word was a word type rather than a word family. Therefore, "books" and "book" were treated separately.
- Only nouns, verbs, adjectives and adverbs were considered as pivot words.
- Each pivot word had to be in the first 1,000 words in the spoken word frequency list by Leech, Rayson, and Wilson (2001).
- Each collocation had to occur at least thirty times within 10 million running words in the BNC spoken corpus.
- Each collocation should not cross an immediate constituent boundary. For example, "I saw you at that place" has five immediate collocational constituents: "I saw you at that place," "saw you at that place," "saw you," "at that place," and "that place." "You at that place" does not meet this criterion.
- Different senses of collocations with the same words and word forms were considered different. For example, "looking up" can mean "to improve" or "to search." These were counted separately. (pp. 342–3)

The final list contained 4,698 collocations indicating there are a large number of grammatically well-formed high-frequency collocations. The list also showed that pivot words that are more frequent have a greater number of collocates. The first 100 pivot words have an average of 20.5 collocations, while the second 100 words have 8.4. In addition, two-word collocations account for 77 percent of the total list.

This collocation list was originally designed for elementary learners of English. Considering the target learners, Shin and Nation concede several weaknesses of their list from a pedagogical perspective. First, many collocations are strongly colloquial and may not be suitable for explicit instruction. Second, frequency is just one of several criteria that should be considered when deciding on what to focus, such as learner need, range of use (spoken and written use), difficulty, teachability, and suitability for the age and background of the learners. Finally, greetings such as "good morning" and "how are you?" do not appear within the 100 most frequent collocations, which indicates frequency alone should not dictate what language to target.

2.3　How collocations are represented in the mental lexicon

In this section, collocations, and more generally "formulaic sequences," are described in relation to the mental lexicon. This section is divided into several parts: how formulaic sequences evolve into developed speech, collocations in the mental lexicon, the cognitive processing involved in speech, collocations in children and L2 adults, problems L2 learners face in regard to collocations and formulaic sequences, and relevant studies.

How formulaic sequences evolve into developed speech

As explained in the previous section, collocation has been defined in many ways and used to refer to different aspects of language. For the purposes of this study, the characteristics associated with "formulaic sequence" are also ascribed to collocation following Wray (2009), who states that features attributed to formulaic knowledge can be attributed to collocations as well.

A collocation's meaning is often described as being more than the sum of the meanings of the individual words. In earlier studies of collocation, Firth (1957) stated that individual words did not have individual core meanings. He believed that collocation established part of the meaning of a word. Sinclair (1987) proposed two possibilities for how meaning is produced: the open choice principle and the idiom principle. The open choice principle sees language as a series of complex choices of individual lexical items (grammar defines how they can be used). The idiom principle claims the language user has a large number of chunks of language available. These chunks represent single choices for the user. Sinclair proposed that the idiom principle takes precedent over the open choice principle (collocational restrictions constrain what words are used in combination). More recently this argument was reinforced by Wolter (2009) who emphasized how truly knowing a word involves more than simply understanding its semantic meaning.

For Halliday (1966), collocations are examples of word combinations; he maintains that collocation cuts across grammar boundaries. For instance, *"he argued strongly"* and *"the strength of his argument"* are grammatical transformations of the initial collocation *"strong argument."* A common pattern for language acquisition is that learners initially use many unanalyzed chunks of language depending on the situation. This language use proceeds to rule-forming processes, that is, grammar (Nattinger & DeCarrico, 1992).

In the process of language acquisition, multiword units are stored and retrieved as holistic units in the mental lexicon (Schmitt & Underwood, 2004; Wray, 2004). Lin and Adolphs (2009) state that "multiword units are believed to be building blocks of fluent speech" (p. 36). Collocational competence is crucial in developing communicative competence. It allows learners to develop new language skills and produce creative utterances.

Collocations in the mental lexicon

The mental lexicon is thought to include more than just individual lexical items (Nattinger & DeCarrico, 1992), but to involve entire phrases as well as individual lexical items. Entire phrases range from individual lexical items that can be combined and subjected to grammatical rules that are very flexible and general (e.g., "He is very tall") to fixed phases that are inflexible and specific (e.g., "Raining cats and dogs"). A formulaic sequence can be thought of as being glued together and stored as a single item (Wray, 2000). It is often originally learned as one whole unit. In addition, formulaic sequences can be created from individual lexical items using grammar. An example of this is "foreseeable future." This noun phrase follows the rules of grammar (adjective + noun) but is more likely to have been acquired and to be used as a chunk of language as opposed to being generated through grammatical rules given the high probability the adjective "foreseeable" is followed by the noun "future." Peters (1983) called this process "fusion."

For many researchers (Bahns & Eldaw, 1993; M. Lewis, 2008; Nesselhauf, 2003) collocation refers to a habitual combination of words. For example, "do" can be used to collocate with "laundry," and "make" to collocate with "a case" but not the other way around. Liu (2010) believes that habitual combination is a fruitful area for research because of its pedagogical value. Knowing collocations requires an understanding of how individual words function together. Wolter (2009) uses the term "collocational productivity" to describe how easily a word can have relationships with other words. High productivity words (e.g., high, powerful) can have relationships with a wide variety of other words, whereas low productivity words (e.g., moot, kindred) can have relationships with a limited number of words. Another useful categorization of collocations was made by O'Dell and McCarthy (2008). They see collocation as being either "fixed," "strong," or "weak." A "fixed" collocation does not vary in structure (e.g., raining cats and dogs), while a "weak" collocation (e.g., strong argument) often varies in structure as described in Section 2.3. "Strong" collocations can vary but to a limited degree.

In addition to considering the "strength" of collocations, researchers have debated whether collocations are arbitrary. Benson (1989) argued that collocations are arbitrary by using a cross-linguistic perspective (comparing corresponding collocations in different languages). Smadja and McKeown (1991) also state that collocations are arbitrarily based on their syntactic and semantic abnormality (the example given is that "strong" and "powerful" are both adjectives and both have similar meanings but they cannot be used interchangeably).

They state that "a collocation is arbitrary because it cannot be predicted by syntactic or semantic rules" (p. 230). This supports the notion that collocations are units of meaning as opposed to the overall meaning being a sum of the individual parts (words). Liu (2010) expands on this point by describing collocations as being "unmotivated" because there is no clear reason for the selection of words in a collocation being based on the meanings. Liu's (2010) study did, however, produce evidence that collocations might not be as arbitrary as initially suspected. This study is described in Section 2.3.

The notion of collocations being arbitrary is evidence that they are stored as individual items in the mental lexicon. Another form of evidence to support this view of collocations is derived from analyzing the phonological aspects of speech. Phonological coherence (pauses and intonation) should show if phraseological units are processed as holistic entities (Lin & Adolphs, 2009). Phonological coherence is based on two criteria: it is always produced fluently as a unit with an unbroken intonation contour and there is an absence of hesitations (Peters, 1983). Phrasological units that are full clauses may have boundaries that also match the intonational boundaries, whereas units that are not full clauses (sentence builders, semantically transparent two-word collocations) have a lower tendency to do this (Lin & Adolphs, 2009). Wray (2002) states that intonation and the speed with which a sequence is articulated is an indication of prefabrication. In addition, a lack of pausing within a sequence can indicate a prefabricated sequence. Lin and Adolphs (2009) believe multiword units that are full clauses may have boundaries that also match the intonational boundaries, whereas units that are not full clauses (sentence builders, semantically transparent two-word collocations) have a lower tendency to show this. They conducted a study that looked at the phraseological unit "I don't know why." For this study, they used the 230,000-word NICLEs-CHN subcorpus that is made up of interview data collected from seventeen Chinese EFL learners studying at a British university. After auditory analysis, they found that the intonational boundary and the phraseological boundary aligned only 55 percent of the time. They concluded that intonation may not be as powerful an indicator of formulaic sequences as originally assumed; however, they stated that it is difficult to determine intonation patterns quantitatively.

The cognitive processing involved in speech

Miller (1956) believed that short-term memory is limited by the number of "chunks" of information and not by the amount of information within each chunk. By changing simple items, like phonemes, into more complex chunks, like words or phrases, memory capacity can be increased. Ellis (2002) argues that collocation learning is similar in that individual words are combined into multiword units that are stored as one item. This process is recursive in that these chunks can then be combined with other chunks to create larger units, which increases the efficiency of communication. This all happens subconsciously. Previous to Ellis, Crick (1979) wrote that the storage capacity of memory is vast but the speed in which it can be accessed is limited. Speakers must create shortcuts to make efficient use of the processing time they have. Ellis' notion of using chunks of language to make communication more efficient is an example of speakers creating shortcuts.

In a similar vein, Bolinger (1975) states that language is stored redundantly; words are stored individually as well as stored as part of longer pre-assembled chunks. Short-term memory holds a limited number of units; however, these units can be made up of more than individual words. They can represent chunks of language that contain more information than single words. Speaking with fluency results from using prefabricated speech, which enables more efficient retrieval and permits speakers (and hearers) to focus on the larger structure of the discourse as opposed to the individual words (Nattinger & DeCarrico, 1992). Wray (2008) expanded on this argument by stating that larger word units combine with each other; however, the amount of grammatical activity is reduced when expressing a complete message as opposed to using individual words.

Wood (2010) reasons that formulaic language is important because speakers have a somewhat limited working memory and, during spontaneous conversations, there are considerable time and attention constraints. He refers to two kinds of knowledge: declarative and procedural. Declarative refers to consciously known content and information. Procedural is knowledge about how to do something. Declarative knowledge can become procedural through repetition/use. This process is often referred to as automatization or proceduralization. Wood (2010) states that "for formulaic sequences, as with all lexical items, it is likely that they are automatized through repeated exposure and frequency in input due to the pragmatic requirements of the communication contexts that learners encounter regularly" (p. 67). He continues by stating:

> The ability of a speaker to produce given sequences is dramatically speeded up
> with time and practice through psycholinguistic mechanisms, and in the process
> the sequences change in nature to phonologically coherent units retrievable as

fixed chunks. Therefore, production becomes faster and there is a qualitative change to the mental procedures underlying speech production. (pp. 68–9)

The benefits of formulaic sequences have been described by various researchers (Schmitt & Carter, 2004; Wood, 2010; Wray, 2000; Wray & Perkins, 2000). They believe formulaic sequences aid speakers by reducing processing load and empowering them to produce a comprehensible utterance. Wray and Perkins (2000) describe four functions of formulaic sequences: they are used as "short cuts," which increase speed and fluency; they are used as "time buyers," which allow speakers to continue their conversation turn; they allow for the manipulation of information, which aids in remembering information that might otherwise be forgotten; and they are used to achieve interactional functions such as apologizing or making a request.

Collocations in children and L2 adults

When describing first language acquisition, Peters (1983) suggests there are two approaches to language learning that happen simultaneously. In the first children use whole chunks of language (the gestalt approach) and in the other they construct sentences one word at a time (the analytic approach). The gestalt approach is similar to collocation acquisition. When children start to communicate orally, they initially use chunks of language that they had been exposed to previously. These chunks of language seem to be unanalyzed and used as a unit in a similar way to how an adult might use a single word from their vocabulary. This unanalyzed language production is also seen on intonational, semantic and syntactic levels. By mimicking language produced by others, children use language that is at a higher level than would be expected through normal linguistic development (Nattinger & DeCarrico, 1992).

Peters (1983) stated that children develop strategies to extract multiword units from conversations. The child can then remember these chunks of language, compare their phonological makeup, and remember them as one piece of language. Later in cognitive development, the child can analyze the structural arrangement and generalize them into patterns. Myles, Hooper, and Mitchell (1998) conducted a two year study of young learners and found the children segmented the formulas, in addition to using them as wholes, to express more complex communication as need required.

Second language acquisition in adults does not develop in the same way. Yorio (1980) found that adults tend to use chunks of language as a way to reduce the effort and attention required during spontaneous communication. Wray (2002) has also emphasized the differences between children and adults; she believes adult L2 learners and child L1 learners approach collocation learning in different ways. While children note chunks of language as a single sequence, adults break down the sequence into individual words. For adults, any pairing of words with a similar meaning would seem equally possible. She also argues that adults need to develop fluency in a different way from children. Barfield (2009b) also states that post-childhood L2 learners break down collocations to their individual components and then have to reconstitute the appropriate pairings. A process of proceduralization through the automatization of chunks into utterances might be the best way for adults to improve fluency.

While Wray and Yorio emphasize the differences between how L2 adults and children process formulaic sequences, Nattinger and DeCarrico (1992) find some similarities. For example, they explain that a large portion of language utterances are highly routine and prefabricated. Children and adults string memorized chunks of speech together when learning a language. Later, they analyze these chunks and break them down into sentence frames that contain slots for various fillers. These structures are used to produce the first conversations. Some researchers (Lewis, 1994; Willis, 1990) believe this process leads to grammar being learned naturally.

Collocation problems of L2 learners

The literature shows that the nature of formulaic sequences causes learners problems when using a second language productively. Initial studies (Bahns & Eldaw, 1993; Webb & Kagimoto, 2009) using small elicitation tests such as cloze and translation tasks found that collocation was highly problematic for L2 learners (Webb & Kagimoto, 2009) and that it accounted for a significantly high proportion of learner errors in L2 writing (Bahns & Eldaw, 1993). Wray points out (2002) that learners, who are in the process of learning a language, tend to be more analytical than native speakers. This results in learners focusing on isolated aspects of the language as opposed to holistic aspects. A reason for the large number of collocation errors is that learners often rely on intuition to determine which lexical items collocate with one another (Chi, Wong, & Wong, 1994). In addition, Fan (2009) believes a language learner's L1 adversely affects collocation production.

Ying and O'Neill (2009) describe three problems learners have due to a lack of collocational competence:

1. Use of longer phrases and utterances because of an inability to express themselves concisely.
2. Odd word combinations – often a result of L1 influence.
3. Overuse of a few general items. Leading to an oversimplified, flat, uninteresting style.

Shih (2000) further investigated this overuse phenomenon and found that collocations of high frequency in learner English tend to be used to express vague ideas when more specific meanings should be conveyed. Shih also found that learners are apt to apply those collocations to cases where more concise expressions are preferred.

Fan (2009) argues that collocation problems are prevalent regardless of the proficiency of the learner. Native speakers acquire collocation knowledge subconsciously and gradually through exposure, but L2 learners do not have this opportunity. While collocations are particularly important for learners who are trying to achieve a high level of proficiency, they are also important for learners with more modest goals as they lead to more fluent and accurate English. However, it is unclear how and which collocations should be taught, especially considering the large number of collocations (Nesselhauf, 2003).

Formulaic sequences and relevant studies

Conducting research into the cognitive processes involved in producing collocations is challenging. However, there are four studies that are pertinent to this challenge and to the discussion in this section. Liu (2010) investigated whether collocations were truly arbitrary (semantically unmotivated). Liu looked at common delexicalized verbs (make, take, have) and adjective + noun collocations commonly nominated to support the claim that collocations are arbitrary (powerful car, strong tea). He used the 360-million-word corpus of Contemporary American English as the data source. In order to investigate the three delexicalized verbs mentioned above, he compiled all the tokens for the query "[v*] a trip" and "[v*] a * trip." The noun "trip" was chosen because it is one of the few verb + noun collocations where the three delexicalized verbs seem to be used interchangeably. By reading through the tokens, it appeared that the three delexicalized collocations were not synonymous. To illustrate, "have a trip" is usually used with an adjective such as "wonderful" or "safe." In these instances "have" means to experience or enjoy. "Take a trip" is most often used for a trip of leisure, whereas "make a trip" is typically used for trips that require effort such as a business trip. Therefore, the results of this study show that most collocations are not arbitrary but functionally motivated, and that understanding these motivations should help students learn the collocations. However, despite Lui's arguments, I believe implementing this approach would give rise to various pedagogical problems, which are discussed in Section 3.5.

Durrant and Schmitt (2010) investigated the theoretical belief that adult language learners process input on a word by word basis, as described earlier in this section. This study carefully controlled the input of targeted word pairs and then tested the retention of those pairs. The participants consisted of eighty-four non-native speakers of English from various countries who were studying at a university in the UK. The university had an entry requirement of 6.0 IELTS or 550 TOEFL, so the participants were considered to be reasonably proficient in English. Participants either received a single exposure, verbatim repetition, or varied repetition. They were then tested by being shown the adjective from an adjective–noun pair, followed by the first two letters of the noun. They were asked to say the noun. For all three conditions, nouns were remembered more effectively when seen together with their paired adjective. This result was weakest for the group that only received a single exposure. The researchers concluded that adults do retain some memory of which words go together in the language to which they are exposed. One criticism made by Durrant and Schmitt was that testing only took place immediately after exposure, so it is unknown how durable these memory traces are. The pedagogical implications of this study are discussed in Chapter 3.

The following two studies analyzed collocational mistakes made by English language learners. Nesselhauf (2003) investigated the use of verb + noun collocations in writing by advanced German speaking learners of English. She looked at all verb + noun word combinations (collocations) from thirty-two essays and classified them as to their degree of restriction. "Free" indicates the verb in the collocation collocates with many other nouns, "restricted" indicates the verb can only be used with a few nouns, "restricted?" is used to classify word combinations where the degree of restrictiveness of the verb is unclear, and "idioms" indicate that both the noun and verb are used in a restricted sense. She also classified the collocations to their scale of acceptability: clearly acceptable C, largely acceptable {C}, unclear CW, largely unacceptable {W}, clearly unacceptable W. She found that: (1) the most common error was the wrong choice of verb, (2) learners need to know more than which lexical items collocate; they need to know complete collocations. This was seen in the large number of mistakes in non-lexical items such as prepositions, and (3) L1 influence on mistakes is especially prevalent in collocations.

The final study (Chi, Wong, & Wong, 1994) focused on delexicalized verbs. The researchers state that "when these verbs are used in conjunction with certain words to form common phrases, the original meanings of these verbs gradually lose their significance" (p. 158). This study was a corpus-based investigation of common verb–noun collocation errors. The participants were first-year university students in Hong Kong. The researchers did not specify the participants' English level. The results showed that "get" verbs were the most common source of mistakes, and students used delexicalized verbs interchangeably. "There seems to be no logical way that may help learners to work out the correct collocations – they either know it, or they do not" (p. 162). By learning delexicalized verb collocations as chunks of language opposed to learning the component words separately, the common source of error found in this study would be minimized. The researchers postulated that a learner's L1 knowledge might be the cause of delexicalized verb errors: "When students do not know, or have not come across, the English verb–noun combinations before, it is highly probable that their L1 knowledge might influence them, while they are searching consciously or unconsciously for a verb to collocate with the nouns" (p. 163).

Pedagogical conclusions

Collocations are represented in the mental lexicon as single choices for a native speaker, so vocabulary acquisition for L2 learners must go beyond teaching individual words in order to allow them to produce fluent speech. Collocation problems are common among L2 learners, but a thorough understanding of the complexities associated with these multiword units provides insight into how language instructors can best teach their students. This knowledge should be viewed as a tool to aid language teachers as opposed to an end in itself.

2.4 Key points of corpus research

While corpora programs did not have a major impact on this study, it is worthwhile to orient my research in relation to the work of corpus linguists. Corpora programs can be used by researchers to analyze language use and find patterns that would have been otherwise undetectable. These programs allow researchers to make generalizations about aspects of language such as speech acts, language usage, and collocation. After a brief description of available corpora programs, I would like to limit the description of corpora to their connection to collocations, common criticisms, and the pedagogical role they have.

Corpora programs, like the Corpus of Contemporary American English (COCA), the BNC, and Time Corpus, have become more readily available and easier to use in recent years. Each corpus program has its own characteristics and can be used to analyze data in different ways. COCA, for example, contains more than 400 million words. The texts used to create this corpus were collected from 1990 to 2009. Several different registers were used to create this corpus including spoken language, newspapers, academic prose and magazines. This corpus has been tagged for parts of speech allowing users to do searches for specific grammatical structures. The BNC contains 100 million words that have been tagged for parts of speech. In addition to written texts, the BNC also includes spoken language. Similarly, the Time Corpus contains more than 100 million words taken from Time magazine. Because the contents are divided by decade, users can see changes in word use and language over time. By having access to various corpora programs such as the ones described above, researchers can analyze language used in different registers, compare written and spoken language, and contrast language produced during different time periods.

As corpus linguistics became more prominent, language was created to aid in its analysis. Halliday (1966) introduced three terms: node, collocate, and span. "Node" is the item (word) that is under study. "Collocate" is the co-occurring item. "Span" refers to the range (the number of words) on either side of the node in which the collocate can appear. Sinclair (1991) built on Halliday's work and used corpora to study the characteristics of collocations. He developed an "integrated approach" where both the grammatical and lexical characteristics of a collocation are considered. Through data analysis, he was able to divide collocations in two categories: upward and downward. "Upward" collocations are where the "node" combines with words that are more frequently used in English than itself. For example, if "back" is the node word under study, it often collocates with words more frequently used such as "into," "from," and "down." These are examples of "upward" collocations. However, "back" also collocates with less frequently used words such as "arrive" and "bring" that form "downward" collocations. The significance of that distinction is that the collocate in an "upward" collocation is usually an adverb, preposition, conjunction or pronoun. Collocates in a "downward" collocations tend to be a noun or verb. Therefore, "upward" collocations form grammatical frames, while "downward" collocations give semantic analysis to a word. In Section 2.2, collocations were described from both a phraseological and statistical perspective. Sinclair's work further aids in this distinction.

In Section 2.2, various definitions for "collocation" were given. A common aspect of these definitions was that the two (or more) words occur together more often than their individual frequencies would predict. Corpora programs can easily be used to identify all collocations in any text if frequency is the sole characteristic of a collocation. Researchers such as Nattinger and DeCarrico (1992) and Sinclair (1991) have relied on these statistical methods for locating collocation through computer analysis.

Reppen (2009) also used a corpus to analyze L1 and L2 writing development through collocations. Reppen uses the term "lexical bundles," which she defines as recurring sequences of words identified through the use of a computer program, in her study. She emphasizes that the lexical bundles come from the corpus and not the researcher. The corpus for this study was compiled over six years and contains essays from students in grades three through six (eight to twelve years old). The students spoke either English or Navajo as their L1. She found that children from both L1s commonly use lexical bundles as frames for beginning their essays. Granger (2009) believes that since most writing is done in electronic form it is easy to compile a learner corpus and identify the collocations that students use and misuse. Another use for corpora programs is to examine the connection between lexis and grammar. As Collentine (2009) notes, "The distinction between grammar and vocabulary is a tenuous one" (p. 454). He is describing how grammar cannot be used as creatively as teachers might expect, and that certain grammatical structures can only be used with a small number of words. The studies and proposals listed above are examples of how corpora programs can be used to research collocations.

In addition to aiding researchers, corpora programs have classroom applications, as recent publications are increasingly pointing out. Reppen (2010) presents several classroom ideas using corpora, although the activities in her book are more suitable for intermediate to advanced level students. O'Keefe, McCarthy, and Carter's (2007) publication, *From Corpus to Classroom: Language Use and Language Teaching*, also proposes potential benefits of corpora programs. However, Trimble (2008) points out it is not as useful for the classroom teacher trying to improve their next lesson as the title implies because it focuses on the researcher as opposed to the student. To their credit, O'Keefe, McCarthy, and Carter (2007) do state that their book "stops at the classroom door" (p. 1). While a valuable tool for language teachers, the pedagogical constraints of corpora programs should be considered, especially for low-proficiency students.

Material from a corpora program is taken out of context, so it is often difficult to understand the usage given only the few words on either side of the target language. Moreover, the source material is often from a piece of writing that would not be considered a useful text for language study. In addition to teachability and learner need, teachers must be knowledgeable and skilled in the use of the corpora programs and have classrooms that offer access to enough computers for the students to use.

In addition to the pedagogical difficulties of using corpora, it is important to understand the limitations of the actual data within these programs. Howarth (1998) states that "phraseological significance means something more than what any computer algorithm can reveal." In addition, Wray (2000) justly points out that a corpus is the amalgamation of spoken and written texts from many different people often from different communities. As a result, a corpus does not represent the language used by any one individual.

Corpora programs have become increasingly available and easy to use. As a result, corpus linguistics has been widely researched, especially in regard to collocation. Moreover, corpora programs offer potential pedagogical benefits to language learners and instructors. However, it is important to also understand and account for their limitations as teaching and research tools. For this study, a corpora program was used as a reference to ensure sensible choices were made (described in Section 5.2) on which collocations to target.

2.5 Conclusion

The pedagogical value of collocation research stems from the cognitive process involved in producing fluent speech. Children, when acquiring their L1, use collocations (chunks of language) to enhance their speaking abilities. They then modify and adapt these chunks of language depending on their communicative needs. L2 adults tend to break down chunks of language and assign meaning to the component parts. This tendency is not surprising given that second language instruction commonly relies on teaching grammatical structures and memorizing word lists. By using techniques and activities inspired by L1 language learning that promote the acquisition of collocations as whole units of meaning, there is potential to improve the efficiency of second language acquisition for adults. This claim is discussed further in the following chapter.

Collocations and Second Language Learning: A Literature Review

3.1 Introduction

In Chapter 3 the pedagogical aspects of collocations are discussed in detail. While Chapter 2 focused on definitions and the cognitive aspects of using collocations to produce speech, this chapter concentrates on the language classroom, as it is the classroom that is the setting for this study.

3.2 Global perspectives

While collocations have not been commonly associated with the debates on English as a lingua franca (ELF), it is worthwhile to address this point. One of the primary arguments, as mentioned in Section 3.3, for studying collocations is that the learner would sound more native-like. It is important to understand though that sounding more native-like is not the same as being more fluent. Furthermore, it is becoming increasingly debatable what constitutes native-like English. In addition, since collocation errors do not hinder comprehension to a great degree, it is relevant to question the value of a collocational focus in the language classroom. A thorough description of the current debates in regard to ELF is beyond the scope of this study, but it is helpful to address some key issues in this debate, specifically in how they affect the pedagogical value of collocations.

English is increasingly used as a second language in numerous countries around the world, such as India, Malaysia, and Denmark to name a few. Halliday (1966) states that there may be as many as six times the number of English speakers in India than there are in England with this disparity continuing to grow. More recently, Graddol (2010) also states that the importance of English is continuing to grow across India. English is also used in countries such as China,

Korea, and Japan as the language for scientific or business purposes. Speakers of English therefore are more likely to be using the language with people from outside the traditional English speaking countries (Burns, 2005a; Dewey, 2013; Sewell, 2013). This prevalence of English around the world is calling into question the relevance of a native speaker norm in language instruction. Dewey states:

> Never has a language taken on such vast proportions as a lingua franca, not only coming into contact with exceptionally diverse languages but in fact being spoken in more lingua franca contexts than "native" ones. This clearly has implications for our continued attachment to "correctness" and "appropriacy" regarding ENL norms. (2013, p. 348)

This notion of ENL norms raises challenging questions for the development of new approaches to teaching English in the classroom.

The debate surrounding ELF often focuses on how English should be taught. Burns (2005a) points out that a focus on the L2 users' needs, as opposed to native speaker norms, accounts for the realities of the global uses of English. However, Sung (2013) states that:

> While descriptions of ELF and other forms of variation can be useful to raise learners' awareness of this aspect of English, they cannot be seen as the sole factor in determining the kinds of linguistic input that may be best for pedagogical purposes, since pedagogy is concerned primarily with attempting to meet language learning needs rather than simply presenting models of language use. (p. 352)

Dewey (2013) expands on this argument by stating the goal should be "research and practice properly brought together in classroom contexts in a way that allows teachers to adopt an ELF perspective when and how they and their learners see fit" (p. 348). Sung (2013) also notes that learners often want a "model" with which they can orient themselves; ELF cannot be used as this model given its emergent and variable nature.

There are undoubtedly linguistic differences between ENL and ELF; however, it is worthwhile to question how large and/or important these differences actually are. Sung (2013) is critical of ELF research when he states there is a "tendency for ELF researchers to essentialize and exaggerate the differences between ELF and English as a native language (ENL), thereby creating a false dichotomy between them" (p. 350). Crystal (1997) also mentions that the differences between New Englishes (varieties of English spoken in non-traditional English speaking countries) is likely to be larger than that between a variety of ENL and a variety of New English. Perhaps a productive way to approach this issue is to identify the differences themselves, and, specifically for this paper, to look at the differences in how collocations are used.

The English spoken in countries such as Britain and America differs from the English spoken in countries where English is a secondary language in regard to phonology, grammar and lexical characteristics (Burns, 2005a); however, vocabulary is cited as being a major aspect likely to show these differences. Crystal (1997) states that "most adaptation in a New English relates to vocabulary, in the form of new words (borrowings – from several hundred language sources, in such areas as Nigeria), word formations, word meanings, collocations and idiomatic phrases" (p. 146). He explains that grammar is more uniform across dialects, but collocations differ to a larger degree depending on the grammatical context in which they are used. He writes, "Collocations, however, are likely to prove one of the most distinctive domains of varietal differentiation" (p. 162). In contrast, the importance of these differences is questioned by Ahulu (1998) when he states that word combinations (collocations) may not show any significant semantic difference between British English and that of English in postcolonial countries. Furthermore, interlocutors are helped by the environment and context of discourse to determine meaning.

ELF researchers have rightly questioned the value of continuing to use ENL as the norm, or model, for English language instruction. However, it is valuable to view ELF as an alternative form of English to which our students should be exposed. As Sewell (2013) states, "Adopting an ELF perspective on teaching does not mean that norms and standards are no longer required, but that these are mutable concepts and that learners need to be introduced to language variation as soon as they are ready" (p. 7). As mentioned above, learners often desire a template to pattern themselves after, and it could be argued that ELF is not yet sufficiently codified because of its variant and transient nature. Sung (2013) recommends:

> While there is a place for enhanced awareness of language variation in ELT, it is important to take into account what is often seen by learners of English as the primary goal of language learning, i.e. mastering the forms of English that are considered widely acceptable and easily understood by the majority of ELF and ENL speakers worldwide. (p. 351)

Delexicalized verb collocations, which are the focus of this study, likely represent an example of the forms that are considered widely acceptable and comprehensible to speakers worldwide given their frequency. Sung (2013) believes that language teachers do not often consider whether the forms that they are teaching are ENL or ELF, and simply target the language that helps their students to communicate effectively. Furthermore, Sewell (2013) states that "the message for learners seems to be that, while ELF rightly emphasizes flexibility, maximizing this still requires the hard work of acquiring something resembling native-speaker competence" (p. 8). Low-level English learners can benefit greatly from an increased level of collocational competence regardless of their future communicative needs.

For this study, I assume that delexicalized verb collocations are suitable as target language for low-proficiency English language learners given the needs of these students, the high frequency with which these collocations occur, and the likelihood that low-proficiency students make errors when using these word combinations. The ELF debate does bring into question what should be considered "correct" in regard to English usage; however, I believe low-proficiency students benefit from having the ability to produce English that can be widely understood. Targeting delexicalized verbs helps students reach this goal.

The terms "native speaker" and "native-like" are used throughout this book. I use this term as a shorthand to signify how people who are exposed to English as a first language likely store and retrieve collocations as holistic units, in contrast to second language learners who are likely to break down the language into individual words.

3.3 Proposed benefits

The practicality of teaching collocations is also subject to debate. Two reasons against a collocation focus in the classroom are the size of the mental lexicon and the belief that mistakes in collocation usage have a limited effect on comprehension. For example, Hill (2000), while suggesting an emphasis on collocations as opposed to grammar in language classrooms, states that the size of the phrasal mental lexicon is enormous, thus making the learning of collocations a challenging task. Bahns (1993) also states that due to the great number, teaching lexical collocations is a challenging task. Conzett (2000) and Woolard (2000) suggest that errors resulting from inappropriate word combination do not hinder comprehension to a great degree. While there is some truth to both of these arguments, others (Bahns & Eldaw, 1993; Conzett, 2000; Handl, 2009; Hill, 2000; Jiang, 2009; M. Lewis, 1994; Reppen, 2010) state that the potential benefits of teaching collocations outweigh the difficulties.

Perhaps the most recognizable benefit is that learners can sound more native-like. This knowledge "allows us to say and write things like a native speaker" (Nation, 2008). To illustrate, a great deal of language that would be considered to be grammatically accurate is in reality not used. Woolard (2000) gives an example of this type of mistake: "Biochemists are making research into the causes of AIDS" (p. 30). This sentence is grammatically accurate in tense, aspect and subject/verb agreement, but native speakers would use the verb "do" as opposed to "make." Because the incorrect verb is used, the reader or listener would know a native speaker did not produce the sentence. Mistakes of word choice also interfere with comprehension. We are able to understand spoken language quickly because we do not focus on the individual words but on chunks of language that we can often predict. Written texts with several collocation errors are often difficult to read, and take additional processing time to understand the intended meaning. Spoken language with collocation errors can hamper comprehension even further as speakers often do not have the luxury of time to review what they heard.

Another benefit, which is particularly relevant to this study, concerns low-level speakers. Nation states that learning multiword units (a term he prefers although he also states it would be possible to use collocation) "allows beginner learners to make productive use of the language without having to know a lot of vocabulary or grammar" (2008, p. 118). He uses the example of survival vocabulary often found in travel phrase books to illustrate this point. This aspect of "productive use" is one of the strongest reasons to focus on collocations as opposed to individual words. While Nation is referring to complete phrases (e.g., Where is the bathroom?), it is not unreasonable to assume that by learning word combinations, especially verb + noun collocations, low-proficiency students find it easier to express themselves. Students who learn lists of individual words, regardless of how carefully selected the words may be, are often unable to use them in conversations or in written texts (Morgan Lewis, 2000; Woolard, 2000).

It has been suggested that studying collocations can help students learn the grammar of a language. By learning chunks of language containing certain grammatical structures, the learner is better able to acquire the contained grammatical pattern (Hill, 2000; Michael Lewis, 2000). It has also been argued that a strict focus on grammar instruction has led to many of the word combination errors mentioned above (Hill, 2000; Morgan Lewis, 2000; Woolard, 2000). This problem occurs because learning grammar is often seen as a question of a simple substitution exercise where different word types can be placed into the correct slot. A better approach would be to teach appropriate word combinations from a lexical perspective and have students come to their own conclusions about the syntax of a language.

In addition to grammar, fluency, both in productive and receptive situations, should improve (Conzett, 2000; Hill, 2000; Morgan Lewis, 2000). Since (or if students are taught that) collocations are multiword units stored as single items in the mental lexicon, they should be able to string longer sequences of words together when producing language and also have an easier time identifying these chunks of language when listening or reading.

Furthermore, collocation study allows students to use what they already know. Woolard emphasizes that "learning more vocabulary is not just learning new words, it is often learning familiar words in new combinations" (2000, p. 31). The first 1000 words of the GSL account for a surprisingly high percentage (according to Nation, 2001, 84.3 percent for conversation, 82.3 percent for fiction, 75.6 percent for newspapers, and 73.5 percent for academic texts) of the items used in written and spoken language in English. However, if students are unaware of how the words fit together, they continue to struggle in listening and reading and more so in speaking and writing.

While these reasons all sound convincing, there is a need to support them with more research. Collocation research has been limited to short studies mostly dealing with advanced level students (these studies are discussed in the following sections). Longitudinal studies focusing on different proficiency levels should provide a clearer picture of the potential benefits. The claims of improvements in grammar and fluency, in particular, need to be researched. The research I have undertaken is a step in this direction and are described in detail in Chapters 4–7.

3.4 Collocations and fluency

This section is dedicated to the role collocations have in fluency. Initially, fluency is described, and an explanation for how using collocations improves fluency is given. This is followed by a description of how fluency and productive collocation use has been measured. Finally, previous research specifically regarding collocations and fluency is presented.

What is fluency?

The connection between collocation knowledge and fluency has been researched, but there have been relatively few studies. In this section, the term "fluency" is defined, and a description is given of the role collocation knowledge has on fluency. This is followed by a discussion of previous studies including different research designs that have been used to measure productive collocation knowledge. This section concludes with a brief discussion of future research possibilities.

The term fluency has been defined differently depending on the researcher. Ur (1991) defined fluency as "receiving and conveying messages with ease" (p. 103). Wollard (2005) states that "fluency is the ability to speak naturally, listen efficiently, read quickly, and write well" (p. 7). Brown (2007) uses a definition that emphasizes producing language when he defines fluency as "a relatively unlimited automatic mode of processing language forms" (p. 64). For this research, fluency has the same performance-based representation as in Lennon's study (1990a) in which "fluency is an impression on the listener's part that the psycholinguistic process of speech planning and speech production are functioning easily and efficiently" (p. 391). Since collocation use is problematic for students, a fluency definition that emphasized the cognitive process involved in speech production was chosen.

Fluency is usually measured by how natural the flow of speech sounds or by the speed in which it is produced (Wood, 2010). The absence of dysfluency markers such as false starts, non-lexical utterances, and fillers contributes to the naturalness of the flow of speech. As Lennon states, "Dysfluency markers, as it were, make the listener aware of the production process under strain" (1990a, p. 391). In Riggenbach's study (1991) it was shown that temporal aspects of fluency such as pauses and speech rate correlated with native speaker judges' perceived fluency of students. Native speakers and highly proficient second language speakers pause between sentences and clauses. Pausing at other points within sentences is a sign of dysfluency. Pausing at these other points within a sentence is likely due to difficulty second language speakers have encoding speech (Wood, 2010). He continues by stating that the mean length of run between pauses is also a good indicator of fluency.

How using collocations improves fluency

The use of collocations affects the fluency level of an utterance. Since fluency can be measured from pauses between clauses and the length of clauses, it stands to reason that fluency can be improved by recalling clauses intact and/or stringing together intact clauses. The use of formulaic sequences may represent a large portion of fluent speech. Prefabricated sequences are a key element of language learning, processing, and production. Consensus is that these multiword units are stored as single choices, similar to an individual word, in long-term memory (Wood, 2010). Fluent speech is not a result of learning rules. It comes from creating shortcuts to use lexical chunks (Skehan, 1998).

A lack of collocational knowledge may result in poor fluency. Language students produce "grammatical" sentences that sound unnatural (Eyckmans, 2009). Henriksen and Stenius Stoehr state that "the main obstacle to speaking English is not lack of knowledge of individual words, but rather ability to link words together in language use" (2009, p. 225). Eyckmans (2009) claims collocations are often comprehensible in the input so learners might not recognize them as problems; however, the errors appear in the production. Collocation errors are a major indicator of being a non-native speaker (Hsu & Chiu, 2008). The researchers' descriptions of errors students typically make ("say the truth" as opposed to "tell the truth") show that collocations are primarily a productive issue.

Through the use of collocations, language learners can speak and write at a more advanced level than they would be able to without this collocational use. Pawley and Syder (1983) state that formulaic sequences make up a large portion of spontaneous speech. Wood (2010) expands on this claim by stating fluency is enhanced by the ability to use formulaic sequences. This improvement can be seen in speech acts that can usually be expressed formulaically. Collocation knowledge allows learners to speak more fluently, sound more native-like and create easier to understand language (Pawley & Syder, 1983; Wray, 2002).

By using collocations, language learners appear to be more proficient than their current level. Researchers (Boers, Eyckmans, Kappel, Stengers, & Demecheleer, 2006) have found that the use of formulaic sequences contributed to perceptions of learners' fluency and range of expression, while Bolander (1989), Peters (1983), and Hickey (1993) all conducted studies that showed learners using formulaic sequences that had grammatical structures well beyond their current proficiency level. Furthermore, Wood (2010) states that more creative utterances can be produced by using a larger number of lexical units and collocations. The positive effect of collocations is also seen in language testing; previous to this investigation studies showed learners who used more phrases scored higher on spoken fluency assessments (Eyckmans, 2009).

Fluent speech is often characterized as having pauses at clause junctions, and between the pauses, there is usually a speech run of a certain length. This rhythm can be achieved more easily by recalling language as a chunk and then stringing these chunks of language together (Wood, 2010). Boers et al. (2006) also mention how using collocations can reduce the number of unnatural pauses within an utterance and increase the length of speech runs.

Producing speech that is more accurate and more native-like is also a result of an increased use of collocations. Boers et al. (2006) believe that accuracy is improved because a language learner is less likely to make a mistake within a chunk of language that has been stored and retrieved as a whole unit. They also state that formulaic sequences help learners to sound more native like because the meaning of a formulaic sequence cannot always be determined by grammar or the sum of the meanings of the individual words.

The use of collocations lessens the cognitive load of producing speech. Peters (1983) characterized formulaic speech as being a short cut. The time created as a result of using multiword units can be used to address issues relating to vocabulary, articulation, and the suprasegmental aspects of pronunciation. Wood (2010) also states that collocations allow the speaker to free up cognitive resources for the other tasks required while speaking. He believes the use of formulaic sequences helps overcome the time and attention constraints of real life communication. Formulaic phrases can be used to express complete functions or clauses that allow the speaker to focus on the next utterance, and lessen the processing load by serving as a structure that the speaker can modify by adding or changing words. Henriksen and Stenius Stoehr state that "collocational knowledge is very important for fluent and idiomatic language use, freeing attentional cognitive resources for higher-order processing" (2009, p. 227).

To summarize, an increased use of collocations can make students' speech sound more natural. Language learners are also able to produce utterances that are more creative and above their current proficiency level. The language they create may also be more accurate and easier to understand. In addition, the speaker's cognitive burden is lessened through the use of collocations.

Measuring fluency and productive collocation knowledge

Before describing the previous studies related to the effect of formulaic sequences on fluency, it is helpful to look at how fluency and productive knowledge of collocations were measured. Collocation studies measuring productive abilities of L2 adults are not common, usually small scale, and unsatisfactory. These studies typically use elicitation or translation tests, and it is questionable if the results can be generalized (Bahns & Eldaw, 1993). Fan (2009) also criticizes studies using elicitation and translation tests by stating that "the major limitation of this category of studies is that they required learners only to produce single collocates of particular words and thus findings of these studies failed to reflect the actual performance of learners in L2 collocational use" (p. 112). Barfield (2009a) also finds fault in collocation research to date. He states that studies have mostly used advanced learners and focused on error analysis and surface forms. For results that can be generalized, researchers need to elicit collocations in more robust ways and not rely on error analysis to determine productive L2 collocational knowledge.

Fluency research has also been criticized in regard to how the speech samples for analysis have been elicited. Wood (2010) states that most fluency studies have used a small number of participants and elicited speech in monologues. He explains that the use of conversational data is not as common as monologic speech because it is difficult to control the cognitive and affective pressures. Researchers have elicited speech in monologues by using picture sequences (Lennon, 1990a) and video narratives (Wood, 2010). Wood acknowledges that other researchers say elicited monologic samples do not represent real-life communication, but Pawley and Syder (1983) state that narrative discourse constitutes a great deal of everyday speech. This claim is valid; however, it does not acknowledge the important role listener feedback plays in everyday speech. They also claim that formulaic sequences and clause chaining are most apparent in narrative retells.

Using monologues to measuring fluency

Fluency has long been considered an important aspect of language proficiency despite it also being a complex issue for language instructors. The qualities of fluency and their effect on assessment were considered in the decision to use monologic speech samples for the spoken fluency assessment. However, there are valid criticisms to be made about this choice. As described earlier, a factor in fluency is the ability to quickly retrieve chunks of language (McCarthy, 2010). The use of these prefabricated chunks of language contributes to fluency and affects both production and perception (Dörnyei, 2009). Wood (2006) contends that by using chunks of language the speaker minimizes pausing within utterances. In addition, Conklin and Schmitt (2008) believe that retrieval and processing time is reduced through the use of chunks of language. The use of chunks of language, such as the collocations under investigation in this study, affects the speech qualities associated with fluency.

Fluency is typically judged by the perceptions of others. However, another approach is to base fluency measurements on temporal features (rate of delivery and pauses). The assessments conducted through this approach correlate with perceptions of informants (McCarthy, 2010). Despite the consistency between the two methods of assessment, there is more to producing a fluent utterance than just the temporal features. While extended pauses within an utterance disrupt fluency (Foster & Skehan, 1999), these pauses are not always the result of communicative failure. They may be the result of cognitive effort and complex planning (McCarthy, 2010). Furthermore, Tauroza and Allison (1990) note that fluency is more than just the rate of delivery. While the temporal features discussed above are captured through the use of monologic speech samples, other aspects of fluency are not.

Rate, smoothness of delivery, and automaticity are qualities associated with fluency that are present in monologic speech, but other aspects of fluency can only be seen in spoken discourse. The beginning of an utterance in a turn-taking situation provides continuity within a conversation and can have a positive effect of perceived fluency (Tao, 2003). McCarthy (2010) states that "one type of automaticity already referred to is the ability of interlocutors to react and respond without delay when it is their turn to speak or when they wish to self-select for the next turn" (p. 5). Turn-taking in multi-party conversation has little overlap or interruption; the ability to speak in this manner is part of spoken proficiency (Sacks, Schegloff, & Jefferson, 1974). McCarthy (2010) also states that "the evaluation of fluency without this interactive dimension, it is argued, gives us only a partial picture of the conversational event" (p. 9). He further explains this point by describing that in turn-taking conversations, longer pauses would not be as prevalent because the interlocutor would intervene and try to help the speaker convey the meaning. Essentially, all parties are responsible for correcting a communicative breakdown within a conversation. Active listeners help the speaker communicate meaning (Bavelas, Coates, & Johnson, 2000). In monologic speech, there is an additional cognitive burden to fill all the silence placed on the speaker.

Despite monologic speech not being able to capture the qualities of fluency described above, it does have advantages for assessment. If fluency was assessed based on a recorded conversation, the interlocutor would positively or negatively affect the speaker's performance for the same reasons described above. Having an active listener as a partner would be advantageous, while an inactive listener could greatly hinder a speaker's performance in an assessment situation. If an instructor served as the interlocutor, it would not only be time consuming (especially for studies with a large number of students like this study) but it would also be difficult to be consistent over the course of the data collection. I felt, for this study, the advantages of using monologic speech (narrative retells) outweighed the disadvantages described in this section.

Previous research

Wood's study (2010) is one of the first to look at the connection between formulaic sequences and speech fluency development in adults. He described this study as being exploratory in both nature and design and that it should be a starting point for future work in this area. Three expert native speakers were used to judge speech samples from the participants. Before the judging, the native speakers had a group session in identifying formulaic sequences in transcripts, and a benchmark was established for what was and what was not a formulaic sequence. The study was conducted at a Canadian university where the eleven participants were full-time students in the English department. The courses in the full-time program did not have any specific focus on fluency or formulaic sequences. The participants were Chinese, Spanish, and Japanese. They were at approximately the same level of oral proficiency based on an interview-based placement test.

This study posed the hypotheses that if the speech rate and/or mean length of runs increase over time, it is likely that more knowledge is being proceduralized. Once per month for six months the students were asked to retell the story in a short animated film that they had just previously watched. This narrative retell was chosen because narratives are traditionally used in fluency research, it is easy to standardize the procedures, and narrative speech leads itself to clause chaining. The animated films were between eight and ten minutes long. The films were silent so the participants could not repeat language that was said during the films. Three films were used during this study, so the students did a retell for each film three times. For example, a student would watch and retell film "A" the first month, and then watch and retell film "A" again in the fourth month.

The judges identified all types of formulaic sequences (FS) in the samples, and SpeechStation 2 software was used to analyze the speech samples. Speech rate (syllables uttered divided by speech time including pauses), articulation rate (syllables uttered divided by total amount of time speaking without pauses), phonation/time ratio (percentage of total pause time of total speech time), mean length of runs (mean number of syllables uttered between pauses), and formula/run ratio (the ratio between the length of runs and the number of FS in the sample) were measured for all of the speech samples collected. The quantitative results showed that the participants' fluency improved significantly as measured by the temporal variables and that more formulaic sequences were used over time. An ANOVA test was conducted and showed statistical significance for all measures except articulation rate. Of the eleven participants, nine increased their ratio of formulas to length of runs. Wood claims this increase indicates this ratio is related to fluency development. In addition, there was no evidence of an effect based on gender or the participant's L1.

Wood cautions that because a small sample was used it is not possible to generalize these results. Furthermore, despite their use in fluency studies, narrative retells are not true indicators of real communicative ability.

Wood also collected qualitative data during his study. Because the same film prompt was used twice, it is possible to compare the use of formulas over time. Wood expected to see instances of dysfluency in earlier retells that were expressed more fluently in later retells. However, Wood noticed that the participants often took different approaches to retelling the same story the second time by using different beginnings, focusing on different aspects, or elaborating on different parts of the story. As a result, he took a broader focus by looking at how different narrative moves were expressed and how formulaic sequences were used to facilitate fluency. Several themes emerged through this analysis: participants used formulaic sequences to extend runs and to give concise descriptions of the events in the narratives. The automatized formulas that were used made the utterances smoother by reducing the frequency and length of pauses. Wood noticed that often an important lexical item was uttered in the second retell, followed by a pause, followed by a coherent quickly uttered formula containing the lexical item. Wood states that "it is clear that the increased use of formulas facilitated the increase in MLR" (2010, p. 162). Five broad categories of formula use could be seen in the second retell. These five categories contributed to the increased length of runs. The five categories are the use of self-talk and fillers, repetition of formulas in a run, use of multiple formulas to extend a run, use of formulas as rhetorical devices and the use of one formula or filler repeatedly (Wood, 2010, p. 162). Wood noticed that the participants tended to use fluent sections of an utterance as a "safe" area, and pauses and areas of dysfluency tended to occur between these sections.

To summarize, Wood supported the following four points with statistically significant data:

- Over time with continued learning and experience, L2 speech is produced faster.
- Learners spend more time speaking as opposed to pausing.
- Utterances contain longer runs.
- In the longer runs between pauses, L2 learners produce more formulaic sequences.

Wood believes the most important finding is that the increased use of formulaic sequences paralleled the improvements seen in the analysis of the temporal measures. He also feels the qualitative analysis gives insight into how and why formulaic sequences are used, though he concedes it is difficult to analyze fluency development through empirical research.

The second study that is discussed investigated the effect of classroom instruction of formulaic sequences on spoken fluency. McGuire (2009) conducted this study at an American university using nineteen mid-intermediate to advanced-level students enrolled in an intensive English language program. The students were Chinese, Japanese or Thai. The control group was taught isolated vocabulary and grammar from the teaching materials. The experimental group was taught formulaic sequences found in the teaching materials. This was supplemented with instruction of additional formulaic sequences. All students completed a pre-test and post-test to measure fluency. The participants were recorded during spontaneous conversation with another student from this study. Each of the recordings was then assessed by sixteen native speaking judges. The judges assigned each recording a grade from 1 to 7: 1 being extremely dysfluent and 7 being very fluent. In addition to the native speaker assessments, formulaic sequence use, speech rate and run length were also measured. McGuire stated that increases over time in speech rate or run length suggest an improvement in spoken fluency.

The participants in the experimental group showed a 16.5 percent improvement on average in regard to speech rate, whereas the control group showed a 0.7 percent improvement. A *t*-test showed this to be a statistical difference ($t_{13.4} = -2.7$, $p = .02$, 90% CI, -26.0, -5.52, $d = 1.28$). The experimental group also showed an improvement of 24.7 percent for mean length of run. In contrast, the control group decreased 4.8 percent. A *t*-test was performed and it showed a statistical difference ($t_{16.4} = -2.9$, $p = .01$, 90% CI, -47.1, -11.9, $d = 1.30$). Similarly, the native speaker assessments had the experimental group increasing by 13.2 percent, and the control group decreasing by 11.9 percent. This difference was also found to be statistically significant through the use of a *t*-test ($t_{16.4} = -2.06$, $p = .055$, 90% CI, -46.4, -3.95, $d = 0.94$). The experimental group increased their use of formulaic sequences by 54.4 percent on average, while the control group increased by an average of 20.5 percent. McGuire states that this study showed a direct link between a classroom focus on formulaic sequences and the increased use of formulaic sequences in spoken discourse. Furthermore, he believes an increased use of formulaic sequences improves student fluency.

Eyckmans (2009) investigated students' receptive knowledge of verb + noun collocations in relation to their productive use of collocations and their fluency. For this study, receptive knowledge referred to the students' ability to distinguish between idiomatic verb + noun collocations and non-idiomatic verb + noun word combinations. The participants for this study were twenty-five English majors at a university in Belgium. Their English proficiency was judged to be at an upper-intermediate level. The treatment was conducted over eight months, and within this period there were 60 hours of instruction. The instructors attempted to maximize the amount of authentic language exposure during the classes and to raise learners' awareness of lexical patterns through noticing activities. The participants oral proficiency was tested in a pre-test and post-test. Both tests used a L1 to L2 retell exercise that required the students to read a story in their L1 and retell it in the L2 using a list of key English words (not phrases) as a memory aid for reconstructing the text. The recordings were graded by three experienced blind judges. Receptive knowledge was measured through the use of the DISCO test (discriminating collocations test), which requires students to correctly select two idiomatic verb + noun word combinations from three choices; the third choice is a non-idiomatic verb + noun combination. Through the use of ANOVA, the results showed that after 60 hours of instruction, the participants' oral production progressed. An ANOVA also revealed a significant difference in the number of phrases produced between the pre-test and post-test for oral proficiency. The participants also made a significant improvement on the DISCO test by improving from a mean score of 29.8 (SD 9.9) to a mean score of 36.08 (SD 4.43). Eyckmans states that 60 hours of input-driven instruction helped improve the students' oral proficiency and phrasal knowledge. The DISCO test also seems to be able to predict a learner's productive phrasal knowledge, but Eyckmans concedes more validation of this test is needed.

The role of collocation knowledge and speaking fluency was also investigated by Hsu and Chiu (2008). The participants for this study were fifty-six Taiwanese English majors at a national university. The students' level was not specifically identified, but the researchers wrote that the students had had eight years of English instruction with many opportunities to speak English. The participants took one written lexical collocation test and two spoken tests. The results indicated that knowledge of lexical collocations (as measured by the written test) were a better indicator of spoken proficiency than the use of lexical collocations (as measured in the spoken tests).

E. Peters' (2009) study examined the effect of attention-drawing techniques on the recall of collocations. Fifty-four advanced EFL students from a Belgian university participated in this study. They were randomly assigned to one of two groups: group 1 focused on unfamiliar vocabulary from a text and group 2 focused on unfamiliar individual words and collocations from a text. The study took place during one session and required the students to take a pre-task vocabulary test, read a 2,100-word text containing glosses of the targeted vocabulary and collocations, complete two questionnaires and a post-task vocabulary test. Both vocabulary tests asked the students to translate the targeted words and collocations from their L1 to English. The results did not show any positive evidence for the use of attention-drawing techniques for the recall of collocations. The questionnaire results showed that students from group 1 also focused on collocations despite not being specifically instructed to do so. Peters believes both the presence of collocations in the pre-test, the marginal glosses of collocations in the text, and the fact the learners were at an advanced level and aware of the importance of collocations contributed to the group 1 participants also focusing on collocations. As Peters notes at the end of this study, it would be interesting to learn if these results would be different for less proficient learners.

Fan (2009) investigated the differences in written collocation usage between L1 and L2 students. This pedagogical study looked at collocational usage in the same narrative writing task. Fan compared two groups: sixty Hong Kong students of mixed English ability and sixty British students. The participants in both groups were 15–16 years old. The results showed that the British students used more types (unique words) and tokens (total number of words) than the Hong Kong students. The Hong Kong students used more general and simple words such as "good" and "big." Furthermore, the Hong Kong students used fewer collocations and an extremely restricted range of collocating words; they overused simple collocating words. Fan believed L1 transfer had a negative effect in the Hong Kong students' use of collocations. Fan also noticed that prepositions used in collocations were a common source of error for the Hong Kong students. The British students, however, used many informal collocations (some kind of, a sort of) whereas the Hong Kong students did not use any. The differences between the two groups of students provides insight into the effect of collocations on written fluency

Summary of collocations and fluency

Researchers have claimed that collocations are crucial for language learners. The researchers claim greater collocational knowledge allows speakers to be more creative when composing utterances. These utterances have fewer mistakes and are easier to comprehend. The use of collocations allows language learners to speak at a higher level and lessens the cognitive burden of producing speech.

The connection between formulaic sequences and fluency needs further research. Webb and Kagimoto (2009) emphasize that little is known of how differences in task type affect acquisition of multiword lexical units despite the fact single word acquisition has been widely researched. Collocation usage and fluency is also an area in need of further research. As Wood (2010) states, "While the link between formulaic sequences and speech fluency makes logical sense, it has not been empirically investigated in much depth, nor has there been much effort to apply this knowledge in teaching materials development" (p. 183). However, some researchers have made progress in this area.

Wood (2010) provides evidence that learners' fluency is improved through the use of more formulaic sequences. McGuire's study (2009) showed that a classroom focus on formulaic sequences leads to their increased use in spoken utterances. Pedagogy is also focused on in Eyckmans' (2009) study, which showed that raising the students' awareness of collocations can help improve their oral proficiency. However, E. Peters' (2009) results raised questions about the merits of using an attention-drawing technique to teach collocations. The final study (Fan, 2009) described in this section provides evidence that L2 learners lack collocational knowledge that hinders their written fluency.

3.5 Teaching collocations

It is unclear why there has been little focus on collocations inside and out of the classroom. Henriksen and Stenius Stoehr (2009) postulate several ideas why there is a lack of attention paid to collocations. They believe:

- it might be because collocation errors rarely cause comprehension problems,
- teachers and students might be unaware of collocations,
- and/or teachers and students might view vocabulary learning as acquiring new words as opposed to restructuring their existing knowledge.

Whatever the reason, language acquisition research and pedagogy would be aided through a better understanding of the reasons why collocations are not acquired efficiently through traditional teaching techniques, what collocations should be taught and how should this be done, and what research there is into the teaching of collocations to date.

Reasons against a traditional approach to language instruction

Second language instruction has tended to rely primarily on the teaching of grammar and individual words as a way to improve a learner's proficiency. While this approach may be beneficial for receptive knowledge, it does not account for the challenges that collocations pose for language students in regard to productive knowledge.

Wray (2002) argues that learners tend to be more analytical when learning a language than native speakers. This results in learners focusing on isolated aspects of the language as opposed to holistic aspects. Instead of processing the chunk of language to which they were exposed as a unit, adult L2 learners break down the chunk and try to understand how the pieces fit together. That approach causes learners to make collocation errors because words do not co-occur freely (Bahns, 1993). Exposure alone is not sufficient for learners to acquire collocational knowledge. Wray (2009) notes that learners might not recognize the subtle irregularity in association between two ordinary words. In Section 3.5, the importance of teaching learners to "notice" collocations is discussed. Wood (2010) also states that since lexical items do not collocate freely, learners have productive problems despite being able to understand the same collocations receptively. For collocations that are not transparent, Henriksen and Stenius Stoehr (2009) point out that learners may misunderstand a collocation if they break it down to individual words. They also note how students often expand their quantity, as opposed to quality, of vocabulary knowledge, and that learning low frequency items is not always useful to expand collocation knowledge. It is better to improve the quality of vocabulary knowledge by focusing on the lexical items already known and expanding productive abilities with these words by understanding their collocates.

Language instructors have often looked to improve learners' productive ability through the teaching of grammar. However, this approach has been criticized. Ying and O'Neill (2009) state that learners can reach a high grammatical proficiency in a short period of time and then plateau, so the learners need to acquire more collocations to reach a higher level of proficiency. Furthermore, syllabuses teach grammatical sequences to enable learners to use them in creative ways (substitution), but it appears native speakers do not do this (Wray, 2000). Other researchers have stated that for L2 adults, a knowledge of collocations and formulaic sequences is enough to replace explicit grammar teaching (M. Lewis, 1994; Nattinger & DeCarrico, 1992).

Native speaking children acquire collocations simply by encountering them several times through their linguistic development. However, adult's lack of collocational knowledge likely stems from a lack of exposure (Durrant & Schmitt, 2010). Even through extensive reading and listening programs, it is unlikely L2 adults are able to overcome this lack of exposure given that learners need to encounter an individual word several times (Horst, Cobb, & Meara, 1998; Waring & Takaki, 2003; Webb, 2007) before they acquire it, and a given collocation appears less frequently than the individual words that make up the collocation. Students rely on a small number of simple items if they do not possess a wide range of collocations resulting in language that is monotonous and repetitive (Fan, 2009). The question of how to teach collocations is addressed in Section 3.5.

Previous research

In comparison to statistical studies using corpora, there has been only a small number of studies focusing on the teaching of collocations. The studies described below can be categorized into three groups: classroom approaches to teaching collocations, concordance programs used to teach collocations, and collocation errors made by second language learners.

To my knowledge there has only been one study investigating how different task types affect collocation knowledge. Webb and Kagimoto (2009) investigated the effects of receptive and productive tasks for receptive and productive knowledge of collocation and meaning. The participants for this study were 145 Japanese first, second, or third year university students. The researchers did not categorize the students as being at a low, intermediate, or advanced level, but they did say the students had on average a receptive knowledge of 1,700 of the 2,000 most common words based on the Vocabulary Levels Test (Schmitt, 2008).

Three weeks prior to the treatment, all participants wrote a pretest. Of the 145 participants, 62 were classified as higher-level learners and 55 were classified as lower-level learners. To ensure the groups were of equal level, the participants were then divided into two experimental groups (receptive and productive treatment groups) and one control group after the pre-test. The groups all had statistically equivalent scores on the pre-test.

In the receptive treatment, the participants read three glossed sentences containing a target collocation. In the productive treatment, the same sentences were used but the participants had to write the target collocations into blanks in the sentences. Both treatments also had L1 translations for the target collocations.

In total, twenty-four verb + noun collocations were used for this experiment. The treatment was done during a single 90-minute lesson that also included all the participants completing the posttest. The posttest measured productive and receptive knowledge of collocation, and productive and receptive knowledge of meaning.

A post hoc, Tukey multiple comparison test revealed that the two treatment groups (receptive and productive) made significant improvement when compared to the control group ($p < 0.05$). There was no significant difference ($p = 0.23$) between the productive group and the receptive group.

Two repeated measure ANOVAs revealed for the higher level students, the receptive group ($F(1,29) = 220.67$, $p < 0.001$) and the productive group ($F(1,31) = 428.62$, $p < 0.001$) had significantly higher scores on the post-test than on the pre-test. Similarly, for the lower-level students, the receptive group ($F(1,25) = 647.07$, $p < 0.001$) and the productive group ($F(1,28) = 528.66$, $p < 0.001$) had significantly higher scores on the posttest than on the pretest. A MANOVA revealed an overall significant difference between the two treatment groups ($F(7,54) = 3.45$, $p < 0.01$) for the higher level learners with the productive group outperforming the receptive group. However, the lower level learners in the receptive group significantly outperformed the productive group ($F(7,47) = 2.57$, $p < 0.05$).

The results are evidence that both productive tasks and receptive tasks are effective for learning collocations. The results showed that lower-level students in the receptive group made more progress than their counterparts in the productive group. The opposite was true for the higher-level students. Three possible explanations were given: (a) the lower-level students, compared to the higher-level students, might have had more difficulty with the increased demands of the productive task; (b) the increased focus on form and meaning in the productive task might have increased learning for the higher-level students, but the increased learning burden may have decreased the amount of time the lower-level students could focus on form as compared with the receptive group; (c) the researchers noticed that many of the higher-level students wrote translations for the sentences in the receptive groups, whereas the lower-level students in the receptive group did not. This strategy might have decreased the amount of time the higher-level students could focus on the collocations.

This study appears to be the first that compares productive and receptive task type in regard to both productive and receptive improvement in collocation knowledge. It also addressed a weakness in the Sun and Wang (2003) study described later in this section by using a greater number of collocations.

However, this study is not without its own weaknesses. The cloze task was quite simple and might not be the best productive task available. To illustrate, Webb and Kagimoto (2009) included this example of the cloze task:

Example

lose touch = 音信不通になる meet demand = 需要を満たす

Set A

- A lot of famous people_____ _____ with their old friends.
- Mick does not want to _____ _____ with his children.
- We mustn't _____ _____ with our family.

Set B

- This is the only way the club can _____ the _____ for tickets from supporters.
- Railways were built to _____ a clear _____ to move people.
- This will allow us to _____ the public's _____ for manufactured goods.
  (p. 62)

The participants had to write one of the two collocations into the three sentences in a set. Given that there were only two possible choices in the productive task and that the results for both the productive and receptive treatments were so similar, it could be argued that the productive task for this study was essentially a receptive task. While it would be more difficult to measure, a task that has the students write sentences using the collocations would measure their productive knowledge more accurately. A speaking task involving the collocations would be even more demanding, but admittedly, much more difficult to design and administer. Furthermore, there was no delayed posttest, which would have given valuable insight into retention rates.

The results indicate that there was little difference between the effects of the receptive and productive tasks on knowledge of collocation and meaning. However, the amount of learning may be dependent on the tasks. Incidental tasks likely result in smaller gains in both types of knowledge (receptive and productive), and these gains are related to the clarity of the meaning in the context, the degree of overlap in L1 meaning and L2 form, and the number and frequency of encounters with the targeted collocations. The results also showed that a manageable number of collocations for students to learn in a short period of time would be twenty-four collocations from twenty-four different known words. In addition, teachers wanting to improve their students' productive abilities should increase the productive demands in a task.

In Section 3.5 proposals for how to teach collocations are discussed. In this respect, Ying and O'Neill (2009) conducted a study into collocation learning using an "AWARE" approach that includes "noticing" collocations (one of the proposals in Section 3.5). In this study, AWARE is an acronym meaning awareness raising of collocations, why should we learn collocations, acquiring noticed collocations, reflection on the learning process and content, and exhibiting what has been learned. The participants for this study were twenty Chinese adult English language learners studying in Singapore, an ESL environment. They were at an intermediate level of proficiency, but were described as having a lack of collocational competence. The study was conducted over a 5-month period and a qualitative methodology was used. The results showed that according to the students' perspectives of the learning process, after some time noticing became automatic and they could not help but notice good expressions while watching TV, reading, or listening to the radio. The participants linked the improvement of their collocational competence to their overall language improvement and created new personal strategies for the acquisition of collocations. The students also felt the oral report using targeted collocations (part of the "exhibiting what has been learned" stage) was particularly useful. For some weaker students, however, there was a feeling that collocations were for more proficient learners, and that they needed to reach a certain standard before they would be able to acquire collocations. Overall, the students had a positive view of studying collocations and considered it to be important for their language proficiency, specifically allowing them to express themselves in a concise and precise manner.

An action research (AR) study done by Jiang (2009) in China focused on material development for improving awareness and productive use of collocations. Jiang examined textbooks used at national level and found vocabulary exercises were an important part, but few tasks were dedicated to word clusters. She designed pedagogic tasks for collocations and had two teachers at different universities use the materials with their students. In total, seventy-five students took part in this study. The students' English proficiency was not specified by Jiang, but the materials suggest the students were at least at an intermediate level. The treatment took place during the students' normal English classes and lasted for 12 weeks. The materials were a combination of speed-reading and collocation tasks. For example, after the students completed a reading, they had to note down good expressions they encountered, use collocations from the passage in different contexts, and then do a retell using words and expressions from the passage. After the 12 weeks the participants completed a questionnaire that elicited both qualitative and quantitative data.

The results showed that the students recognized the importance of studying collocations in English learning and responded positively to the collocation awareness tasks. However, the majority of students still relied on memorizing individual words as opposed to word clusters to expand their vocabulary.

The open-ended questions on the questionnaire showed that prior to the treatment the students did not pay much attention to collocations, were never told the importance of collocations and were unaware of the value of a collocation dictionary.

The first concordance study to be considered was undertaken by Sun and Wang (2003) and focused on inductive and deductive teaching approaches. A concordance program was used to evaluate the effectiveness of the two approaches at two different levels of difficulty. In the study, eighty-one Taiwanese high school students were put into two groups (inductive and deductive). The students had studied English for an average of four years and were all of high enough ability to understand the concordance output. The participants completed a pretest, underwent training, and then completed a posttest. Both the pretest and posttest were error correction tests. This entire procedure lasted for 100 minutes spread over two class periods.

The training for the inductive group involved a three-step process where the participants first found three instances of the collocation on a web-based concordance. They then tried to induce the underlying patterns and made notes. Finally, they corrected sentences based on what they had perceived previously. This process was modeled for the students at the beginning of the treatment. The target procedure for the deductive group was also modeled in the beginning of the training. They were given the necessary rules to make corrections and then completed a series of proofreading problems similar to what was done in the inductive treatment. Both groups (inductive and deductive) were given the answers to the proofreading problems at the end of the treatment. They then wrote the posttest.

The results showed the inductive approach to be superior to the deductive approach ($F = 10.43$, $p = .002$). When considering level of difficulty, the inductive approach was statistically superior ($F = 10.49$, $p = .002$) to the deductive approach for "easy" collocation patterns. There was no statistical difference between the two approaches for "difficult" collocations.

There were several weaknesses in this study, however. As Sun and Wang note themselves, the study was carried out over a short time. A longitudinal study would have been more effective in measuring student progress. A follow-up study by Chan and Liou (2005) also noted that there was a limited number of collocations used in the Sun and Wang study and that the way the collocations were divided into difficulty level was arbitrary. In a separate study done by Webb and Kagimoto (2009), described above, they also noted this weakness of the Sun and Wang study.

The Chan and Liou study (2005) also used a computer-assisted language learning (CALL) classroom and web-based concordancing for collocation learning. Their study investigated the effects of using five web-based practice units on verb–noun collocations. The web-based practice units included several types of activities including multiple choice and gap-fill exercises.

The study consisted of thirty-two Chinese college EFL students who were not English majors. The students' English proficiency level was not mentioned by the researchers. The students took a pretest, two posttests, a background questionnaire, and an evaluation questionnaire. The results showed that the students initially made significant ($p<.05$) collocation improvement. This was seen on the first posttest. A second posttest given two and a half months later showed that the students regressed; however, their performance was still better than on the pretest and was still statistically significant ($p < .05$). This study also looked at four types of verb + noun collocations that are common error types for Chinese college students. The four types as described by Chan and Liou (2005) are:

a. synonymous verbs (e.g., construct/build/establish);
b. hypernym (e.g., create/compose) and troponym (e.g., break/damage) verbs (see Chapter 2 for a more detailed explanation of these verb types);
c. delexicalized verbs (e.g., make, do); and
d. English V–N collocations in lack of translation equivalents in Chinese (e.g., brew tea, "pao cha" in Chinese). (pp. 236–7)

The results showed that the participants made greater improvement for types "c" and "d" than for types "a" and "b."

This research focused on the effectiveness of the concordancer on collocation study and did not look at what effect the different activities included in the web-based practice units had. The inclusion of a delayed posttest was an excellent addition to the Sun and Wang study (2003), as it showed that the participants' collocation improvement regressed after two-and-a-half months.

An obstacle for teaching collocations is the sheer number of them. Bahns (1993) argued that by conducting a contrastive analysis between the L1 and the target language this number could be greatly reduced. He feels that for a considerable portion of collocations there is a direct translational equivalent. These collocations would not need to be taught, and the learner could focus on collocations that do not have a direct translational equivalent and would commonly be misused. In his contrastive analysis of German–English noun + verb and verb + noun collocations, he found many translational equivalents such as "show" + "interest," which in German is "interesse" + "zeigen." He stated that the majority of collocation errors result from L1 influence and that collocation learning materials should account for a student's L1.

Another study focusing on learner errors was undertaken by Wray (2008). In this case study, a beginner language learner was given the task of performing a language interaction in Welsh after only five days of tutorials. Given the short period of time, the tutorials emphasized memorization of complete phrases and sentences. The learner had correctly memorized the material, but during the language interaction, she made several errors typical of a beginner student. These errors happened significantly more often at boundaries between memorized units than within the units. Wray postulated that a beginner could memorize many of these interactions and often appear to be linguistically competent.

Due to the limited number of studies dealing with approaches to teaching collocations, research-based knowledge that can be applied in the classroom is lacking. However, future studies, including this one, can use the experiments described above as a starting point.

Which collocations should be taught?

As mentioned earlier, one of the problems about teaching collocations is the large number of them. Furthermore, choosing collocations from a text can also be problematic because it is difficult to rank them in terms of importance. Henriksen and Stenius Stoehr (2009) explain that if the input is rich, it is difficult to choose on which collocations to focus. However, researchers have made several proposals such as frequency, discourse in the target language, transparency, translational equivalents and learner need as being useful criteria for deciding which collocations to target.

Handl (2009) compares L1 learning to L2 acquisition. She proposes that since acquiring collocations in the L1 is a natural process resulting from constant exposure, for L2 acquisition "the teaching/learning environment and materials have to compensate for the lack of linguistic input" (p. 69). She continues by saying that frequency can be used to rank significant collocations. Wood (2010) also mentions teaching materials when he states that there are gaps in the collocations used in target language discourse and those found in language textbooks. He proposes using "authentic" language in the teaching of collocations.

In order to reduce the number of collocations learners need to focus on, Wray (2008) recommends separating transparent collocations since students are likely able to construct these from their lexical and grammatical knowledge. Another suggestion made in the previous section, is to separate collocations that have direct translational equivalents in the mother tongue (Bahns, 1993).

Learner need should also be considered. Wood (2010) mentions that different collocations should be targeted for different syllabi. Fan (2009) ranks learner need as being the most important criteria to consider by saying:

> While it is important to teach, for example, collocations which are "more restricted" or which occur "more frequently," teachers should have confidence in focusing on collocational use they see as relevant to the making of meaning in a particular context, taking into account the language needs of their students irrespective of whether such use concerns only lexical words or both lexical and grammatical words. Nobody understands the needs of L2 learners better than their teachers. (p. 121)

To summarize, teachers should choose collocations that are frequent, non-transparent, and authentic. Also, teachers can further reduce the number of collocations to be targeted by considering L1 transference. Learner need is perhaps the most important criteria though. Rundell (1999) states that identifying suitable collocations is an important productive need of our learners.

How to teach collocations

Collocations are both problematic and crucial for language learners. Researchers have identified collocations as being a common source of error, while also being crucial for fluency development (Bahns & Eldaw, 1993; Nesselhauf, 2003). Webb and Kagimoto (2009) state that very few empirical studies have addressed the issue of how collocations can be most effectively taught in the language classroom. However, researchers have suggested several guidelines for how teachers can approach collocation instruction in the classroom.

Advocates of an increased focus on collocations in the classroom often mention language use as being important for collocation acquisition. "Students need to learn words and sentences not as isolated, planned answers to classroom exercises, but rather to learn how to use these structures to create the flow and purpose of a spontaneously unfolding conversation" (Nattinger & DeCarrico, 1992, p. 113). First language learners benefit from large quantities of comprehensible input to determine how and when a particular collocation is used. L2 adults' lack of exposure likely causes their lack of collocational knowledge (Durrant & Schmitt, 2010). Language instructors must compensate for this impediment.

Explicit instruction in collocations is one possible way to make up for the lack of exposure. Laufer and Paribakht (1998) note that the majority of words are learned through direct instruction with relatively few gains being made incidentally in an EFL context. Webb and Kagimoto (2009) make a similar claim by stating:

> In the ESL context, it may be enough to make learners aware of the importance of learning collocation, and to teach them to notice words that regularly appear together in context. This method may, in turn, lead to incidental gains. However, in an EFL context, in which incidental gains tend to be relatively small, it may be useful for teachers to not only make their learners aware of collocation, but also to teach it. (p. 71)

Nesselhauf (2003) also states the importance of explicit instruction: "It seems indispensable that a number of collocations be taught and learnt explicitly" (p. 238). Collocation acquisition is mentioned by Durrant and Schmitt (2010): "Explicit focus on target collocations would dramatically improve their acquisition" (p. 181). Language instructors must incorporate explicit activities for collocations if acquisition is to be expected.

Students know that learning new vocabulary can improve their receptive and productive knowledge. However, students are often not familiar with collocations and the important role they play in language acquisition. Ying and O'Neill (2009) state that teachers need to raise student awareness of collocations. Fan (2009) similarly states that raising students' awareness is important because collocation use is arbitrary. Willis (1990) believes that for collocation acquisition students need to notice and speculate about patterns of language within a text. Teachers should start this process by using the most common patterns containing the most common words, which will create a useful learning experience (Wray, 2000). For awareness raising of collocations, Henriksen and Stenius Stoehr (2009) believe language instructors must overcome several challenges: they must develop pedagogical tools for raising student awareness, they must support the students' ability to notice patterns in the input, and they must increase their students' understanding of the need to develop collocational knowledge of frequently occurring lexical items. Ying and O'Neill (2009) also claim that learning is most effective if students see the significance of what they have learned and are able to exhibit it. The characteristics of productive activities for collocations are discussed in the next paragraph.

In Section 3.5 Webb and Kagimoto's study (2009) about learning word pairs was described. They believe that productive ability is improved through the use of productive tasks, while receptive tasks mostly lead to receptive gains. Fan (2009) states that teachers should create the need to productively use collocations in the classroom. Repetition is also commonly mentioned as a key component of productive collocation activities. Durrant and Schmitt (2010) claim repetition is effective for improving learning. They state fluency-based rereading exercises are particularly effective and there is a need for substantial exposure. Wood (2010) believes activities with repetition of formulaic sequences are important for automatization, which is crucial for fluency. In addition to repetition, he continues by stating that fluency development activities should impose speed constraints and force the production of speech in chunks. Fan (2009) also mentions that effective activities require repeated use of collocations, in addition to being communicative, authentic, and focusing on everyday events.

Wood (2010) explains in depth how collocations should be taught. He advocates the use of models of speech from fluent speakers. The students should be encouraged to notice formulaic sequences within these models and determine their meaning and discourse function. For this process, teacher and peer feedback is valuable. He also believes students can benefit by learning entire chunks of language (including articles and prepositions) and not just which words collocate with other words. For verb + noun collocations, teachers and students should focus on the verb because it is the more common cause of mistakes. He makes a final recommendation of targeting collocations based on the students' L1. This recommendation is similar to Bahns' study (1993) described in Section 3.5. For beginner students and learners who are not proficient, Wray (2008) suggests that memorization may be more beneficial than using other methods for acquiring collocations. Hill (2000) also suggests rote learning by stating that collocations should be learned in such a way that "we can retrieve them from our mental lexicon just as we pull a phone number or address from our memory" (p. 53). The majority of researchers argue for an explicit approach to collocations.

An alternative to explicit instruction for collocations is made by Liu (2010) in his study described in Section 2.3. A cognitive approach is proposed when he stated that students should be taught why collocations use a particular combination of words. He believes some potential benefits are that using cognitive analysis can help students use collocations productively because there are too many collocations to memorize. It may also help the students use the verbs more accurately since they understand the motivation for the verb in the collocation.

By understanding the semantic differences between "make a trip" and "take a trip" students might understand "make" and "take" collocations better. However, he tempers his claims by stating that "although I see strong benefits of cognitive analysis in learning collocations, based on the new research findings, I also understand the need for students to notice, memorize, and repeatedly practice collocations to attain a good grasp of them" (p. 24). He also concedes this approach is probably not suitable for young children, students of different learning styles, and students of low language proficiency. In addition, not all collocations require the same level of cognitive analysis. Wray (2000) has cautioned against approaches that overgeneralize the characteristics of a formulaic sequences. She believes it is impossible to present only grammatically and semantically regular sequences because subtle restrictions arise as a result of idiomaticity. She states that "this makes all formulaic sequences potentially unreliable for analysis" (2000, p. 485).

To summarize, researchers propose an explicit approach to collocation instruction, which partially compensates for L2 learners' lack of exposure to the target language. It is also important to raise students' awareness for collocations. Learners need to understand the importance of collocations for developing their productive abilities and fluency. Productive tasks are seen as being more effective for improving a learner's speaking and writing ability, and repetition is a key element that should be present within these tasks. Finally, cognitive analysis may help with collocation acquisition, but it is important to carefully choose the targeted collocations and consider the characteristics of the students before devoting class time to this approach.

Testing collocation knowledge

Tests for collocations have been developed (Eyckmans, 2009; Gyllstad, 2009; Revier, 2009), but in creating these tests the developers faced the challenge of defining the construct of "collocation" and demonstrating that the tests actually measure collocational knowledge. A thorough summary of these tests and the studies conducted to measure their reliability and validity is beyond the scope of this study. However, it is useful to discuss general principles for testing collocation knowledge.

Wray (2009) believes teachers should consider both productive and receptive ability when testing collocation knowledge. She explains learners often overestimate their productive abilities using language to which they have been exposed. They do not see the gap between what they understand and what they can use productively. The ability to productively use collocations is an aspect of the CONTRIX test developed by Revier (2009). He states that "testing of L2 collocation knowledge needs to focus on the recognition and production of whole collocations" (p. 126). He believes tests should measure productive knowledge of whole verb + noun chunks by eliciting these collocations without requiring a long text to establish context and be suitable for learners at different proficiency levels.

Gyllstad (2009) developed two tests for collocation knowledge: COLLEX and COLLMATCH. He believes there is a lack of properly validated tests for collocation knowledge and that researchers have been making conclusions based on tests that have not been measured for validity and reliability. The COLLMATCH and COLLEX measure knowledge of verb + noun collocations that are problematic for learners and constitute the communicative core of utterances. Both of these tests measured out to be valid and reliable.

To summarize, there is a lack of properly validated collocation tests, and this shortcoming has negatively affected collocational research. In addition to being reliable and valid, collocation tests need to measure productive ability as there is often a gap in what students can receptively understand and what they can productively use. This study measures productive collocational knowledge through a spoken assessment, which is described in more detail in Sections 5.3 and 6.2. The participants describe a picture sequence before and after the intervention. The same sequence of pictures are used in both assessments, so it is possible to determine if the students are able to use collocations in the second description that they were unable to use in the first.

Criticisms of a collocational focus in language classes

The nature of collocations, the challenges of learning English in an EFL environment, and gaps in the research all contribute to the difficulty language instructors face when teaching collocations. Bahns (1993) believes the large number of collocations is the main challenge for teaching them in the classroom. Thus, researchers (Handl, 2009; Shin & Nation, 2008; Wood, 2010; Wray, 2008) have emphasized that there is a need to target collocations based on student need, teachability, frequency, and transparency as stressed previously. In addition to the pedagogical challenges that exist because of the large number of collocations, materials with a collocational focus have not been researched enough in regard to how learners use and evaluate these resources (Barfield & Gyllstad, 2009). Another challenge is described by Liu:

[collocations] are currently taught mostly as prefabricated chunks using primarily noticing–memorization strategies. This noticing- and-memorization-only approach is problematic not only because it ignores the motivated nature of most collocations but also, and more importantly, because it takes away from the study of collocations any cognitive and linguistic analysis, a very important and useful part of the language-acquisition process. (2010, p. 22)

As described in Section 3.5, most researchers recommend noticing and memorization for collocation instruction, but Liu questions the value of this approach. Wray (2000) also questions the claims of researchers such as Lewis (1994), Nattinger and Decarrico (1992), Hill (2000), and Hill, Lewis, and Lewis (2000) about the ability of learners to make generalizations about the grammar from formulaic input. She states that teaching syllabuses tend to assume the learner's ability to generalize, but this assumption is not supported by research. In Section 3.5, Webb and Kagimoto's (2009) study into the effects of task type on collocation acquisition is described. They believe there is a need to research acquiring collocations through other vocabulary learning tasks. Liu (2010) also states that researchers need to further examine the nature of collocations and the approaches used to teach them. These gaps in the research make the teaching of collocations problematic. However, this study should address some of the pedagogical challenges of teaching collocations.

3.6 Conclusion

Through the use of collocation instruction, learners can sound more native-like, learn the grammar of a language, and sound more fluent by stringing multiword units together. Furthermore, low-level learners can make productive use of the language by using what they already know. Using collocations also improves fluency by reducing the pauses within clauses, by allowing language learners to speak above their current level, and by helping students to produce more accurate utterances. In addition, collocation use lessens the cognitive load of producing speech.

To maximize these benefits, instructors should choose collocations based on frequency, translational equivalents, transparency, and learner need. The targeted collocations can be taught through the use of explicit instruction to compensate for the L2 learner's lack of exposure, consciousness-raising activities to demonstrate the importance of collocation knowledge, productive tasks to improve fluency, and repetition within tasks to aid language intake. However, if the teaching and learning of collocations are to be more influential in future approaches to second language instruction, more evidence is needed to support these perceived benefits.

4

Methodology

4.1 Introduction

This chapter describes the interpretive paradigm and the methodology of AR. For this study, I chose to mainly use a qualitative research design. However, quantitative data was also collected, so mixed method methodology and how it can be incorporated within an AR study is also illustrated.

4.2 Interpretive paradigm

For this book, the term "paradigm" refers to a general set of beliefs that governs the choices made throughout a study by a researcher. This set of beliefs can also be described as a researcher's ontological (beliefs about what knowledge is) and epistemological (beliefs about how we understand knowledge) standpoints (Brooke, 2013). McGregor and Murnane (2010) state that "it is common knowledge that a paradigm is a set of assumptions, concepts, values, and practices that constitutes a way of viewing reality for the community that shares them" (p. 419). They further this description by explaining that paradigm encompasses a philosophical and technical aspect; however, for this book, it is used exclusively in the philosophical sense.

In order to understand a study, it is necessary to consider the researcher's beliefs in regard to paradigm. Mackenzie and Knipe (2006) affirm that "it is the choice of paradigm that sets down the intent, motivation and expectations for the research. Without nominating a paradigm as the first step, there is no basis for subsequent choices regarding methodology, methods, literature or research design" (p. 194). Creswell (2003) also emphasizes the importance of clearly stating a paradigm because the reader can understand the researcher's assumptions regarding how they expect to learn and what they expect to learn over the course of the investigation.

In addition to understanding what paradigm governs a study, it is also necessary to understand what the word (along with other words) actually represents and how it can be distinguished from other terms often used as synonyms by different researchers. Mackenzie and Knipe (2006) explain that "the most common definitions suggest that methodology is the overall approach to research linked to the paradigm or theoretical framework while the method refers to systematic modes, procedures or tools used for collection and analysis of data" (p. 198). Consequently, for this book, paradigm, methodology, and method are used with this interpretation in mind.

Paradigms can be divided into two expansive categories: positivism and interpretism. Brooke (2013) describes that "these research traditions and methods can be broadly described as those pertaining to a scientific model or positivist approach preferring quantitative research methodology and those of the naturalistic or interpretative approach, which predominantly apply qualitative techniques for study" (p. 430). A review of the literature shows there is some conflict in the terms used to describe specific paradigms. For example, McGregor and Murnane (2010) divide paradigms into positivism (associated with quantitative research) and post-positivism (associated with qualitative research). However, Mackenzie and Knipe (2006) align both positivism and post-positivism with quantitative methods of data collection and analysis. Furthermore, they use the terms interpretivist, constructivist, transformative and pragmatic to further divide paradigm. In the following paragraphs, the positivism paradigm is first briefly described before a fuller characterization of the paradigm for this study, interpretism, is given. In addition, the pragmatic paradigm (Mackenzie and Knipe, 2006) is explained as it was also influential over the course of this investigation.

As mentioned in the previous paragraph, positivism is associated in research with the quantitative methodology. Watson-Gegeo (1988) characterizes this paradigm branch as a nomothetic (formulation of general or universal laws) science from an outsider perspective. Brooke (2013) expands on this by describing positivism as "centering on probabilities through the collection of (commonly) large scale, quantifiable data in an objective and controlled way" (p. 430). Furthermore, he distinguishes this paradigm from interpretism by saying the findings are considered invalid if they cannot be applied to different contexts from which the research was conducted.

Researchers using interpretive paradigms, as used in this study, are equally concerned with the process (the why and the how) as they are with the facts (the where, what, who, and when) or outcome (Brooke, 2013). Interpretive paradigms offer an insider perspective and are inherently subjective. The findings are an interpretation as opposed to universal truth. Hammersley and Atkinson (1995) characterize the research conducted under interpretive paradigms as representing a "slice of life" that provides insight into human opinion and behavior. A criticism of this paradigm (more specifically of AR, the methodology used in this study) is that it does not attempt to validate its findings. When describing AR in TESOL, Brooke (2013) concedes this point by stating that "up to a point this may be true because action research does not posit that it holds assumptions regarding the value-free nature of its results" (p. 433). However, McGregor and Murnane (2010) support this quality by stating "research should not be value-free and unbiased but be value-laden, subjective and intersubjective, even value-driven within the critical paradigm" (pp. 423–4). The findings can be considered trustworthy if the reader can audit the events and understand how the researcher's background and experiences were accounted for. This trust is achieved through rich description of the research process. In addition, interpretive paradigms can be distinguished from positivism by the importance placed on the participants' views of the situation being investigated (Creswell, 2003).

As previously mentioned, the main methodology use in this investigation was AR; however, this study can also be characterized as employing aspects of a mixed-method methodology that is associated with the pragmatic paradigm. The pragmatic paradigm prioritizes the research problem and uses all approaches to understanding the problem (Creswell, 2003). The research problem is addressed through "data collection and analysis methods . . . chosen as those most likely to provide insights into the question with no philosophical loyalty to any alternative paradigm" (Mackenzie and Knipe, 2006, p. 197). The research problem is considered most important and all approaches are utilized to better understand the problem. Creswell (2003) explains that "inquirers draw liberally from both quantitative and qualitative assumptions when they engage in their research" and "pragmatists do not see the world as an absolute unity. In a similar way, mixed methods researchers look to many approaches to collecting and analyzing data rather than subscribing to only one way (e.g., quantitative or qualitative)" (p. 12). Pragmatism shows how methodologies can be successfully mixed (Hoshmand, 2003) and that "research approaches should be mixed in ways that offer the best opportunities for answering research questions" (Burke Johnson & Onwuegbuzie, 2004, p. 16).

Given the pedagogical nature of this study and the practical research questions, a paradigm that embraced subjective interpretation from an insider perspective was deemed appropriate. Furthermore, it was thought that the research questions could best be addressed through the collection and analysis of both quantitative and qualitative data. Consequently, the paradigm used for this study is largely interpretism; however, elements of the pragmatic paradigm were also influential.

4.3 Qualitative research

A predominately qualitative research design was a suitable choice for a research methodology for several reasons. Primarily, at the initial stages of this investigation, it was uncertain which direction the study would take. Second, the initial research questions that were introduced in Chapter 1 focused on subjective interpretations from both the learners' and my own perspective. In addition, I wanted to collect a range of data to support my findings, and I believe for the reasons described below a qualitative research methodology addressed these concerns.

From the beginning stages of this investigation it was clear a flexible research design would be needed. Dörnyei (2007) characterizes qualitative studies as having an emergent research design. He explains that during the process of conducting an investigation, the research design can be adapted as new information is learned. The researcher does not set out to test a preconceived hypothesis. Davis (1995) explains that "different paradigms [methodologies by my terminology] are used for different purposes" (p. 448). Given the purpose of this study, the flexibility and adaptability of qualitative research would be needed throughout the process of conducting this exploratory study.

The initial research questions focused on the learners' attitudes toward an alternative approach to vocabulary instruction. I felt a qualitative study would be appropriate for addressing this issue because it would allow for an in-depth analysis of the issues and produce subtle findings that might be missed through the use of a quantitative methodology. Dörnyei (2007) describes one of the strengths of qualitative studies as being grounded in the participants' responses. He expands on this point by explaining that qualitative studies can explore the participants' views of the situation under investigation and can elicit subjective opinions. Researchers can attain a fuller understanding of a context because they can seek to answer "why" questions. Qualitative studies are of the most value when prior to their undertaking the researcher carefully considers the purpose of the investigation to determine if qualitative research is the most appropriate methodology to use. Lazaraton (1995) cautions that "the purposes, assumptions, and methods of qualitative research are still debated, misunderstood, and/or ignored by some in our profession" (p. 456).

By using multiple sources of data, researchers can examine a situation from several perspectives, which ultimately can strengthen their findings. This triangulation is endorsed by Davis (1995) when he states that "another essential procedure in ensuring research credibility is to triangulate by utilizing multiple sources, methods, and investigators" (p. 446). Dörnyei (2007) also notes that the wide range of data sources within qualitative studies is a strength; however, the outcome of these studies is ultimately dependent on the researchers' interpretation of the data.

In the following sections, I describe the specific methodology within qualitative research that is used for this investigation – AR. The discussion is of the literature of AR, specifically for what AR and qualitative research represent along with a justification for their use given the goals of this study. Davis (1995) states that "the failure of researchers within the field of SLA to make explicit the philosophical and theoretical perspectives guiding their studies has created other problems of definition as well as those involving research legitimacy" (p. 434), while Lazaraton (1995) notes that "perhaps consensus on the definitions, principles, and value of qualitative research is not necessary, desirable, or even possible" (p. 468). It is not the goal of this chapter to fully describe the intricacies of the methodology of AR; however, I feel a characterization serves the reader well in order to understand the research design and findings from this investigation.

The methodology of AR

AR is a methodology within the interpretivist paradigm, which is particularly effective in TESOL (Brooke, 2013). Burns (2005b) explains that:

> In contrast to basic and applied studies, AR takes an explicitly interventionist and subjective approach. Because it is centrally situated in the local concerns and problems of the research participants, its aims are to investigate issues of practical importance, using systematic data collection procedures. (p. 60)

Within this paradigm, research should be conducted in the daily lives of participants in their natural settings as opposed to experimental settings (McGregor & Murnane, 2010). Burns states that "action research confronts rather than minimises the variables present in the research context and attempts to seek explanations inclusive of those variables" (p. 67).

Action researchers seek improvement through change in an aspect of the research situation. Kemmis and McTaggart (2008) explain that "participatory action researchers are embarked on a process of transforming themselves as researchers, transforming their research practices, and transforming the practice settings of their research" (p. 293). Creswell (2003) also emphasizes change by stating that "the research should contain an action agenda for reform that may change the lives of the participants, the institutions in which individuals work or live, and the researcher's life" (pp. 9–10). In AR, the researcher is an integral part of the process. Improvement and involvement are the two defining characteristics of AR (Burns, 2007). Kemmis and McTaggart (2008) state that "classroom action research typically involves the use of qualitative interpretive modes of inquiry and data collection by teachers (often with help from academics) with a view to teachers making judgments about how to improve their own practices" (pp. 273–4). The involvement of the researcher is not seen as a negative because AR does not attempt to produce findings that are universally true (Brooke, 2013). Researchers within this methodology investigate an issue within their context and seek to improve the situation. The findings are then presented through rich description allowing the reader to critique the researcher's interpretations. The reader can then judge whether the findings are applicable to their context.

AR is often characterized by a spiral of self-reflection, which is described in Section 4.3; however, Kemmis and McTaggart (2008) also describe AR as being: a social process in which students and teachers work together; participatory in that research is done on themselves, either individually or collectively; practical and collaborative; emancipatory; critical of inefficiencies in the research context; reflexive to what has been learned previously; and transformative in both theory and practice. Kemmis (1993) offers that

> Social research is always (in one way or another) connected to social action and social movement. It sees the connection between social research and social life as intrinsic to research as an activity, not extrinsic, or instrumental, or as a question of the enlightenment of individuals who will later set about changing the world – though these things may give clues to important aspects of a deep critical understanding and practice of action research. (p. 3)

Kemmis and McTaggart's description of AR emphasizes the close relationship between the researcher (teacher) and the participants (students) in educational contexts. They elaborate on this point by stating that "three particular attributes are often used to distinguish participatory research from conventional research: shared ownership of research projects, community-based analysis of social problems, and an orientation toward community action" (p. 273). Burns (2005b) emphasizes the role of participants in AR studies when she describes participant involvement as being a pillar underpinning AR. McGregor and Murnane (2010) articulate this involvement and collaboration when stating that "humans are seen as central to the research process, rather than isolated from it. They are not controlled and studied but are participants in the process, even instigating and benefitting from the research" (p. 424).

Given the involvement of students in educational AR and the desire to affect positive change within a teaching context, AR is well suited for investigating pedagogical issues. This can be seen by the fact "there is now a variety of traditions of educational action research, each with its own potential and limitations, and, increasingly, with its own literature. And each, one supposes, is more or less suited to the distinctive cultural and historical conditions under which it has evolved" (Kemmis, 1993, pp. 1–2). However, Brooke (2013) notes that there is a gap in TESOL research between applied linguistics and the pedagogy of the classroom with theoretical papers being more prominent than case studies based on situated learning. Somekh (1993) also comments on the fact that abstract research is held in a higher regard than practical studies. Brooke (2013) concludes that "there is a need for more action research conducted by teacher-researchers; and the development of this approach to better understand TESOL and its complexities" (p. 434). This study is step in that direction.

What is AR?

AR is described in different ways by various researchers; however, there are also commonalities in the various descriptions for AR. By summarizing how AR is viewed in this investigation, I hope to illustrate the research principles that influenced the goals, the process, and the procedures used during this study. Part of the appeal of AR as a methodology for this study is its adaptability over the research process. When examining the findings and procedures presented in the following chapters, the emergent nature of AR and its ongoing characteristics should be considered. By doing so, the reader can orient themselves within the overall process and understand the motivations for the procedures and changes that were implemented.

The primary purpose of AR is to contribute to knowledge from the perspective of practice. AR is about working toward practical outcomes and creating new forms of understanding (Reason & Bradbury, 2008). In addition to practicality,

AR also emphasizes how the research is connected to the professional context. In educational settings, AR can be defined as a teacher's structured thorough enquiry into their own professional context (Dörnyei, 2007; Nunan, 1992; Wyatt, 2011). For teachers, the classroom is where AR is usually conducted and where the initial motivation to investigate a phenomenon occurs. The process "starts with the observation of a number of events for which there is no obvious and immediate explanation and for which there is a desire to gain a coherent explanation" (Stephens, Barton, & Haslett, 2009, p. 471). In educational AR these events could be an area of concern to the teacher or an aspect of her or his practice that could be better understood through investigation. The researcher then initiates a process of understanding the innovations and developments that are occurring and uses the new knowledge for further development. During this process in the classroom, the researcher systematically records the information that is later reflected on and analyzed. Further actions are then based on the evidence gained from the initial actions (Burns, 2009b). AR can be described as a series of steps or stages. A more thorough description of these stages is presented in Section 4.3.

Stages of AR

While AR is flexible and exploratory, it can also be viewed as a series of stages in which each stage is part of a larger process aimed at improving an aspect of a teacher's practice. Brooke (2013) states that "the AR approach provides an essential structure to direct processes of practical situated research combined with focused reading or deliberative reflection in the field under study" (p. 432). Wallace (1998) characterizes a reflective cycle as structured reflection "which will help us to make sense of our experiences, and perhaps through such structured reflection come to a solution" (p. 14). Each stage thus gives structure to the overall investigative process.

The first step in an educational AR study is to identify an area for investigation. As mentioned earlier, this can stem from a problem in the classroom, but it can also be an aspect of teaching that is not fully understood. Wallace (1998) states that "[action research] nearly always arises from some specific problem or issue arising out of professional practice" (p. 15). Burns (2007b) similarly states that "interventions in practice are in response to a perceived problem, puzzle, or question that people in the social context wish to improve or change in some way" (p. 987). This leads to a process of trial and error investigation (Brooke, 2013) that is initiated by reading around the topic, attending conferences, and/

or conferencing with colleagues (Wallace, 1998) to gain a better understanding of the situation. The teacher can then apply this knowledge through a change or intervention in one's teaching practice. The "action" in action research refers to putting deliberate practical changes into one's teaching practice with the hope of improving, modifying or developing the situation (Burns, 2009a). The teacher researcher then observes and collects data, which can later be used for reflection. This process is repetitive and fluid, meaning the teacher researcher will likely be simultaneously engaged in different stages and aspects of a particular study. In regard to this investigation, this series of stages was followed, but it should also be noted that in reality the process is not as distinct as it might appear from the preceding description. I was often engaged in different stages concurrently.

AR involves one or more cycles of activities (Davison, Martinsons, & Ou, 2012). These cycles are flexible and used responsively and reflexively by participants. Brooke (2013, p. 432) expands on this point by stating that "it is a process of exploratory change with spiral of planning, action, observation, and reflection. This is then followed by further-planning and so round the spiral once more." During a research project, it is essential to repeat interventions to improve or confirm these changes in strategy that were used to obtain the research goals (Brooke, 2013). In this study, four reflective cycles were conducted each of which was motivated through an examination of the previous cycle's data.

While various researchers refer to the steps in the investigative process differently, action researchers typically follow a process similar to the one illustrated in Figure 4.1. For the purposes of this chapter, all future references to a reflective cycle signifies the series of steps seen immediately below. I describe each stage specifically as it relates to this study in the following paragraphs.

As seen in Figure 4.1, the AR reflective cycle is flexible and repetitive. However, I tend to follow a process that involves a series of stages. At any given time I might be engaged in more than one stage, but in general each reflective cycle follows the pattern seen above.

At the beginning of each reflective cycle, the topic is researched during the "plan" stage. Burns (2007b) states that "the action aspect requires some kind of planned intervention, deliberately putting into place concrete strategies, processes, or activities in the research context" (p. 987). This planning is especially needed for the first reflective cycle in which the initial area of concern is investigated through reading around the topic, attending conferences, and discussing the issue with colleagues. For later reflective cycles, this stage becomes a more focused investigation due to what has been learnt through the previous reflective cycle.

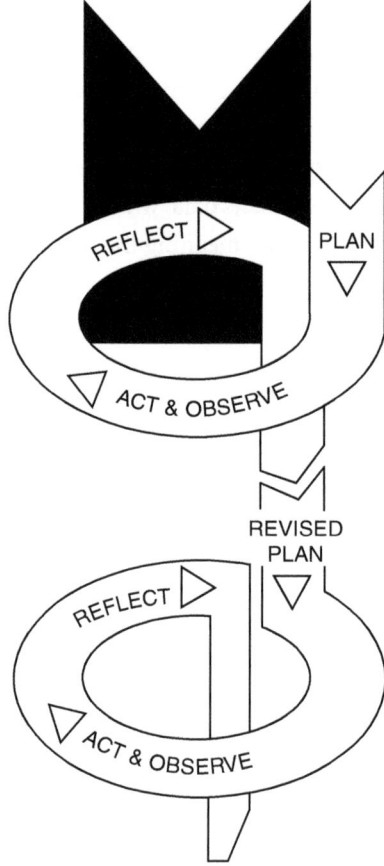

Figure 4.1 The AR spiral based on Kemmis and McTaggart (2008, p. 278)

Based on the knowledge gained, I develop an action plan with the goal of improving and/or gaining insight into the original area of concern. For this study, the "act and observe" stage is an intervention into my teaching practice. For the initial reflective cycle the intervention represented a change from teaching individual words from the GSL to frequent collocations. In later cycles, the intervention was refined and different structures were targeted using various techniques. During the intervention stage of this study, I collected data through the use of questionnaires, audio-recordings and field notes. The justification for using these specific tools is seen in Section 4.6.

The next stage, "reflect," is an assessment of the intervention in which the change in procedure is analyzed from various viewpoints using the data collected in the previous stage. For this study, questionnaires provided insight into the learners' feelings about studying collocations, field notes illustrated the teacher's perspective (my perspective), and the audio-recordings were used to judge the effectiveness of the intervention. Burns (2007b) explains that "the research component of action research means systematically collecting data about the planned actions, analyzing what they reveal, reflecting on the implications of the data, and developing alternative plans and actions based on data analysis" (p. 988).

The following stage depicted in Figure 4.1, "revised plan," is preparation for the subsequent cycle. This stage is similar to the "plan" stage; however, the decisions made are based on the previous findings of the study as opposed to outside resources. In this stage, I decided on the necessity of conducting a subsequent reflective cycle.

This overall process then repeats for the next cycle. Burns (2005) notes the importance of this repetition when she states that

> Iteration is a further principle of AR that contributes to enhancing rigour and reducing subjectivity. Iterations of the AR cycle enable initial insights and findings to give way to deeper, new but related, questions. Further data collection then serves to: i) build on evidence from previous cycles; ii) expand the scope of the study; iii) triangulate the data across different episodes, sites and subjects through multiple data sources; iv) test new findings against previous iterations of the cycle; and v) avoid the bias inherent in cross-sectional research. (pp. 67–8)

While Kemmis and McTaggart's (2008) model appears to be structured, the actual process is more labyrinthine. While describing their depiction of the AR cycle (Figure 4.1), they explain that

> In reality, the process might not be as neat as this spiral of self-contained cycles of planning, acting and observing, and reflecting suggests. The stages overlap, and initial plans quickly become obsolete in the light of learning from experience. In reality, the process is likely to be more fluid, open, and responsive. The criterion of success is not whether participants have followed the steps faithfully but rather whether they have a strong and authentic sense of development and evolution in their practices, their understandings of their practices, and the situations in which they practice. (p. 277)

As shown in the above quote, the stages are not easily compartmentalized as one stage often melds with the next.

AR, like any other methodology, needs forethought to be successful. There is a need to adopt a systematic approach (Somekh, 2006). Researchers need to be explicit about their approach, research aim, theory, and methods at the beginning of their study through to its publication. This is as true for AR as it is for other methodologies (Avison, Lau, Myers, & Nielsen, 1999). For an exploratory investigation such as mine, it is a challenge to balance the need for a structured approach with an emergent research design. However, one of the strengths of AR is its ability to adapt to new understandings of the teaching/learning dynamic. Therefore, if AR projects are to cover an extended period of time, given the exploratory and emergent nature of this method, it is unnecessary to have a very detailed intervention plan (Davison et al., 2012). The methodology itself is difficult to characterize. Reason and Bradbury describe that "action research cannot be programmatic and cannot be defined in terms of hard and fast methods" (2008, p. 3). To summarize, there is a need for structure and a sound research design, but within this design, researchers should have the flexibility to change course when a better understanding of the situation is gained through data analysis. This apparent disconnect is a challenge that is ever present in AR studies.

Reflection within AR

While the initial action plan for the intervention in my vocabulary instruction was quickly conceived, it was clear that this issue was complex and would require in-depth analysis and assessment. Only through the process of data collection and analysis, would a better understanding of this issue be gained. Reflection, which is a crucial aspect of AR, would also have an important role in my study.

Reflection involves emotions, passions, intuitions and logical thinking processes. Teachers must be open-minded, responsible, and wholehearted (Stanley, 1998). Later in this section, several areas of concern regarding AR are discussed including the introspective nature of reflection, which is a possible source of concern of which teacher researchers should be aware. Reflectivity on teaching is mainly discussed in regard to its definition, the process involved, and the investigation of evidence gathered from reflection (Stanley, 1998). Drawing conclusions based on the evidence, as opposed to preconceived ideas, is crucial for AR to yield valuable findings. Stanley (1998) describes

> The process of developing a reflective teaching practice can be represented as a series of phases: (a) engaging with reflection, (b) thinking reflectively, (c) using reflection, (d) sustaining reflection, and (e) practicing reflection. The phases do not represent a sequence that is followed but rather moments in time and particular experiences that constitute a particular phase. (p. 585)

The reflection must involve active, persistent, and careful consideration.

Reflection within AR is also a possible source of weakness. The quality of AR depends on the sensitivity of the researcher whose data collection, analysis, and interpretations are influenced by their sense of self and identity (Somekh, 2006). Stanley (1998) believes teachers often find it difficult to accept evidence in their classroom teaching of pedagogical issues. This is especially true if these findings are unsettling or unflattering. At these times, teachers can continue the reflective process through readings, workshops, and conversations with other teachers. A teacher's initial beliefs may be especially influential. Burns (2009a) explains that "as the research proceeds, it's important not to be swayed by your initial interpretations but to keep an open mind and to see how further data collection provides new information and interpretations" (p. 124). However, in AR studies, such as this investigation, the teacher researcher is often investigating their own classroom. This dynamic makes objective observation difficult. Reason and Bradbury explain that "action researchers agree that objective knowledge is impossible, since the researcher is always a part of the world they study" (2008, p. 8).

Researchers must balance a research imperative to generate knowledge and a practical imperative to ensure a positive outcome for the student (Davison et al., 2012). However, AR has several stages (described in Section 4.3) each of which presents a challenge for the teacher researcher. The initial identification of an area of concern can be difficult. Teaching/learning situations can be complex and involve many problems and processes that are not easily identified (Davison et al., 2012). After a problem is identified, an action plan based in theory is implemented. AR must include both action and research, but this can be accomplished in many different ways using many different theories (Davison et al., 2012). Changes in one aspect of a project affects other aspects of the situation, which may then also need to be addressed (Brooke, 2013). The observations and responses made by teacher researchers lead to a deeper understanding of their situation and personal methodology. This personal development occurs even if the teacher finds it difficult to make satisfactory improvements in the initial problem area (Brooke, 2013). The reflective stage is a core element of AR but also a skill that needs to be developed. Teachers can use reflection as a tool after they understand what reflection is and how to do it (Stanley, 1998). Researchers might investigate these complexities and lose sight of the research objectives, or they might focus on the research objectives and fail to deal with the practical complexities (Davison et al., 2012). Burns (2009b) described the write up of AR studies as telling a research story. Therefore, it is important to document how the AR was undertaken and methodological problems that arise (Davison et al.,

2012). For AR to grow as a methodology, published studies need to address the process undertaken as well as the findings.

Throughout the process of conducting this study, I was conscious of the issues described above. Reflection was not only used as a tool to influence the direction the research would take, but it was also used to orient myself to the original goals of the study and to raise my consciousness for the actions I was undertaking as they related to the overall research story.

Theory in AR

AR's appeal as a methodology for second language acquisition stems from its ability to bridge the gap between theory and practice. Proponents of AR claim it lessens the divide between theory and practice (Crookes, 1993). Theory alone has a limited impact on classroom dynamics. Theories only benefit classroom practice if they bring to the surface, alter, and strengthen beliefs already present in the mind of the teacher (Johnson, 1996). These preconceived beliefs are generated through a teacher's experiences, both inside and outside the classroom. Expressing these beliefs helps teachers gain a better understanding of them and to alter their approaches to teaching (Johnson, 1996). In addition, teaching situations vary greatly and cannot easily be generalized. Teaching requires teachers to determine how to convey a topic to a specific group of students in a particular time and place (Johnson, 1996). Another contributor to this gap might be the lack of research into language teacher education classes (Bartels, 2002). Given the inconstant nature of teaching, there will always be a gap between what is taught in teacher education programs and what happens in the classroom. However, educators agree that AR minimizes the gap between theory and practice and that this gap needs to be bridged (Rainey, 2000).

Second language acquisition has been widely investigated using both qualitative and quantitative research methodologies. While it is typically considered a form of qualitative research, "AR gave substance to a paradigm shift about how research might be conducted in and about organizations" (Stephens et al., 2009, p. 469). In educational research contexts, AR is closely connected to the classroom and is therefore "particularly effective in TESOL (Teaching English to Speakers of Other Languages) settings" (Brooke, 2013, p. 432) because it is unique in how it associates research and practice. The research goals of this study are practical and consequently necessitate a methodology that bridges the gap between theory and practice. Reason and Bradbury (2008) believe a theory without action is meaningless. Furthermore, a strength of AR is that the research informs practice and vice versa (Avison et al., 1999). It is a "cycle of activities, including problem diagnosis, action intervention, and reflective learning" (Avison et al., 1999 p. 94).

As mentioned earlier, AR is particularly suitable for TESOL because it can be a pedagogical methodology. Researchers are now realizing that a teacher's knowledge about teaching is more than facts and theories, but this knowledge comes from experiences and classrooms to which teachers have been exposed (Johnson, 1996). Theories only influence classroom practice if the teacher makes sense of the theory. For this to happen, the theory must be situated in a context similar to their own (Johnson, 1996). AR is highly contextualized within a teacher's practice and provides an opportunity to look into, question, and investigate realities of one's practice (Burns, 2009a). AR provides the necessary structure to help teacher researchers through an investigative process.

In the early stages of AR, theory is used to justify an action plan. In AR, a researcher tries out a theory in a real classroom, gain insight from this experience, modify the theory based on the insight, and try it again. Each of these cycles adds to the theory (Avison et al., 1999). Theory guides the action plans. It must also form the basis for evaluating the outcomes. However, theory itself can be questioned and reflected upon. If a theory is inappropriate, it should be replaced by one which better explains the situation and predicts the outcomes of change (Davison et al., 2012). What is learned then leads to a new theory that is the basis for more experimentation and/or action taken. This leads to differences between what the theory can explain and what is seen through observation (Stephens et al., 2009). In addition, the teacher develops new abilities to create knowledge (Reason & Bradbury, 2008). Burns (2009a) describes this development by stating that "action researchers are interested in understanding what their explorations reveal and so developing personal practitioner knowledge and 'practical theories' is a central focus of this type of research" (p. 114).

The role of theory within AR, specifically the notion of AR being a generator of theory (Baskerville & Wood-Harper, 1996; McKay & Marshall, 2001), is also a possible source of concern. It can be difficult to develop a precise and holistic understanding of a teaching/learning situation and as a result, identifying a suitable intervention plan can be recondite. Even if the change is based on theory, you need a strong practical justification to implement these changes. The implemented change should be based in theory in regard to how it can improve the teaching/learning situation (Davison et al., 2012). However, one of the strengths of AR is its exploratory nature. Initial theories might need to be changed in subsequent cycles if they are found to be inappropriate (Davison et al., 2012). For this study, the initial theories (described in Chapter 3) were mainly proposals for how an alternative approach to vocabulary instruction could potentially benefit my students.

For this investigation, the theory used to justify the initial intervention (see Chapters 2 and 3) mainly consisted of a series of proposals and/or empirical evidence generated through investigations of higher proficiency language learners than the population under investigation in this study. By investigating an alternative student population and testing the proposals made in an authentic language classroom, new theories based in practice may be generated.

Mixed methods within AR studies

As mentioned in Section 4.1, this study used aspects of the mixed methods methodology to address the research questions. Johnson, Onwuegbuzie and Turner (2007) define mixed methods research as:

> Mixed methods research is the type of research in which a researcher or team of researchers combines elements of qualitative and quantitative research approaches (e.g., use of qualitative and quantitative viewpoints, data collection, analysis, inference techniques) for the broad purposes of breadth and depth of understanding and corroboration. (p. 123)

Creswell (2003) notes that mixed methods researchers believe that the research problem is best understood through the collection of diverse types of data. He also states that both quantitative and qualitative information are represented in the final database thus providing the best understanding of a research problem. Mackenzie and Knipe (2006) note that approaches to research design have become more complex while also becoming more flexible in their application of methods resulting in mixed methods becoming more common and accepted.

As described in Section 4.2, mixed method methodology is associated with the pragmatic paradigm that is considered to be consequence-oriented, problem-centered, and pluralistic (Creswell, 2003). Burke Johnson et al. (2007) state that "mixed methods research is, generally speaking, an approach to knowledge (theory and practice) that attempts to consider multiple viewpoints, perspectives, positions, and standpoints (always including the standpoints of qualitative and quantitative research)" (p. 113). The justification for using the mixed method methodology is rooted in the epistemological and ontological qualities of the pragmatic paradigm along with the flexibility and open-mindedness of the methodology itself.

Perhaps the most compelling reason for employing the mixed method methodology (or aspects of it) is the ability to better triangulate data sources. Themes that emerge through the process of qualitative data analysis (described in Section 4.6) can be compared against quantitative findings. Qualitative findings can also provide further insight and a deeper understanding of what is learned through the application of statistical measurements such as those used in this study. Jick (1979) asserts that the limitations of one method can be neutralized through the use of another method. Webb, Campbell, Schwartz, and Sechrest (1966) believe the use of two or more independent measurement processes reduces the uncertainty in the interpretations made during data analysis. This belief is also shared by other researchers (Burke Johnson et al., 2007; Creswell, 2003).

Triangulation is just a part of the rationale for utilizing a mixed method methodology. Sechrest and Sidana (1995) identified the following four advantages: for verification purposes; for estimating possible error in the underlying measures; for facilitating the monitoring of data collected, and; for delving into a data set to gain a better understanding of its meaning. Tashakkori and Teddlie (1998) also note that mixed method approaches provide greater insight into data analysis. Creswell (2003) that the use of this methodology allows the research problem to dictate the data collection process implemented.

The flexibility of AR is described throughout this chapter, and mixed methods can be incorporated into AR studies to address research problems when appropriate. Brooke (2013) shares a similar conviction when he writes that "the commitment to do what seems to be right for oneself and significant others should be the essence of educational action research with its multi-voiced and multi-methodological approach" (p. 434). He also states that "action research is well-suited as an approach in the TESOL environment. This is because, first, it is founded on humanitarian characteristics, second, it seeks more multi-voiced and multi-methodological findings and third, it strives to find solutions to real life problems" (p. 434). His second point endorses the use of both quantitative and qualitative data collection and analysis within AR studies. Kemmis and McTaggart (2008) also distinguish AR from strictly qualitative research when they state that "the participatory action researcher will differ from the one-sidedly qualitative approach that asserts that action can be understood only from a qualitative perspective" (p. 290). Similarly, Burke Johnson and Onwuegbuzie (2004) write that epistemological beliefs should not limit the data collection methods a researcher utilizes. Mackenzie and Knipe (2006) express the notion of incorporating the most appropriate data collection tools regardless of the overriding research paradigm or methodology when they state:

> researchers are not quantitative, qualitative or mixed methods researchers, rather a researcher may apply the data collection and analysis methods most appropriate for a particular research study. It may in fact be possible for any and all paradigms to employ mixed methods rather than being restricted to any one method, which may potentially diminish and unnecessarily limit the depth and richness of a research project. (p. 200)

In educational research, particularly in AR studies that seek improvement through change, the use of different methodologies (Kemmis, 1993), specifically the use of a variety of data collection tools, should not be restricted. This pluralism allows for more effective research (Burke Johnson and Onwuegbuzie, 2004). In Section 4.6, a more detailed description of quantitative research is given as it relates to this study.

4.4 Why AR was chosen for this study

AR was chosen for this study because of the important role reflection has, the relationship AR has with theory and the ability to triangulate the data collected. In addition, AR is suitable for the topic under investigation in this study because of its emergent nature. Furthermore, AR is an appropriate choice of methodology for research that has the ultimate goal of improving a pedagogical situation from both the teachers' and students' perspective.

The findings from AR studies are not generalizable, but the initial goal of this investigation was to produce findings that would ultimately help teachers improve a pedagogical situation. However, it was unclear how this would be accomplished, so this study needed a flexible research design that would allow knowledge to be gradually accumulated.

By using AR, the researcher is part of the process and can collect data from their own perspective. This firsthand access to information is unavailable through the use of other methodologies. Most methodologies encourage the researcher to distance themselves from the study to avoid influencing the results. However, in studies that are strongly pedagogically based, such as this investigation, it would be unnatural for a teacher researcher to be removed from the process. This close proximity to the intervention and data collection should be viewed as an advantage in this research context. Somekh (2006) described AR researchers as "insiders" with access to information typically unavailable through the use of other methodologies.

AR is a form of professional development in which the primary purpose is to learn more about what is happening in the classroom in order to improve the situation (Burns, 2009b). Teachers who engage in AR are able to address important concerns related to their classroom teaching (Avison et al., 1999; Wyatt, 2011). AR is a viable methodology for the context of this investigation because it is cyclical, and can fit into normal teaching activities. The cyclical aspect of AR can be easily readjusted for the university semester system, and the techniques and exercises that I use in everyday teaching routines can be adapted to become data collecting tools and intervention procedures.

Reflection is part of the AR process. The structure of the AR design accepts that researchers go through a process of self-understanding. Reflection encourages teachers to be open-minded. It also enables teachers to better understand the theories, knowledge gained through experience, and criteria they use to make classroom decisions (Somekh, 2006; Wyatt, 2011). At the beginning of the study, it was thought that this personal introspection would provide valuable insight throughout this investigation.

AR's strongest attribute might be that it bridges the gap between theory and practice. AR generates both practical and scholarly knowledge through a change or intervention (Davison et al., 2012). The research is connected with the classroom more so than with other methodologies. Teaching situations vary, so a theory cannot easily be generated to cover all situations. However, the initial action plan is based on theory, and the subsequent reflective cycles either support or bring into question the original premise. AR's primary purpose is to learn more about what is happening in the classroom in order to improve the situation (Burns, 2009b). The research goals for this study are largely pedagogical, so AR's close connection to the classroom is appealing.

While AR is not typically associated with statistical testing, quantitative analysis was possible within the research design for this study. This numerical data collection allows for a triangulation of the findings. This triangulation can strengthen or bring into question the findings of a study. Furthermore, the data collection tools that are available for AR also provide triangulation of findings in that this study can use both observational and non-observational methods and collect data from the students and the teacher.

Given the subject under investigation, the research context, and the resources available to the teacher researcher, AR was determined to be particularly suitable for this study. AR is an exploratory methodology, and the subject under investigation in this study requires a trial and error approach. While a great deal of forethought was put into the research design, the direction the study would go in is largely unknown at the initial stages. The cyclical nature of AR allows the researcher to recalibrate and incorporate newly discovered information. In addition, AR is particularly suitable for TESOL. It encourages the telling of the whole research story. This is especially useful for this study because it is such a long process and much is learned and changed at each stage. Finally, AR requires a stable teaching situation for the researcher. However, it is not overly burdensome because the time demands of conducting research can be managed and a great deal of the intervention procedures and data collection overlaps with the responsibilities of normal teaching.

AR is also an appealing choice of methodologies because of its potential influence on a researcher's teaching abilities. As described earlier, an investigation starts from an area of concern. It is a structured look into a change in procedures. The second stage (see Figure 4.1) is similar to what a teacher would normally do when trying to solve a classroom problem. Going through the stages in an AR study increases a teacher's awareness of their own teaching practice. They may enhance their self-efficacy and find the experience empowering. It may also make all future instruction more effective, and teachers may become more confident and autonomous. They could also improve their ability to create lessons based on student need.

The final reason AR was chosen as the methodology is its focus on the participants in the study (Avison et al., 1999; Somekh, 2006; Wyatt, 2011). AR is a partnership with the students: the researcher attempts to improve their teaching practice, which is also in the best interest of the students. The researcher acknowledges the students' desire to succeed, and the ultimate goal of the study is to improve the situation. AR takes into consideration the notion that students are not interested in theory, and that they want their time and effort to be utilized in the most efficient way possible. Furthermore, AR does not seek to produce findings that are universal. The researcher can focus on their students and what is best for them.

To summarize, AR was chosen for this study because of its distinctiveness as a methodology, the value it places on reflection and its connection with theory. In addition, AR allows for results to be triangulated through the use of a variety of data collection tools and quantitative analysis. It was also chosen because it is particularly suitable for the topic under investigation in this study. Finally, conducting AR can help me gain a better understanding of my teaching practice and ultimately benefit my students.

4.5 Participants and context

The data collection for this investigation was conducted over a 3-year period. During this time, three separate groups of participants took part in the study. While the three groups of participants were of a similar level in terms of (low) English proficiency, there were some important differences in regard to their experiences studying collocations and vocabulary. The three groups henceforth are referred to as Toyo 1, Toyo 2, and HUE 1. In the Japanese university system, there are two semesters per year, with the "spring" semester beginning in early April and finishing at the end of July and the "fall" semester begins in early October and finishes at the end of January. There are typically 15 weeks of instruction per semester, and each reflective cycle for this study was conducted over one university semester.

As a way of providing a background to the English educational experiences of these students I briefly describe the approach used for English instruction in Japanese schools. All of the participants in the three groups studied English in Japanese elementary school (for three to six years depending on the school), junior high school (three years), and senior high school (three years). In Japanese elementary schools, English is taught as a second language, where students typically take only two classes per week, which meet for 40 minutes per class. The classes focus on simple greetings and basic vocabulary, and the classes are largely conducted in Japanese and are not very communicative (Matsuura, Chiba, & Hilderbrandt, 2001; Ryan, 2009).

In Japanese junior and senior high school classes, the students usually study English twice a week for one hour per class. The classes focus on English vocabulary that is thought to be useful on university entrance exams (Benson, 1991; R. Berwick & S. Ross, 1989; Brown & Yamashita, 1995; Ryan, 2009), and grammar translation is still used as the major approach to English instruction. As a result, the students' receptive knowledge of English can be at a much higher level than their productive abilities (Ryan, 2009). However, it is common for Japanese high schools to employ native speaking assistant language teachers (Kubota, 2002; Matsuura et al., 2001; Scholefield, 1996). Typically, the Japanese homeroom instructor decides how often and in what capacity to use the assistant language teacher (ALT). Some ALTs simply read dialogues and provide a "native voice" to the text, while other ALTs are given the freedom to conduct their own classes, which tend to be more communicative (Scholefield, 1996).

While there are some exceptions, Japanese students usually have a limited ability to communicate in English when they enter university despite having studied it since elementary school. Nakata states (2006) that "there is a general consensus that the educational system has resulted in Japanese learners with weak English communication ability and low motivation to learn the language" (p. 166). The students are familiar with grammar translation but have had limited experience in communicative English classes. Vocabulary has been emphasized during junior and senior high school, but the targeted words are chosen to aid the students in preparation for entrance examinations. Japanese students entering college often display decreased levels of motivation or confidence to speak English (Gilfert & Croker, 1997 as cited in Kubo 2009). Kubo (2009) states thus, "Generally [Japanese university students] do not possess the confidence to speak despite having studied the target language for six years or more" (p. 40). For the reasons stated above, I use the term "low proficiency" throughout this book to describe the students level. A discussion of the students' previous experiences studying is given in Section 5.3.

Toyo 1 participants

The students who participated in the first reflective cycle in this study were all low-proficiency Japanese university students (TOEIC scores 210–425) from a private university in Gunma prefecture. The students were in their second year and were all science majors. The majority of the students were 19 or 20 years old at the time of the intervention, and the students who participated in this reflective cycle were evenly divided over two classes (twenty-one students in each class). Each class also had approximately the same number of male students as female students.

In their first year of university, every student had taken two communicative English classes: one in the "spring" semester and one in the "fall" semester. I taught both of these classes that met once per week for 90 minutes per class. It was during this first year that I used the approach based on the general service list, described in Chapter 1. This approach was largely unsuccessful in the goal of improving the students' productive abilities and is the motivation behind this current study. To paraphrase, the area of concern (as described in Section 4.3) for this investigation was the students' lack of productive ability using previously taught individual words from the GSL.

In total, forty-one students out of a possible forty-two chose to participate. I was conscious of creating, as close to possible, a pressure-free research environment, so I did not enquire into the one student's reason for not taking part in the study. As mentioned above, the participants' ESL proficiency was low but they were, for the most part, friendly and willing to engage in classroom activities. In brief, the important difference between this group and subsequent groups was the fact that I had previously taught these students individual words from the GSL.

Toyo 2 participants

The second group of students was from the same private university as the Toyo 1 group. This group participated in the second reflective cycle. They were also science majors, but this group consisted of only first-year students, so the majority of the students were 18 or 19 years old with approximately an equal number of male and female participants. The students were divided over six classes with the largest class having thirty-two students and the smallest class having twenty-four. The overall English level was thought to be similar to the Toyo 1 group, but this level assessment could not be confirmed through TOEIC scores because only a few of the students in this group had taken the test at that time. The data collection took place during their first university semester, the spring semester. The treatment period was therefore the first time I had taught this particular group of students (as opposed to the Toyo 1 group).

In total, 153 students chose to take part in this investigation. However, only 135 students completed the second questionnaire that was administered after the intervention period. Overall, this group of students, while not at a high English proficiency level, was friendly and engaged throughout the intervention period.

HUE 1 participants

The final group of participants, involved in the third and fourth reflective cycles in this study, was from a public university in Hokkaido, Japan. While the change in research contexts was not originally anticipated, it was advantageous in that I was able to investigate the same topic but collect data from a different group of students. I believe this change adds an increased level of robustness to the findings. The students were all in their first year and majoring in education. The students were mostly 18 or 19 years old with approximately 60 percent being female. There were also two female students who were slightly older (22 and 25 years old). The students were evenly distributed over two classes.

The first intervention period (reflective cycle 3) was during the spring semester (their first university semester), so it was also the first time I had taught this particular group of students. The fourth reflective cycle was conducted in the following semester, the fall semester. The students were also at a low proficiency level. TOEIC scores were not available, but having taught this group and the Toyo 2 group with similar materials, I estimated their English proficiency to be at a similar level.

Initially forty-three students agreed to take part in this study, but the post-intervention questionnaire was completed by only twenty-one participants for reflective cycle 3 and thirty-eight participants for reflective cycle 4 for unknown reasons. However, the students were friendly and willing to participate in the activities during the treatment period.

4.6 Data collection

AR avails itself of a wide range of data collection tools, and by including quantitative analysis within the AR methodology, numerical data can be collected and used to support or question findings as well as offer a level of triangulation.

For this study, triangulation of the data is achieved by utilizing different collection tools to investigate a common research question. Data collection techniques for qualitative research can be divided into two groups: observational and non-observational (Borg, 2011; Burns, 2009b). Observational methods include field notes, journals, recordings and transcripts of conversations that take place in a natural setting. Non-observational methods include questionnaires, interviews and student work (Brooke, 2013; Burns, 2009a). I believe another level of triangulation is achieved through the inclusion of data collection tools from both groups. For this study, field notes, questionnaires and audio-recordings were used; the justification for each of these data collection tools is given in Section 4.6.

Traditional methodologies emphasize that by collecting data through the use of multiple tools, researchers can maximize the chances of producing credible results. AR can also be enhanced in this way by using several data collection techniques (Burns, 2009a). Some researchers also encourage that quantitative data collection tools be used in collaboration with qualitative methods when they state that "evaluation demands the use of a variety of research tools, . . . including both quantitative and qualitative research methods" (Brown & Rogers, 2009, p. 248).

AR, while accepting of quantitative data, still relies on detailed qualitative analysis. Thick rich description is common in AR (Burns, 2009a). Burns encourages action researchers to tell their "research story" in chronological, selective, particular, or conceptual form (Burns, 2009a). This narrative aspect is not common in other methodologies.

Quantitative analysis within AR

This AR study uses quantitative measures to juxtapose the qualitative data. To justify this approach, criticisms of AR is described from a quantitative perspective, and reasons for including quantitative analysis within research projects are presented. The final paragraph presents some criticisms of quantitative data of which researchers should be aware.

While AR is viewed as being excellent for small-scale investigations, its appropriateness for other types of studies have been questioned by researchers who believe larger studies suitable for publication in peer-reviewed journals should use advanced analysis techniques, such as statistical measurements (Sholdt, Konomoto, Mineshima, & Stillwell, 2012). Quantitative researchers are critical of qualitative methods because they do not seek to prove the validity of their findings (Brooke, 2013). However, by incorporating measures found in quantitative research into qualitative studies, the strengths of one method compensate for the weaknesses of another. This combination can be accomplished by researchers using qualitative methods to quantify some data sets or by using research designs that integrate fieldwork and survey research; however, this approach is atypical (Jick, 1979).

While AR is not commonly associated with statistical results, I believe the findings from this AR study can be strengthened through their use. AR may incorporate quantitative measures of performance where change is proposed because these tests allow researchers to measure the improvements in performance resulting from the change (Davison et al., 2012). Researchers often choose only one form of data analysis; however, there are advantages to using an approach that incorporates aspects of different methodologies. To gain a deep understanding, research should be multi-methodological or triangulated. The data can then be compared to see if they corroborate one another (Brooke, 2013). Similarly, qualitative and quantitative methods should be viewed as being complementary. By using both methods together, the weaknesses found in a single method design are minimized (Jick, 1979). The research design for this investigation uses quantitative measures to determine both the initial and resulting levels of spoken fluency. Evaluations should consider the pre-intervention state in order to determine the success of the implemented change (Davison et al., 2012). In addition, the desired end-state should be formally identified in the planning phase. Quantitative measure can then be used to determine if the objectives have been met (Davison et al., 2012). Language teachers undertaking quantitative research need to use appropriate research designs, accurately interpret statistical results, and draw measured conclusions from these results (Sholdt et al. 2012).

Quantitative analysis has also received criticism as it relates to AR. AR presents several challenges for the quantitative researcher. AR is exploratory, so pre-ordinate planning is difficult because researchers cannot determine where an AR project will lead (Ross & Bruce, 2012). Furthermore, quantitative research relies on the randomization of professional learning strategies that is difficult to implement in AR projects (Ross & Bruce, 2012). While presenting numbers may be a part of data analysis, statistical calculations are not common (Burns, 2009a). Furthermore, incorporating statistical tests into a study involves more than collecting quantifiable data. Bachman (2004) explains that "in order to analyse quantitative data appropriately and meaningfully, we need to understand the specific assessment procedures or instruments we have used to collect the data, and the properties of the numbers these procedures provide" (p. 13). The difference between quantitative and qualitative research is that the two research methodologies represent different ways of thinking (Brooke, 2013). However, since qualitative research methodologies are accepted as equal in value to quantitative approaches (Avison et al., 1999), there is an opportunity to utilize the strengths of both approaches within a single study, in this case, an AR study.

Data collection tools

As described in Section 4.4, a strength of the qualitative research methodology is the ability to triangulate by using multiple kinds of data from different sources. Consequently, I have chosen to use questionnaires, field notes, and audio-recordings as data collection tools for this investigation. The following sections describes each tool and its appropriateness for this study.

Questionnaires

Questionnaires are a versatile data collection tool that can target specific data through the use of explicit questions and can be used to collect both subjective qualitative data and quantitative data. Dörnyei (2007) explains that "[questionnaires] are relatively easy to construct, extremely versatile and uniquely capable of gathering a large amount of information quickly in a form that is readily processible" (pp. 101–2). Furthermore, Brown and Rogers state "you may need to use a survey in order to understand better how things are really operating in your own, personal environment – in your classroom or other learning setting" (2009, p. 117). Qualitative data can be collected via a questionnaire through the use of open-ended questions. These questions can yield unexpected data and "provide a far greater richness than fully quantitative data" (Dörnyei, 2007, p. 107). Turner (1993) believes open-ended questions allow respondents to express attitudes and opinions that are not offered through the use of closed questions and that they may be a more accurate measurement of their opinions. One approach to analyze open-ended data is to look for emerging themes or patterns. Categories should emerge from the data and be supported by quotes that are used to demonstrate the concepts (Burns, 2009a).

For this study, questionnaires were chosen with both the research context and research questions in mind. Questionnaires are a useful data collection tool in studies investigating a large number of participants. Dörnyei (2007) notes that they are efficient in both time and effort required for administration and data processing. The research questions initially focused on the learners' opinions and the anonymity of questionnaires was therefore seen as being advantageous to maximize the chances of honest responses. Brown and Rogers (2009) state that "typically, survey studies focus on a group's attitudes, opinions, and/or characteristics" (p. 3). Furthermore, as Busch (1993) notes questionnaire items employing Likert type scales are commonly used for investigating opinions, beliefs, attitudes and beliefs about language learning. In addition to Likert scale items, open-ended questions were included because they are necessary when we do not fully know the range of possible answers (Turner, 1993) that, for an exploratory study such as this, is beneficial.

In order for questionnaires to yield useful data, careful consideration must be a part of their creation. An ill-constructed questionnaire can provide unreliable data (Dörnyei, 2007). Questionnaires should be short with clear instructions, examples on how to respond to the contained items, and translations for respondents who might not fully understand what is expected of them. Turner (1993) states that "when questionnaires are presented in a language that respondents are engaged in learning, limitations in their language ability may prevent them from responding in a manner that accurately reflects their true opinion or attitude" (p. 736). Piloting a questionnaire beforehand, with a similar group to the target participants, can help address these issues. Furthermore, if an online questionnaire is used, they should be easy to complete, be easy to access and provide anonymity for the participants (Lefever, Dal & Matthíasdóttir, 2006). I have responded to these issues by constructing and piloting a short questionnaire with a Japanese translation for all instructions and items. Dörnyei (2007) also notes that for qualitative research, questionnaires have a weakness in that the respondent only has a superficial and brief engagement with the topic. To address this issue, I believe questionnaires should be used in conjunction with other data collection tools.

Several of the research questions for this study are suitably addressed through the collection of data via a questionnaire. From reflective cycle 1, all four research questions focus on the students' opinions of the collocation focus. As described above, questionnaires are useful for collecting data pertaining to attitudes and opinions. In the subsequent reflective cycles, open questionnaire items were added to enable the students to expand on their responses about their perceptions of the collocation focus. This study was exploratory in nature, and the open questionnaire items added richness to the data collected and allowed me to better address the research questions pertaining to the students' opinions about the intervention procedure.

For reflective cycle 1, a paper version of the questionnaire was given to the students in the final class, and the findings were compiled manually. A description of the procedure used to administer this questionnaire, to pilot the questionnaire, and to ensure an accurate translation of the questionnaire can be seen in Section 5.2. For the final three reflective cycles, the questionnaire was administered online to make data analysis more efficient. In reflective cycle 2, the questionnaire was completed in class, while for the final two reflective cycles, the students were instructed to complete the questionnaire online after class. For the final three questionnaires, the students were instructed that they could answer the open items in Japanese, and an experienced Japanese professor translated their responses into English before data analysis.

Field notes

Data collected through the use of field notes can juxtapose the data elicited from questionnaires. Wallace (1998) describes field notes as being flexible and easily implemented, and Dörnyei (2007) writes that an orderly set of field notes can be a valuable source of data. Field notes do not require anyone else besides the researcher, and for the purposes of classroom research, they can be collected during lessons, while the students are engaged in an activity. Wallace (1998) explains that field notes provide a self-evaluation of a lesson or activity, and they allow the teacher/researcher to focus on a particular aspect of a class. Field notes enhance awareness of one's practice and are an excellent resource for reflection.

A concern with using field notes is the ability of the researcher to record her/his observations without delay. Wallace (1998) cautions that fleeting observations are easily lost and that fatigue can impair recall if the researcher does not record their thoughts in a timely manner. Nunan (1992) presents several techniques for documenting classroom interaction, but researchers need to consider their teaching context and research goals when deciding on how to record observations and what is relevant.

The process of writing field notes has not been examined closely enough. While it is not practical to have universal guidelines for writing field notes, researchers can develop a specific set of guidelines to better understand their particular research context through their use (Emerson, Fretz, & Shaw, 2011).

There are many possibilities for how an event can be captured through field notes. How researchers understand and recount events varies, so different researchers write different notes depending on variables such as their area of research interest, their personality, mood, and background. Field notes transform observed events into words on paper and thus selection is required. The writer omits certain things while focusing on others. Some researchers emphasize certain aspects while ignoring others (Emerson et al., 2011). Geertz (1973) mentions how field notes allow a research to revisit a passing event. The researcher will have a written account of an event, which at first may appear innocuous but later prove relevant.

Given their proximity to the participants, researchers using field notes cannot be completely neutral. Field researchers actively participate in the context and cannot be completely detached from the observed phenomena. This immersion gives the researcher a deeper sensitivity to the process under investigation and the interactions that take place during the process (Emerson et al., 2011). The first-hand interactions with the participants may provide a greater understanding that would not be available through observation alone. However, Karp and Kendall (1982) believe that the researcher, despite being part of the observed event, still differs from the participants in commitment and constraints.

For this study, the data collected through the use of field notes was not of the same quantity or quality as the data collected through the questionnaires and audio-recordings. However, this data did provide another perspective on the intervention, and when considered alongside the data collected through the other tools, offered some insight into the area under investigation. Field notes were chosen as a data collection tool because they could be used to characterize the students' development of competence in using collocations as assessed by the teacher throughout the course (research question three for the final three reflective cycles). I wrote the field notes immediately after the classes finished and focused on creating a weekly log that captured the events that took place and their sequence. An excerpt from my field notes can be seen in Appendix 8.

Audio recordings

The final data collection tool described here is audio recordings. For this study, participants create a narrative from a picture sequence. This procedure was chosen because it had been previously used in fluency research (Hansen, Gardner, & Pollard, 1998; Lennon, 1990a, 1990b). Furthermore, for this investigation a picture sequence was appropriate for the students' level and standardized the speech sample during data collection (Wood, 2010). The recording elicited through this procedure is also advantageous for assessing fluency when compared to a speech sample taken from an interview or conversation because it avoids the variance created through different interlocutors and ensures the ability for all students to express themselves. In addition, Pawley and Syder (1983) state that narrative discourse constitutes a great deal of everyday speech.

Audio recordings have been used in previous fluency studies. Kluge and Taylor (1999), Kubo (2009), and Kessler (2010) used audio-recordings in their studies and found them useful for fluency development. Kessler noted that most of the students enjoyed the taping procedure. Similar to my study, these three studies used an initial audio-recording of a speech sample and compared it with a post-intervention recording. While fluency was the focus of these studies, during the intervention, the students did additional recordings throughout the intervention.

The Kluge and Taylor study (1999) focused on fluency, but they also emphasized the importance of developing a procedure to implement an outside of class taping process for their students. Their fluency assessment used the average words per minute for the initial and post-intervention speech samples. Their findings showed an improvement, but they did not conduct a statistical analysis (aside from calculating the mean and standard deviation) to determine if the improvement was significant.

Kubo (2009) also used words per minute to measure fluency. His study investigated if students who engaged in outside of class pair taping exercises would improve their spoken fluency and confidence in using English orally. His results showed the audio-recording task had a positive effect on both measures.

Kessler's fluency study (2010) used a similar length audio recording (about 2 minutes) to my study. However, in his study, rate, pausing, utterance length, and volume were measured individually on a six-point scale, while in my study, I compiled these variables under a general heading of listener perception and used a seven-point scale. Kessler compared audio-recordings for the aspects of fluency mentioned above in relation to the observable influence of anxiety on fluency for audio-recordings taken in two different environments: recorded in a laboratory setting and recorded using mobile audio devices (MP3 players). The recordings made using mobile devices such as MP3 players were ranked more positively for the fluency variables described above than using an audio laboratory. I chose a setting similar to the laboratory in Kessler's study, so I could ensure completion of the speaking tasks. In Kessler's study, the students identified their self-consciousness and anxiety resulting from the presence of other students in the laboratory. In my study, the students completed the recordings in an empty classroom, hopefully, minimizing the negative effects of anxiety.

Previous fluency studies (Griffiths, 1991; Lennon, 1990a; Riggenbach, 1991; Schmidt, 1992) have identified rate, pausing, utterance length, and volume as characteristics of fluency. Listener perceptions are also important to consider when assessing fluency. The use of audio-recordings in fluency studies is suitable as it accounts for these characteristics. However, Kessler (2010), when referring to the use of audio-recordings taken outside of class, notes that "students may be more inhibited" (p. 362). He also writes that "speaking can heighten anxiety and anxiety negatively affects fluency" (p. 362). The pressure of doing the audio-recording might add to this anxiety. Similarly, Emerson et al. (2011) contend that audio-recordings do not capture everything that is occurring. The speech sample is dependent on when, where and how the recorder is used. The participants might be negatively influenced in their performance depending on how they react to the recorder's presence.

For this study, audio-recordings were used in the second and third reflective cycles to address the research questions pertaining to differences seen in the students' spoken fluency between an initial and a summative spoken assessment task. The procedure used to administer the pre-intervention and post-intervention spoken assessments for reflective cycles two and three is described in Section 5.3.

The three data collection tools described above were each chosen with careful consideration of their strengths and weaknesses in regard to addressing the research questions for this study. Their use in conjunction should minimize their respective weaknesses and offer the quality of triangulation to my findings. A summary of research questions initially targeted through the use of each data collection tool can be seen in Table 4.1.

Table 4.1 Data collection tools for the research questions

	Questionnaires	Field notes	Audio-recordings
Reflective cycle 1 research questions (Section 5.2)	1, 2, 3, and 4	Used, but did not address any specific research question	Not used
Reflective cycle 2 research questions (Section 5.3)	1, 2, and 6	3	4 and 5
Reflective cycle 3 research questions (Section 6.2)	1, 2, 4, and 6	3	5
Reflective cycle 4 research questions (Section 6.3)	1, 2, 4 and 5	3	Not used

Approach to analysis

The research design for this study did not strictly adhere to any one methodology. Consequently, a range of data collection tools (described in Section 4.6) were available and were selected based on how well they could address the research problems under investigation in this study. The qualitative data underwent thematic analysis (TA) as it was thought this process would reveal underlying themes present in the field notes and student responses from the questionnaires. Braun and Clarke (2006) note TA's flexibility when they state "thematic analysis is not wed to any pre-existing theoretical framework, and so it can be used within different theoretical frameworks (although not all), and can be used to do different things within them" (p. 85). They also mention that TA is relatively easy to conduct and provides core skills for qualitative analysis. TA is flexible in that it can be used in different ways to determine themes as long as the researchers are consistent in their approach within any particular analysis. Furthermore, it can provide a rich and detailed report of the qualitative data while still uncovering complex elements to consider (Braun & Clarke, 2006).

As mentioned above, TA is flexible in how it can be conducted; however, there are commonalities in how it is commonly used by various researchers. Brooke (2013) describes the overall process as being

> commonly done using a word or phrase to amalgamate data segments which inform the research objectives. Once coding is accomplished, analysis often consists of: summarizing the predominance of codes, presenting similarities and differences in related codes or comparing one or more codes. (p. 432)

Unlu and Wharton (2015) emphasize that coding can be done progressively to reveal salient themes. A thorough description of the process is given by Braun and Clarke (2006). They identify the following six phases of analysis:

Phase 1: familiarising yourself with your data.
Phase 2: generating initial codes.
Phase 3: searching for themes.
Phase 4: reviewing themes.
Phase 5: defining and naming themes.
Phase 6: producing the report. (pp. 92–9)

They also emphasize that the themes should emerge from the data and not simply from the questions that were asked during the data collection.

While the process appears linear as presented using the six phases, in actuality, it is iterative. Braun and Clarke (2006) explain that "analysis is not a linear process where you simply move from one phase to the next. Instead, it is more recursive process, where you move back and forth as needed, throughout the phases" (p. 92). The recursive nature thematic analysis is also present when considering themes that emerge over several reflective cycles. Burns (2005b) states that "research themes that link prospectively and retrospectively through different iterations of the research serve to strengthen explanations that are developed over periods of time" (p. 67). Kemmis and McTaggart (2008) emphasize that the goal of identifying themes within data sets is to identify problems and issues that can be improved upon. The importance of a theme is not determined by the number of times it occurs within the data set, but it is ascertained by how the theme relates to the research questions.

Burns (2005b) states that "the aim of the research is to provide rich descriptions and practical solutions that might have resonance for other practitioners in comparable situations" (p. 67). McGregor and Murnane (2010) add that "the role of researchers is to create an audit trail showing the thinking behind their interpretation of the participants' accounts of their world" (p. 423). Consequently, the following paragraphs describe the thematic analysis process I used when examining the qualitative data.

The qualitative data from both the questionnaire and my field notes were analyzed through a procedure in which each student response was assigned one or more "tags." The tags referred to possible themes or categories of responses. After a data set was completed, all the responses for a particular tag were considered as a whole. From this analysis, further sub-themes emerged and the tagging procedure was repeated. This process was muddled, and responses often had to be reclassified; however, I believe it exposed the themes present within each data set. To exemplify, the following student response (taken from Table 5.13) was initially given the tag "problems with vocabulary study":

> I had trouble when I had to figure out how I can use the words in a particular situation.

After this data set was analyzed, all of the responses with this tag were considered together. These responses were then assigned a sub-category tag such as "differences from their L1" or "semantics." The response given above was assigned the tag "use." While this entire process was time consuming, it did allow for a structured analysis of a large data set.

The surveys used in the four reflective cycles also elicited quantitative data that were subjected to statistical analysis. For each questionnaire administered over the course of this study, there were several Likert scale items. The initial research questions (Section 1.6 or 5.2) focused on the students' attitudes toward a change in procedure for vocabulary instruction. The inclusion of these questionnaire items was appropriate because "Likert scales are generally useful for getting at respondents' views, judgments, or opinions about almost any aspect of language learning" (Brown & Rogers, 2009, p. 120). By using a numerical scale, Likert scale responses represent a form of interval data that can be used to calculate percentages, means, and standard deviations (Bachman, 2004; Brown & Rogers, 2009; Larson-Hall, 2010). These findings could then be compared over the course of the four reflective cycles.

For the audio-recordings, native speaker judgment was used to measure fluency. Three expert judges assessed the voice recordings blind on a seven-point scale with a score of one representing extreme dysfluency and a score of seven representing extreme fluency. This scoring procedure was chosen for two reasons. First, it has been previously used in past fluency research (McGuire, 2009). Second, I believe this scoring procedure dovetails well with the previously mentioned (Section 3.4) definition for the term "fluency," which is from Lennon's study (1990a) in which "fluency is an impression on the listener's part that the psycholinguistic process of speech planning and speech production are functioning easily and efficiently" (p. 391).

Prior to the assessment period, the three expert judges took part in a benchmark session to standardize the assessment criteria. The benchmark session procedure was based on Wood's (2010) study in which expert judges were used to identify formulaic sequences in spoken discourse. Initially, I sent each judge an information package including the spoken assessment task completed by the students and the fluency definition described above. I also included three different voice samples that I had personally assessed at the following three scores: two, four and six. After the judges had read through the information package and listened to the three recordings, I sent each judge six voice recordings for them to assess. Each judge received the same six recordings, and these recordings were different from the initial three that I had assessed. Three of the six recordings were graded differently by the judges; however, in each case the grades only differed by one point on the seven-point scale. We briefly discussed the three recordings that received different scores via Skype, and a second set of three recordings was sent to each judge. These recordings were all given the same scores. All voice recordings used for the benchmark session were excluded from further analysis. This overall approach to analysis was implemented with the goal of minimizing the potential problems with data collecting described in the next section.

Data collection concerns

AR studies have a potential weakness in regard to both the data collection and analysis. Specifically, the researcher needs to be aware of the quality of the data collected, the influence conducting an AR study has on the results, and the applicability of the results for other situations.

Perhaps the greatest potential area of concern is in regard to the data collected during an AR study. In this study, AR relies on the collaboration between myself as the researcher and the students as participants in the investigation. The nature of the power relationships affects the data (Somekh, 2006), so as the researcher, I need to account for and minimize this effect. Furthermore, AR teachers need to assure the quality of the data they collect; otherwise, their findings are not of value (Borg, 2011; Dörnyei, 2007). AR is exploratory and the research goals might change over the course of an investigation; however, researchers should have a plan for data collection that allows for the greatest amount of objectivity. Researchers need to identify and use appropriate metrics of performance to objectively evaluate the outcomes of the intervention (Davison et al., 2012), since it can be difficult to assess the effectiveness of the change. After the intervention period, the reflective stage is another potential quagmire because a challenge for AR researchers is to make sense of the data in order to show what is revealed (Burns, 2009a). The quality of data is crucial for any methodology; however, action researchers need to be especially vigilant in this regard given their close proximity to the participants. Given the practical goals of my study, I focused on the well-being of the students and adjusted the research goals accordingly while collecting data to determine student improvement.

The teacher researcher is an influential part of an AR study. Others note that "traditionally scientific enquiry takes place in a closed system where the influence of the environment is minimized whereas in AR the influence of the environment is part of the experiment" (Stephens et al., 2009, p. 471). They expand on this point by stating "AR recognizes and integrates the influence of the environment into the enquiry process" (Stephens et al., 2009, p. 473). For the purposes of this investigation, my influence on the data collection helps ground the findings by connecting the research to practice.

Traditionally research has strived to produce findings that are applicable to other situations. Burns (2009a) notes that "one point to remember is that action research does not set out to answer questions that can be generalised to other classrooms. Nor does it aim for the kind of objectivity required in experimental quantitative research" (p. 128). Wallace (1998) presents a similar point when he states "[other methodologies] are much more concerned with what is universally true, or at least generalizable to other contexts" (p. 17). For this study, the goals (as seen in the research questions presented in Chapter 1 and Sections 5.2, 5.3, 6.2, and 6.3) focus on improving my own teaching practice in order for my students to more effectively use the target language to improve their productive abilities.

Ethics

The ethical aspects of conducting an AR research study with Japanese university students were considered prior to the undertaking of the data collection period of this study. This process focused on the principles that should be considered for conducting research in language classes, the issue of informed consent, the consent form given to the students, and the review process conducted by the Aston University ethics committee.

Wiles, Heath, Crow and Charles (2005) state that "social research ethics are closely aligned with medical research ethics" (p. 6) and that "principle-based approaches involve adherence to moral principles that can be outlined as follows:

- Autonomy: people must be free to make their own informed decisions about participation in research
- Non-maleficence: research must not inflict harm
- Beneficence: research should benefit others
- Justice: people must be treated equally within the research process." (p. 7)

Given the anonymity in the data collection, the research goals, and the pedagogical nature of the research design, I believed the later three moral principles listed above would be accounted for throughout this study. However, the first principle, autonomy, needed to be addressed.

Wiles et al (2005) write that there is a "need to provide sufficient information to enable participants to make informed decisions about participation" (p. 12) and that "information provision generally comprises written information in conjunction with, or followed by, oral information" (p. 12). The student population under investigation in this study were low-proficiency English language learners, so I compensated for the students' lack of English comprehension by providing a Japanese translation on the consent form described below. I also enlisted the help of a Japanese member of the English faculty at both universities in which I conducted this study. These professors were well informed about the nature of my research and both agreed to serve as intermediaries if any students had questions or concerns. However, to the best of my knowledge, no students approached these professors over the four reflective cycles. The students were also made aware that they were free to withdraw from the study at any time. I am confident that through my oral description and the Japanese translation the students were well aware of what was expected of them.

The use of consent forms is subject to some debate as there is a greater chance that having a signed consent form could compromise confidentiality and anonymity (Coomber, 2002). However, I believe that the benefit of receiving informed consent outweighs this potential risk. When designing the consent form, I considered the advice of other researchers and provided the information in a user-friendly way (Wiles, Crow, Charles & Heath, 2007). I also tried to "avoid information sheets that look too official" (Truman, 2003). For the issues of informed consent and consent forms, Wiles et al. (2005) state that "the important message emerging from work in this area is that it is crucial that researchers understand the information needs of the group that they want to research and that they use this knowledge to provide information in a way that will enable potential study participants to understand what participation will involve" (p. 13).

The final issue described here involves the review process. For research proposals, Stanley and Wise (2010) state that "it takes a knowledgeable expert assessor to evaluate the appropriateness of the stance adopted" (p. 7). They also state that professional bodies "are the fundamental focal point for ensuring good practice across many aspects of professional conduct" (p. 8). Accordingly, prior to the treatment period for this first study, the Languages and Social Science (LSS) research ethics committee at Aston University approved my proposal for data collection. Each participant signed a consent form that described the nature of the research and explained that her or his participation was on a voluntary basis. The consent form was translated into Japanese to ensure the students fully understood what was being asked of them. The LSS research ethics committee recommended the use of a drop box for the consent forms, so the students would not feel pressured into participating; this suggestion was followed, thus ensuring both anonymity and voluntary participation. A copy of the consent form used for this study can be seen in Appendix 19.

4.7 Intervention procedures

The intervention procedures, along with the results, for reflective cycles 2 and 3 are described in Chapter 5, while Chapter 6 presents the intervention procedures and results for reflective cycles 3 and 4. By describing what occurred in each reflective cycle in turn, the emergent nature of how the research progressed over time and the reasons for changes to the procedures can be illuminated. As is common in AR, the findings from one reflective cycle influenced the intervention procedures in the next reflective cycle.

In order to illustrate the progress of the research over the four cycles, Table 4.2 summarizes the participants at each stage, the focus in the collocation list, the intervention activities, the initial purpose and the data collection tools used.

4.8 Conclusion

AR was chosen for this study because it is flexible, exploratory and pedagogical. AR studies investigate an issue that directly affects the students, as was the case

Table 4.2 Summary of the progress for the four research cycles

Reflective cycle	Participants	Collocation list	Intervention	Initial purpose	Data collection tools used
1	Toyo 1	Frequent verb + noun	Writing sentences	Exploratory Viability of teaching collocations	Field notes Post-treatment questionnaire
2	Toyo 2	Delexicalized verb + noun	Matching exercises Receptive vs productive tasks	Receptive vs productive tasks for collocations in regard to spoken fluency	Field notes Initial questionnaire Post-treatment questionnaire Audio-recordings
3	HUE 1	Delexicalized verb + noun	Productive tasks	Highly demanding productive tasks for collocations in regard to spoken fluency	Field notes Initial questionnaire Post-treatment questionnaire Audio-recordings
4	HUE 1	Frequent adjective + noun	Productive tasks	Comparing students' feelings toward adjective + noun collocations compared to verb + noun	Field notes Post-treatment Questionnaire

in this study that began with my realization that my approach to vocabulary instruction was flawed. My ultimate goal is to produce findings that can shed light on this issue and offer a solution, and an AR design can help me accomplish this aim.

The First and Second Reflective Cycles

5.1 Introduction

This chapter, along with Chapter 6, presents the findings of this investigation in chronological order. This chapter conveys the findings of reflective cycles 1 and 2, while Chapter 6 focuses on reflective cycles 3 and 4.

5.2 First reflective cycle

As is frequently the case in AR, the research questions in this reflective cycle were different from those that emerged in the subsequent cycles. As I explained in Chapter 4, one of the reasons for choosing AR as a methodology was its exploratory nature. It was therefore likely to be the case that my focus and key concerns would change over time. When I started this investigation, I was unsure of how to proceed. My first goal for the first reflective cycle in the AR process was to determine if there was potential in an increased focus on collocations in my classes. My second goal was to develop a set of procedures and activities to introduce the students to collocations. My teaching approach would ultimately need to be efficient in regard to class time and seen as worthwhile in the opinion of the students. If I dedicated too much time to teaching collocations, I would not be able to cover the other required components of my curriculum. I also wanted to use an approach that would parallel approximately the same amount of time as my former instruction using the General Service List (GSL) did in the previous semester. Furthermore, if the students did not recognize the value of the new approach, they would not be receptive to the change in procedure and the move away from the GSL instruction (described in Chapter 1). Therefore, I decided to focus on the learners' responses to studying collocations and to gauge the amount of class time required for this new form of instruction. I believed the experiences gained through collecting the data and the insights I would gain would provide a template on which future reflective cycles could be based.

Why are learners' responses important?

When designing lessons and instructing classes, teachers often put value in their own experiences as language learners; they express their views and beliefs about techniques, methods and/or approaches that were successful for them (Prentice, 2010). However, the teacher's view does not necessarily account for learners' personality, aptitude, culture or many of the other factors that can determine if a learner is successful or not.

Learners' responses refer to how effective a certain approach to teaching is in their opinion. In terms of language learning, the learner puts more value on, and in turn be more willing to engage in, activities they feel improve their L2 proficiency. Specifically for this study, the relevant question was whether students felt that a focus on collocations improved their productive ability in spoken English.

Learners' responses can help teachers understand the underlying beliefs students possess toward language learning. Learner beliefs are an important aspect of the language learning experience (Oxford & Lee, 2008; White, 2008). For language learning, learner beliefs are similar to learners' responses because they refer to how learners view language, language learning, and the contexts they participate in as language learners. White states, "Beliefs are important because learners hold their beliefs to be true and these beliefs then guide how they interpret their experiences and how they behave" (2008, p. 121). Beliefs affect the effort students put into their work. If learners feel a new approach is superior to what they have experienced in the past, they may be more willing to partake.

Research questions for reflective cycle 1

The research questions I developed directly influenced the items used in the questionnaire. At this point in the research, I understood that reflective cycle 1 would be the first in a series of steps to investigate the area of concern of this study. Therefore, I decided to embrace the exploratory nature of AR and seek data that would further justify the direction of my research and provide insight into how to proceed.

The research questions focused on the learners' responses to the activities that I used to teach the targeted collocations from list 1 (described in Section

5.2 and included in Appendix 1). I was primarily interested in eliciting their responses to the following five issues:

- if studying collocations was worth their time and effort,
- if they felt able to productively use the targeted collocations in conversations,
- if this approach was superior to targeting individual words,
- if writing sentences was helpful,
- if 15 collocations per week was a suitable number.

In later reflective cycles, these learner responses would need to be reconfirmed, especially in regard to their perceived ability to use the targeted collocations productively. However, I felt that the responses to these initial research questions would rationalize my line of inquiry and provide insight into how to progress.

The research questions for reflective cycle 1 were as follows:

1. What are low-proficiency Japanese university students' responses to studying collocations?
2. Will the students feel capable of using the collocations in conversation?
3. In the students' opinion, is the productive task of writing sentences helpful?
4. From the students' perspective, how many collocations should be targeted each week?

Procedures for reflective cycle 1

The research was carried out during the students' communicative English classes that met once a week. The collocation intervention (which are described in the following paragraph) was presented to the students as part of their normal class work. The participants for this reflective cycle (the Toyo 1 group described in Section 4.5) spent a similar amount of class time and did a similar amount of homework in the vocabulary component of their first year communicative English class, which I taught the previous year. This previous in-class experience, which focused on individual words taken from the first 500 words of the GSL, was used as a comparison for considering their responses to my new teaching approach.

The intervention consisted of giving the students fifteen collocations from collocation list 1 (see Appendix 1 for collocation list 1) a week. For explicit instruction, ten to fifteen vocabulary items is seen as being a suitable number for low-proficiency students (Morgan & Rinvolucri, 2004). The process and criteria used to create the collocation list are described in more detail in Section 5.2.

Before the first set of collocations was given to the students, I briefly explained the term "collocation." So as not to confuse the students, I simplified the definition for collocations to the following: two or more words often used together. The students wrote the weekly collocations (the collocations targeted each week) into a vocabulary notebook, and their homework was to write a Japanese translation for each collocation and a sentence using the given collocation. Researchers have endorsed the use of L1 for vocabulary instruction (Lewis, 2008; Morgan & Rinvolucri, 2004; Nation, 2008; 2004; Ur, 1991). Morgan and Rinvolucri (2004) state that "the mother tongue is the launch pad for the second language (p. 8). The following week a short activity using the previous week's collocations was given to the students; typical activities recommended for vocabulary instruction used during this intervention include matching the verb and noun components of the collocations (Morgan & Rinvolucri, 2004), completing a cloze activity (Nation, 2001; Ur, 1991), or having pairs of students exchange their vocabulary books and quiz each other (Lindstromberg & Boers, 2008). The researchers mentioned above recommended these activities for the teaching of individual lexical items, but the activities were easily adapted for the teaching of collocations. Furthermore, by using a follow-up activity in the following class the overall procedure repeatedly exposed the students to the targeted collocations, which is also seen as being an effective strategy for acquiring new vocabulary (Lewis, 2008; Schmitt, 2008; Ur, 1991). Lewis (2008) asserts that "we acquire an individual word by meeting it a number of times . . . meeting it frequently with no explicit teaching is both a necessary and sufficient condition for its acquisition" (p. 51). The students then wrote the next week's collocations into their vocabulary notebooks. The total class time each week for this process was approximately 15 minutes. Every week I collected the notebooks at the end of class and corrected the students' sentences (described in the following paragraph). The students were able to collect their books later that day or any time after. Both Brown (2007) and Ur (1991) have advocated that vocabulary should be taught in separated, spaced sessions. Ur (1991) states that "it is better to teach vocabulary in separate, spaced sessions than to teach it all at once" (p. 67).

The feedback consisted of reading the students' sentences, and identifying the type of errors present (missing words, verb mistake, spelling, wrong word choice, etc.). Each kind of error was assigned a symbol, which would then be written (in red) on the sentences. For each sentence containing an error, the students had to rewrite the sentence and try to correct any errors present. If the student were unable to correct the error in this second attempt, I would write the correct sentence. Occasionally, class time was available to have the students work in pairs and help each other with error correction.

This routine was repeated for four weeks. In the next week's class, the students engaged in activities targeting the fourth set of collocations, but I did not introduce a new set of collocations to the students. Thirty minutes of the following week's class, the sixth class, was dedicated to reviewing the first four sets of collocations. During the next week's class, the first sixty collocations were tested. The test lasted 20 minutes and consisted of three sections: matching verb and noun components, completing a cloze activity, and writing sentences. The actual test for the first four sets of collocations can be seen in Appendix 5. The test sections were similar to the class activities and homework.

This whole procedure was then repeated for the second half of the semester. However, I made one change in procedure for the sets of collocations targeted in these weeks. Instead of having the students write Japanese translations for the collocations as part of their homework, I created a matching exercise that required the students to match the English collocation with its Japanese translation. The students completed this exercise in class as they copied the targeted collocations into their notebooks. After three or four minutes, I showed the class the correct answers for the matching exercise. An example matching exercise can be seen in Appendix 6. The reasoning for this change in procedure is described in Section 5.2. Table 5.1 summarizes the weekly activities and intervention procedure for reflective cycle 1.

In total, the collocation component accounted for 30 percent of the students' final grade (15 percent per test). This whole procedure was identical to that of the previous year with the only difference being that the students studied collocations as opposed to individual words from the first 500 words on the GSL.

Collocation lists

Over the four reflective cycles that constitute this investigation, three different collocation lists were used with the students in the study. The first collocation list was a collection of frequent verb + noun collocations (henceforth referred to as "Collocation list 1"). This collocation list was used in reflective cycle 1, but subsequent reflective cycles used a different list due to the findings of the first cycle, which are discussed in Section 5.2. The second collocation list, which was used in reflective cycle 2, is a collection of delexicalized verb + noun collocations. This list was also used for the third reflective cycle. The third collocation list was

Table 5.1 Summary of procedure for reflective cycle

Week	In-class collocation work	Class time required in minutes	Homework
1	There were no collocation exercises done during the first class.		
2	Explain the term collocation. Students copied the first set of collocations into their notebooks.	5	Write a Japanese translation for each collocation in the first set. Write a sentence for each collocation.
3	Class activity using the first set of collocations (see Section 5.2 for examples of the activities used). Students copied the second set of collocations into their notebooks.	15	Write translations and sentences for second set of collocations. Make corrections for the first set sentences.
4	Class activity using the second set of collocations. Students copied the third set of collocations into their notebooks.	15	Write translations and sentences for third set of collocations. Make corrections for the second set sentences.
5	Class activity using the third set of collocations. Students copied the fourth set of collocations into their notebooks.	15	Write translations and sentences for fourth set of collocations. Make corrections for the third set sentences.
6	Class activity using the fourth set of collocations.	15	Make corrections for the fourth set sentences.
7	Collocation review for set 1, 2, 3, and 4.	30	Study for the test.
8	Collocation test for set 1, 2, 3, and 4. Students copied the fifth set of collocations into their notebooks while doing the Japanese translation matching exercise.	25	Write sentences for the fifth set of collocations.
9	Class activity using the fifth set of collocations. Students copied the sixth set of collocations into their notebooks while doing the Japanese translation matching exercise.	15	Write sentences for the sixth set of collocations. Make corrections for the fifth set sentences.
10	Class activity using the sixth set of collocations. Students copied the seventh set of collocations into their notebooks while doing the Japanese translation matching exercise.	15	Write sentences for the seventh set of collocations. Make corrections for the sixth set sentences.

Week	In-class collocation work	Class time required in minutes	Homework
11	Class activity using the seventh set of collocations. Students copied the eighth set of collocations into their notebooks while doing the Japanese translation matching exercise.	15	Write sentences for the eighth set of collocations. Make corrections for the seventh set sentences.
12	Class activity using the eighth set of collocations.	15	Make corrections for the eighth set sentences.
13	Collocation review for set 5, 6, 7, and 8.	30	Study for the test.
14	Collocation test for set 5, 6, 7, and 8.	20	
15	Questionnaire.		

a collection of frequent adjective + noun collocations. This list, which was the fourth reflective cycle's target language, is used primarily to investigate a different type of collocation (adjective + noun collocations as opposed to verb + noun collocations). The procedures used to compile each list are described below.

Collocation list 1

In total, 120 collocations were covered over the course of reflective cycle 1. All of the collocations were of the verb + noun variety, chosen on the basis that use of only verb + noun collocations would provide a clear definition of what a collocation is for the students (Woolard, 2000). For this first cycle of research, I assumed that by using this type of collocation my students would be better able to write sentences and use the collocations in productive ways.

The collocation list used in this cycle was almost entirely comprised of medium-strength collocations. Medium-strength collocations have the following characteristics:

- account for a large part of what we say and write,
- are more restrictive than freely combining words (old house) but less restrictive than words where you strongly expect a second word based on the presence of the first word (foreseeable future),
- contain individual words that most learners are familiar,
- each collocation can be stored in a learners mental lexicon as a single item,
- learners, especially low-proficiency students, are often unfamiliar with the specific combination.

Hill (2000) and Conzett (2000) recommend initially targeting this type of collocation, and therefore this principle was also adopted for this study.

In order to compile this list, I started by creating a pool of possible collocations that could be targeted. I collected collocations from the "Elementary/ Pre-intermediate" level activities in the "Collocations Extra" workbook (Walter & Woodford, 2010) and from the "Study pages" of the *Oxford Collocations Dictionary: For Students of English* (2009). When I was unsure of how restrictive a certain collocation was, I referred to the *LTP Dictionary of Selected Collocations* (1999). This dictionary states that the contained collocations are not combinations of freely combining words, are combinations of words that are useful for English language learners, and are likely to cause some comprehension problems for these learners. The final stage of this process was to compare the individual words that comprised the collocations against the GSL.

The individual words that made up the collocations came largely from the first 1,000 words on the GSL (84.4 percent). Researchers (Durrant, 2009; Handl, 2009; Shin & Nation, 2008) recommend using frequency as a guide when determining which collocations to target. It should not be the only factor but is a useful criterion when compiling a collocation list. The words not included in the first 1,000 were usually associated with computers (software, password, website, etc.) or school (homework, essay, exam, etc.). It was felt that these words, while not being highly placed on the GSL, still represent the most useful words for university-aged students.

A certain amount of professional judgment based on the previous experience of teaching students at this stage of learning was also used when choosing the collocations; I tried to include the most useful collocations in regard to the students' interests and future needs, based on my previous experience of teaching vocabulary.

As mentioned in Chapter 1, the GSL (West, 1953) was used to compile the list of the individual words that were targeted in the vocabulary component of my classes. The GSL was also used to measure the frequency of the individual words that are contained in collocation list 1. However, the GSL has been criticized for using a corpus that is dated and too small (2.5 million words). Consequently, the individual words contained in collocation list 1 have been compared against the New General Service List (Browne, Culligan, & Phillips, 2013), which is based on a 273-million-word subsection of the Cambridge English Corpus. The findings showed that 80.98 percent of the individual words from collocation list 1 are represented within the first 1,000 words of the New General Service List

(NGSL). Consequently, I do not feel the use of the original GSL is a major source of concern for this study.

Collocation list 2

The second collocation list for this study focused on delexicalized verb + noun collocations (see Appendix 2 for the collocation list). As mentioned above, the reasons for using a different collocation list from the first reflective cycle are described in more detail in Section 5.2. It should also be noted that there is considerable overlap between the collocations used for this list and collocation list 1. Of the 120 collocations from list 1, 58 are also included on list 2.

This collocation list was used for the second and third reflective cycles. As with collocation list 1, there are 120 collocations on this list. The list was compiled by investigating the most common collocates for delexicalized verbs. Delexicalized verbs are common sources of error for language learners (Chan & Liou, 2005; Chi, Wong, & Wong, 1994; Sinclair & Renouf, 1988). In order to create this list, I started by including the fifty-eight collocations from list 1 that contained a delexicalized verb and were problematic for the students in reflective cycle 1. I then used the delexicalized verb as the node word and found other common collocations using the *Oxford Collocations Dictionary: For Students of English* (*OCD*) and the *LTP Dictionary of Selected Collocations*. The *OCD* also provided some delexicalized verbs not included in collocation list 1, which were used as node words for list 2. The first 1,000 words of the New General Service List contain 78.31 percent of the individual words contained in list 2. Of the 120 collocations on this list, 83 (69.2 percent) contained a delexicalized verb that is within the 100 most common words on the GSL (exactly the same for the NGSL). In addition to frequency, student need and teachability were criteria used in the selection process. As with the first collocation list, a certain amount of intuition based on previous experience was used to meet these criteria. This collocation list was used in the second and third reflective cycles.

Collocation list 3

The third collocation list was used in the fourth (final) reflective cycle (see Appendix 3 for the collocation list). This list is comprised of 120 highly frequent adjective + noun collocations. By using a list of 47 problematic nouns for second language learners, I was able to compile a list of adjective + noun, which are highly frequent and address the criteria of student need. The original list of nouns was compiled by Hill, Lewis and Lewis (2010) and entitled "Problematic

But Really Useful Words: 47 Nouns Whose Meanings Depend on the Adjectives Used with Them." The researchers did not specify if any other criteria, aside from intuition, was used to create this list. From the list of forty-seven nouns, thirty-three were chosen based on frequency. Each of these 33 nouns is within the first 1,000 words of the GSL.

Using these nouns as pivot words, I used frequency to determine which adjective + noun collocations to include. All of the adjectives used in the collocations on this list are also from the first 1,000 words of the GSL (West, 1953). I used five criteria to find collocations in the corpus:

- Nouns from the "list of 47" that were not within the first 1000 most frequent words were not investigated (33 nouns met this cutoff).
- All adjectives are within the first 1000 most frequent words except if the adjective plus noun collocation occurred at least 200 times within the BNC.
- All collocations must occur at least 50 times within the BNC.
- Only the five most common adjectives for each noun were included.
- However, all collocations that have 200 or more occurrences within the BNC are included. (Antle, 2014, p. 301)

The final criterion enabled nouns that have many highly frequent collocations to be fully represented. It was thought that excluding these highly frequent collocations would be counterproductive.

The "Phrases in English" concordancer (Fletcher, 2011), which incorporates a database from the BNC, was used to conduct the analysis. All of the collocations on list 3 are two grams (sequences of two words). Each of the thirty-three nouns was investigated individually by entering "adjectives: all" into the first position and the noun under investigation into the second position. The concordancer produced a list of all the adjectives that collocated with the noun from the BNC. The criteria described above were then used to select the most appropriate collocations to target. After the thirty-three nouns were investigated, the resulting list had 154 collocations. I then reduced this number to 120 collocations in total by considering student need and teachability.

Data collection for reflective cycle 1

Building on the advice of Jiang (2009) and Nesi (2009), the main data collection tool I used during this phase of the research was a questionnaire (see Appendix 4 for the questionnaire). The questionnaire was piloted with five students who were at a similar level to the participants, but who did not partake in this study. With the aid of another Japanese professor, I asked the five students if the instructions and questions were clear, if they were able to answer all of the questions, and if they found any of the questions objectionable or irrelevant. The five students completed the questionnaire in less than five minutes.

I administered the questionnaire to my students at the end of the semester. It consisted of several statements posed as Likert scales. Five of the statements (listed below in the results section) were related to the research questions for this study and the results for these questions are shown in Table 5.2 and 5.3 in the following section. Due to the students' low proficiency in English, it was decided that all parts of the questionnaire would be accompanied by a Japanese translation. The term collocation was likely familiar to the students because I explained the term during the second class. However, the questionnaire also provided an explanation as well as an example to ensure comprehension. The translation was done by a Japanese English teacher and was checked by another Japanese member of the faculty. Both were confident that the students would not have any trouble understanding the term collocation, the instructions for the questionnaire, or how to respond to each question.

Quantitative results for reflective cycle 1

A total of forty-one students completed the survey, in which they indicated the degree to which they agreed with the following statements. A Likert scale was used and a point value was assigned to each response (strongly agree – 5 points; agree – 4 points; neutral – 3 points; disagree – 2 points; strongly disagree – 1 point). I used the five-point scale, so the findings from this reflective cycle could easily and concisely be compared with the findings from future reflective cycles. The four statements were:

1. Studying collocations has been useful.
2. I am able to use the collocations we studied in conversations
3. Studying collocations is more helpful than studying individual words
4. Writing sentences using the collocations was helpful.

Table 5.2 shows the results for four of the statements from the survey.

In addition to the four statements above, a fifth question was posed in order to determine if the number of collocations targeted each week was a suitable number for low-proficiency students. Table 5.3 shows the results for the statement:

Each week we studied 15 collocations. That was . . .

Table 5.2 Students' responses of studying collocations

Question	Likert		Positive responses (%)		Neutral responses (%)	Negative responses (%)	
	Mean	SD	5	4	3	2	1
1	3.44	0.84	7.3	41.5	41.5	7.3	2.4
2	2.90	0.77	0.0	22.0	48.8	26.8	2.4
3	3.54	0.78	4.9	53.7	34.1	4.9	2.4
4	3.73	0.78	12.2	53.7	31.7	0.0	2.4

Table 5.3 Students' responses in regard to the number of collocations covered each class

Question	Negative responses (%)		Neutral responses (%)	Negative responses (%)	
	Way too many	Too many	Just about right	Not enough	Not nearly enough
5	2.4	12.2	85.4	0	0

The results shown in Table 5.2 were evidence that the alternative approach was seen as successful. The first and third statements indicated that the students had a favorable impression of studying collocations: 48.8 percent of responses agreed or strongly agreed studying collocations was useful, and 58.6 percent of responses agreed or strongly agreed studying collocations was more helpful than studying individual words. The majority of students (65.9 percent) also agreed or strongly agreed that the task of writing sentences was useful. However, the second statement showed that the students still did not feel confident in their ability to use the words productively: 78.0 percent of the participants strongly disagreed, disagreed or gave a neutral response to the statement "I am able to use the collocations we studied in conversations." The results shown in Table 5.3 (85.4 percent thought fifteen collocations per week was just about right) indicated that fifteen collocations was a manageable number for the low-proficiency students to handle for the procedure described in Section 5.2.

Qualitative findings for reflective cycle 1

The questionnaire for this reflective cycle did not contain open-ended questions, so the qualitative data are drawn from my field notes. Table 5.4 presents the

Table 5.4 Insights from the reflective cycle

Category	Subcategory	Examples from the data
Difficulties for the students	Delexicalized verbs	The students have a lot of trouble with the delexicalized verbs.
	Collocation meaning	The majority of errors stem from a misunderstanding of the collocation's meaning. The students are more able to write sentences that show they understand the collocation's meaning since I implemented the matching exercise.
Student participation	In-class	The students are more engaged during the in-class activities than they were during the in-class activities for the individual GSL words the previous semester.
	Homework	The students are putting more effort into their homework. They seldom copy sentences from a dictionary or each other.
Procedural challenges	Teacher feedback	Marking the students' sentences is very time consuming.

themes from the data that were especially relevant to the continuation of the procedures I used in the research. The examples from the data are actual quotes taken from my field notes, which influenced the decisions made in regard to targeted language and procedures used.

Each of these categories is addressed in the following two sections: "Discussion for reflective cycle 1" and "Changes in procedure implemented for reflective cycle 2."

Discussion of reflective cycle 1

The data collected provided me with enough information to address the research questions for this reflective cycle and also to reflect on the implications of the data for taking the process of AR further. Specifically, the field notes were helpful in that they provided a great deal of information that would help shape future reflective cycles.

The first research question, "What are low-proficiency Japanese university students' responses to studying collocations?" was specifically addressed by the first and third questionnaire items. The students had a positive impression of studying collocations (3.44 mean for questionnaire statement 1) and felt studying collocations was more helpful than studying individual words (3.54 mean for questionnaire statement 3). The students' responses on the questionnaire indicated they felt this alternative approach to vocabulary instruction to be more useful than targeting individual words. However, the results also showed that the majority of students are still not confident in their abilities to productively use the collocations. Questionnaire item 2 asked if the students feel capable of using the collocations in conversations, and the mean response was 2.90. This indicated, in the students' opinion, that the approach used in the first reflective cycle needed to be adapted if the students were to improve their spoken fluency with the targeted collocations. In addition, the findings from this questionnaire item only elicited the students' self-assessment of their abilities with the targeted collocations; there was no evidence collected during this reflective cycle to support or question the students' opinion.

The questionnaire item eliciting responses about the value of writing sentences indicated this activity to be beneficial in the students' opinion. Item 4 on the questionnaire had a mean of 3.73, which indicated the students' positive feelings toward the productive activity of writing sentences. However, it is interesting to consider why this item received such a positive response and item 2 did not. I believe there are two possible reasons for this disparity. The first is that the students valued improving their written fluency even if this improvement did not help their spoken fluency. The second possibility is that the students were underestimating their ability to use the targeted collocations in conversations. It was clear that I needed to address this problem in reflective cycle 2.

The final research question, "From the students' perspective, how many collocations should be targeted each week?" was addressed by questionnaire item 5. Overall, the students felt fifteen collocations was a suitable number per week for the activities and homework in reflective cycle 1.

Based on the observations recorded in my field notes, the alternative approach to the vocabulary component was a success, as evidenced by quotes such as the following:

> The students are more engaged during the in-class activities than they were during the in-class activities for the individual GSL words the previous semester.

> The students are putting more effort into their homework.

An example of how this increased level of engagement and effort was manifested could be seen in the students' homework. Specifically, I noticed that the students seldom copied sentences from their dictionaries; this was a common problem during the semester when individual words were taught from the GSL. The students probably did not know how to find sentences with a certain collocation in a dictionary and were left with no other option but to write the sentences themselves. Furthermore, since the student sentences were original and contained mistakes, they provided an excellent opportunity for individual and pair revision based on my feedback. During the pair revision tasks, the students actively helped their partners and would often ask me questions about specific mistakes, which collectively they were unable to solve. However, despite the productive exercise of writing sentences appearing to be beneficial, it was time consuming for both the students to complete as homework and for my revisions. A more time efficient approach for teaching collocations needed to be investigated in reflective cycle 2 (see Section 5.3).

After the first collocation test in week eight, I addressed a weakness in the procedure for the first reflective cycle: the students often misunderstanding the meaning of the collocations. The matching exercise described in Section 5.2 (see Appendix 6 for an example of this matching exercise) helped in this regard. In subsequent reflective cycles, I decided that the students would have access to a "collocation dictionary" that I prepared, which included a Japanese translation of each collocation, an example sentence, and a picture. I predicted that this dictionary would provide the same assistance as the matching exercise.

As I mentioned in Section 5.2, I decided to use a different collocation list for reflective cycle 2. The reason for this change was that based on the sentences the students wrote throughout the intervention period it was apparent that collocations containing delexicalized verbs were the most problematic collocations. The errors made by the students when using delexicalized verb collocations were numerous and fundamental. To illustrate one fundamental error, a common student sentence for the collocation "get lost" was the following:

I get lost my keys.

This exact same sentence was submitted by six of the students and several others made a similar error with this collocation. I did not believe the students copied each other because I had warned them not to and the other sentences for this homework assignment were not the same. I considered this to be a fundamental error because it violates the form, meaning, and use of this particular collocation. This error appeared to be made because the students understood one possible definition for "lost" and did not realize that the collocation "get lost" had a different meaning. The students' use of this error strengthens the argument that students should learn how to use the words they already know as opposed to simply acquiring new individual lexical items (Hill, Lewis, & Lewis, 2000; M. Lewis, 1994; Morgan Lewis, 2000; Wollard, 2005). While this was the most

common error, other delexicalized verbs were also misused in a similar way as
seen in the following sentences taken from student workbooks:

> I make time for 12 clock.

> I catch fire matches.

> I go bad and my mother is angry.

There were of course many other errors within the sentences for different collocations, such as the following:

> I apply for a job for money.

> I went quickly because I miss the bus.

However, the majority of sentences written by the students for non-delexicalized
verb collocations, such as the examples presented above, indicated they understood the collocations' meaning.

To summarize, this reflective cycle provided me with useful data that
addressed the initial research questions. Specifically, the knowledge gained
through my field notes also influenced the procedures for future reflective cycles.

Changes in procedure implemented for reflective cycle 2

The first reflective cycle proved to be a worthwhile undertaking. The data I collected encouraged me to continue with this line of investigation, but during this
cycle I became aware that I needed to make procedural changes. The changes
made between the first and second reflective cycles were more numerous than
between any other subsequent cycles. As mentioned earlier, the first reflective
cycle was exploratory. As I progressed through the AR process, the procedures
I used became more refined. As a result, I did not need to make as many procedural changes as I did between the first two reflective cycles.

As mentioned in Section 5.2, the initial intervention for reflective cycle 1
involved the students writing an example sentence for each collocation. This
procedure for subsequent reflective cycles was changed for two reasons. The first
reason was the amount of time required to edit all of the students' sentences
each week. Each week I had to edit the fifteen new sentences and check the
revisions for the previous set of sentences. I was able to complete this task for
the forty-two students I was teaching at the time, but I felt I would be unable to
accomplish this level of feedback for the larger group of participants (153 students) involved in reflective cycle 2. The second reason was that students often

wrote short sentences, while grammatically correct, which did not illustrate if they actually knew how to use the collocation correctly. An example of this type of sentence is:

I will break the rules.

While writing sentences is a productively demanding activity, I felt it was unsuitable for teaching the correct usage of the target collocations. In addition, I feel having the students write sentences is only a worthwhile exercise if the sentences are checked by their teacher. I base this assumption of the fact my students tended to misunderstand the collocation's meaning while writing sentences, and that they often wrote simple sentences, like the example given above, which did not illustrate a productive ability for the targeted collocation. Therefore, for reflective cycle 2, I decided to compare the receptive and productive tasks described in Section 5.3 (also seen in Appendices 10 and 11). Since the students felt unable to use the collocations in conversations, there was a need to identify the tasks that enabled them to improve their productive abilities.

The second part of the students' homework for reflective cycle 1 was having the students write a Japanese translation for each collocation. However, it was difficult for me to check the accuracy of the Japanese translations. After the first collocation test, I provided the translations myself through a matching exercise and I found that this change in procedure addressed this issue. For the next reflective cycle, I decided to provide an online collocation dictionary that had a Japanese translation, an example sentence, and a picture that depicted the given collocation. This dictionary should provide a similar function as the matching exercise. An example page from this dictionary can be seen in Appendix 7.

In the first reflective cycle, I targeted fifteen collocations per week for 8 weeks. I decided to reduce this number to twelve per week for ten weeks for reflective cycle 2. In the second reflective cycle, I planned to introduce the targeted collocations during the last 15 minutes of each class. Given the nature of the productive and receptive tasks for reflective cycle 2, I felt twelve collocations was a suitable number. However, just as in reflective cycle 1, 120 collocations were taught to the students in the next reflective cycle.

The collocation list for the second phase also needed to be adjusted. The original list included collocations that were thought to be highly useful for the students as well as being highly frequent. The second list included collocations that have these characteristics, but focused on collocations with a delexicalized verb (do, make, take, etc.). The reasoning for this change was presented in the previous section. These collocations are very common in spoken and written English and are problematic for students (Chan & Liou, 2005; Chi, Wong, & Wong, 1994; Nation, 2001; Nesselhauf, 2005; Sinclair & Renouf, 1988). Students have also shown the ability to make greater improvements with these collocations as opposed to collocations with synonymous verbs, hypernym verbs, and troponym verbs (Chan & Liou, 2005).

The second reflective cycle (described below) included a spoken assessment that measured fluency. This addition was time consuming to administer and assess, but I felt it was necessary if improvements in spoken fluency were to be confirmed.

Initial feedback from the students on their previous experiences of studying vocabulary was not collected during the first reflective cycle. However, I realized that this data would provide further insight into the students' responses. Thus, the second reflective cycle included an initial questionnaire that elicited the learners' responses about the usefulness of studying vocabulary and strategies they used previously.

The final changes are related to how the collocations were introduced to the students and the tasks the students undertook. These activities are described in the procedure section for reflective cycle 2 (Section 5.3).

5.3 The second reflective cycle

The research goals for this reflective cycle were pedagogical and stemmed from the findings of cycle 1. I collected evidence in the preceding reflective cycle indicating that the students would benefit from a focus on delexicalized verb collocations. I also realized that while the productive exercise of writing sentences is beneficial if there is teacher feedback, it is not a plausible activity for larger groups of students. Therefore, this reflective cycle investigated if receptive exercises alone can help improve the students' spoken fluency. Productive tasks were also investigated for spoken fluency using a different group of students. Both groups completed pre-intervention and post-intervention spoken assessments, so statistical analysis could be conducted.

I was interested in finding an approach to teaching collocations that improved spoken fluency. Changes in procedure were looked at in the light of whether they were efficient in regard to class time and beneficial in regard to improvements in spoken fluency.

Research questions for reflective cycle 2

The research questions for this reflective cycle were developed based on the data collected during reflective cycle 1. Research questions 1, 2, and 6 were also questions from reflective cycle 1. These questions were included to determine if the changes in procedure for the intervention affected the learners' responses. Research question 3 was largely answered through my own observations and field notes. The fourth and fifth questions required that two spoken assessments (pre-intervention and post-intervention) were measured for fluency.

1. What are the low-proficiency Japanese university students' responses to studying collocations?
2. Will the students feel capable of using the collocations in conversation?
3. What characterizes the students' development of competence in using collocations as assessed by the teacher throughout the course?
4. For the students undertaking receptive tasks, what differences can be seen in the students' spoken fluency between an initial and a summative spoken assessment task?
5. For the students undertaking productive tasks, what differences can be seen in the students' spoken fluency between an initial and a summative spoken assessment task?
6. From the students' perspective, how many collocations should be targeted each week?

Procedure for reflective cycle 2

This reflective cycle was carried out over the course of one university semester. This semester was from April through July and was the students' first semester at university. The intervention was presented to the students as part of their normal course work. The participants for this reflective cycle, the Toyo 2 group, are described in Section 4.5. In total, 153 students chose to partake in this reflective cycle.

During the second class, the students completed an initial questionnaire eliciting information about their previous experiences studying vocabulary. This questionnaire can be seen in Appendix 14, and the findings are presented in Section 5.3.

After the students completed the questionnaire, they were randomly assigned to group A (the receptive task group) or group B (the productive task group).

I gave a brief description of the term collocation. To avoid confusion, I explained that a collocation was two or more words often used together with the first word being a verb. I also gave several examples of collocations that fit the description. During this same class, the students completed the initial spoken assessment task. The assessment task required the students to record themselves describing a series of pictures. A narrative retell was chosen for the spoken assessment because of its use in previous fluency studies (Hansen et al., 1998; Lennon, 1990a, 1990b). I told the students that this voice recording would have no impact on their final grade and asked that they simply try their best. The picture sequence is included in Appendix 9. To ensure the students understood what was expected of them during the spoken assessment, I demonstrated how to describe a picture sequence by using a different set of pictures. Following my demonstration, I used yet another picture sequence and had the students practice with partners. After both students had the opportunity to describe the pictures, I did the exercise myself in front of the class. I repeated this last step one final time with another picture sequence.

For the weekly exercises, the students in group A completed receptive tasks targeting the collocations. Receptive tasks were investigated because researchers had questioned whether receptive tasks lead to productive abilities for targeted vocabulary (Nation, 2001). Each week twelve collocations were targeted, and the students did these exercises on a computer at the end of class for approximately 15 minutes. There was a test in the seventh class that covered the first five sets of collocations. This process was repeated for another five sets of collocations with a test covering collocation sets six to ten. In total 120 collocations were targeted over the course of the semester. The students in group B undertook the same process with the same collocations. The only difference was that their exercises had a productive aspect. The two tests accounted for 30 percent of the students' final grade. The second of these two tests can be seen in Appendix 12. Table 5.5 summarizes the weekly activities and intervention procedure for reflective cycle 2.

The receptive tasks followed the same pattern for each set of collocations. There were three parts in each receptive task. In part A, the students were given a list of twelve collocations and instructed to use the collocation dictionary to search for the meaning of each collocation. The collocation dictionary was placed on a website I created, and the definitions were listed alphabetically. Other researchers have stated the merits of having students use a dictionary for vocabulary acquisition (Morgan & Rinvolucri, 2004; Nation, 2001, 2008; Schmitt, 2008; Ur, 1991). In part B, the students read example sentences containing the collocations, whereas in part C, the students answered questions based on the sentences from part B. Each question contained one of the targeted collocations. An example of the receptive tasks can be found in Appendix 10. The answers for the part C questions were made available before the next class.

The productive tasks followed the same pattern for each set of collocations; however, there were only two parts in each productive task. In part A, the students used the collocation dictionary to search for the meanings of the targeted collocations. This step was identical to part A in the receptive tasks and targeted the same collocations. In part B, the students completed a cloze exercise using the same collocations and sentences from part B of the receptive tasks. An example of the productive tasks is included in Appendix 11. The students checked their own answers for the part B cloze activity. When designing both the receptive and productive tasks, I attempted to include an aspect of need, search, and evaluation. Laufer and Hulstijn (2001) believe each of these aspects contribute to the amount of involvement while processing new words, which in turn affects their acquisition.

In the penultimate class, I administered the post-intervention spoken assessment. As with the initial voice recording, I prepared the students by having them describe the same example picture sequences with partners. I explained that this voice recording would be used with the initial recording as a before and after comparison. I explained again that the recording would not influence their grade and encouraged the students to try their best. The final questionnaire, which was translated using the same procedure as reflective cycle 1, was administered in the final class. A summary of the weekly activities can be seen in Table 5.5.

As mentioned in Section 5.2, there were several procedural changes made for this reflective cycle. These changes were made to address a different set of research questions and to make the data collection more efficient. A summary of these changes is presented in Table 5.6.

Data collection for reflective cycle 2

I collected data for this reflective cycle using questionnaires, field notes, and audio-recordings of a spoken assessment. Both quantitative and qualitative data were collected during the treatment period.

A second questionnaire was given to the students following the intervention period. This questionnaire asked the participants to compare their previous experiences of studying individual words to that of studying collocations. The participants were specifically asked if they felt able to use the targeted

Table 5.5 Summary of intervention activities for reflective cycle 2

Week	Activities for group A (receptive group)	Activities for group B (productive group)	Class time required
1	No collocation activities were done in the first class		
2	Initial spoken assessment Vocabulary questionnaire Randomly assigned to group A or B Receptive activities for set 1	Initial spoken assessment Vocabulary questionnaire Randomly assigned to group A or B Productive activities for set 1	35
3	Receptive activities for set 2	Productive activities for set 2	15
4	Receptive activities for set 3	Productive activities for set 3	15
5	Receptive activities for set 4	Productive activities for set 4	15
6	Receptive activities for set 5	Productive activities for set 5	15
7	Collocation test for sets 1 to 5		30
8	Receptive activities for set 6	Productive activities for set 6	15
9	Receptive activities for set 7	Productive activities for set 7	15
10	Receptive activities for set 8	Productive activities for set 8	15
11	Receptive activities for set 9	Productive activities for set 9	15
12	Receptive activities for set 10	Productive activities for set 10	15
13	Collocation test for sets 6 to 10		30
14	Post-intervention spoken assessment		12
15	Questionnaire		10

collocations productively. This questionnaire was similar to the one used in the first reflective cycle (described in Section 5.2). However, the data collected from this questionnaire was both quantitative and qualitative. A Japanese translation also accompanied all instructions and questions.

At the beginning of the intervention, the participants completed an initial spoken assessment recorded using a voice recorder. This procedure was repeated at the end of the intervention period. The audio-recordings were then assessed blind by three judges for spoken fluency. The judges were experienced English language instructors. These results were subjected to statistical analysis. A description of the procedure used to implement the audio-recording is given in Section 5.3, and a justification for the use of an audio-recording for assessing fluency is given in Section 4.6.

Throughout the intervention period I also used field notes. These field notes documented how engaged the students were in the collocation exercises from

Table 5.6 Procedural changes made between reflective cycles 1 and 2

	Reflective cycle 1	Reflective cycle 2
Participants	Toyo 1 group	Toyo 2 group
Number of collocations targeted each week	15	12
Collocation dictionary	No	Yes
Homework	Writing sentences and translations	No collocation homework
Number of groups	1	2 (receptive and productive)
Intervention activities	Matching collocations with their translations Writing sentences	Receptive group – answering questions Productive group – cloze activity
Initial questionnaire about previous vocabulary experience	No	Yes. Contained both closed and open-ended questions
Post-intervention questionnaire	Yes. Contained only closed questions	Yes. Contained closed and open-ended questions
Spoken assessments	No	Yes. An initial and post-intervention assessment

my (their teacher's) perspective and were also used to compare differences in how the students completed the receptive and productive tasks.

I believed that these data collection tools were suitable for this reflective cycle given the research questions for several reasons. The research questions regarding the learners' responses and feelings (research questions 1, 2, and 6) could be addressed by the data collected from the closed questionnaire items. The fourth and fifth research questions could only be investigated through the use and analysis of a spoken assessment. Field notes and the open-ended questionnaire item addressed the research question about characterizing the students' collocation development.

Quantitative and qualitative data about the learners' previous vocabulary experiences

During the first reflective cycle, I realized I needed to collect information about the effectiveness of the students' experiences studying vocabulary. The primary goal was to test the argument that the students were not sufficiently improving their productive abilities with previously targeted individual words (see

Section 1.1 in Chapter 1 for a detailed description of the motivation for this study and for a description of the communicative English class in which this problem was identified). This questionnaire also provided the opportunity to collect data about the strategies used by the students and their feelings about vocabulary instruction in general. Before analyzing the findings, I was unsure of what trends would be identified in the data.

The initial questionnaire eliciting information about the students' previous vocabulary experience is included in Appendix 14. The participants completed this questionnaire prior to the intervention period. As stated above, the purpose of the questionnaire was to learn about the participants' experiences studying vocabulary, and in general, the experiences for low-proficiency first-year Japanese university students. The initial questionnaire was completed by 153 participants at the beginning of their second semester. As mentioned in Section 4.5, the second Japanese university semester begins in October and continues through January. The questionnaire elicited both quantitative and qualitative data, and due to the students' low level in English, a Japanese translation for each question was given. The following discussion reports the quantitative and qualitative findings.

The following four statements had the participants assess their receptive and productive abilities with the targeted vocabulary they had previously studied. I assigned each response a point value so mean and standard deviation could be calculated. A response of "strongly agree" was assigned a value of 5, "agree" had a value of 4, "neutral" had a value of 3, "disagree" had a value of 2, and "strongly disagree" had a value of 1.

Statement 1: "I can usually understand the words I studied when I hear or read them."

The following statement was designed to have the students assess their productive ability with previously taught vocabulary.

Statement 2: "I can usually use the words I studied when speaking or writing."

Statement three is similar to the first statement, however, the focus is on the students' retention of their receptive ability for previously taught vocabulary.

Table 5.7 Receptive knowledge of previously studied vocabulary

Statement (n = 153)	Likert		Positive responses		Neutral responses	Negative responses	
1	Mean	SD	5	4	3	2	1
	2.88	0.90	4 (2.6%)	33 (21.6%)	65 (42.5%)	43 (28.1%)	8 (5.2%)

Table 5.8 Productive knowledge of previously studied vocabulary

Statement (n = 153)	Likert		Positive responses		Neutral responses	Negative responses	
2	Mean	SD	5	4	3	2	1
	2.51	0.84	0 (0%)	19 (12.4%)	55 (35.9%)	64 (41.8%)	15 (9.8%)

Table 5.9 Retention of receptive knowledge of previously studied vocabulary

Statement (n = 153)	Likert		Positive responses		Neutral responses	Negative responses	
3	Mean	SD	5	4	3	2	1
	2.60	0.81	1 (0.7%)	16 (10.5%)	70 (45.8%)	53 (34.6%)	13 (8.5%)

Table 5.10 Retention of productive knowledge of previously studied vocabulary

Statement (n = 153)	Likert		Positive responses	Neutral responses	Negative responses		
4	Mean	SD	5	4	3	2	1
	2.33	0.81	0 (0%)	14 (9.2%)	42 (27.5%)	78 (51.0%)	19 (12.4%)

Statement 3: "After several weeks, I can still understand the words I studied when I hear or read them."

The following statement was designed to have the students assess their productive ability with previously taught vocabulary after a period of several weeks.

Statement 4: "After several weeks, I can still use the words I studied when speaking or writing."

The fifth Likert scale statement from questionnaire 1 asked the participants to rank their level of agreement (similar to statements 1 to 4) to the following statement:

Statement 5: "Studying individual words in my previous classes has been useful."

The final closed question from questionnaire 1 had the students identify the various techniques/tools they had used to study vocabulary either in class or on their own. This question allowed the participants to choose more than one answer, so the total percentage is greater than one hundred.

Statement 6: "I have used the following methods to study vocabulary (please check all that apply)."

Table 5.11 Students' perception of the usefulness of their previous vocabulary study

Statement (n = 152)	Likert		Positive responses		Neutral responses	Negative responses	
5	Mean	SD	5	4	3	2	1
	3.99	0.70	30 (19.7%)	98 (64.5%)	17 (11.2%)	7 (4.6%)	0 (%)

Table 5.12 Techniques used for studying vocabulary by participants

Technique/Tool for Studying Vocabulary (n = 153)	Number of participants who have used this technique	Percentage of participants who have used this technique
Word cards	81	52.9
Vocabulary notebooks	129	84.3
Memorizing word lists	66	43.1
Writing sentences	65	42.5
Fill-in-the-blank exercises	75	49.0
Writing translations from a dictionary	107	69.9
Memorizing words from reading passages	68	44.4
Other	4	2.6

The following section presents the qualitative data collected from the open-ended questionnaire item. Since this set of data was collected before the students undertook their respective receptive or productive tasks, I did not feel it was necessary to separate the responses based on their group. The students' comments about their previous vocabulary experiences are classified into several categories. The questionnaire item elicited responses about the students' likes and dislikes, and also what the students found easy or difficult in regard to studying vocabulary. As a result, the majority of the responses could be classified as being positive or negative. Table 5.13 presents the positive responses and Table 5.14 presents the negative responses. The full data set is included in Table A.1 and Table A.2 in the Appendices.

The procedure used to analyze the qualitative data involved a categorizing process in which each response was given one or more tags relating to possible themes or patterns. After all learner responses were tagged, each theme was investigated individually. Within a theme, a second cycle of tagging was often conducted to identify sub-categories. By grouping the responses in this manner, the patterns within the data were identified.

The themes that emerged from the data through analysis indicated the learners had beliefs for how vocabulary should be introduced, what words should be targeted, what techniques were effective for acquiring the targeted structures, and how this targeted vocabulary should be reviewed. In addition, the learners identified components of English vocabulary that were problematic and aspects of vocabulary instruction that were not enjoyable.

Discussion of the findings about experiences studying vocabulary

Based on the findings presented above, it is clear that overall the learners felt studying vocabulary was useful. Statement five shown in Table 5.11 had a mean score of 3.99 indicating that the students' overall impression of their experiences studying vocabulary is positive. However, they did not feel confident in their ability to productively use the targeted vocabulary, especially after several weeks. Statement four (Table 5.10) had a mean score of 2.33 with 51 percent of the students disagreeing with the statement that they felt able to use previous taught vocabulary after several weeks.

The findings from statement four and five are contradictory to a certain degree. The students felt their previous vocabulary study was useful, yet they also felt unable to use the words that were targeted. However, I believe the students' positive response to statement five was due to their appreciation of the potential value an improved vocabulary could have on their overall English proficiency. These findings were consistent with the original area of concern described in Chapter 1 (I described how the students struggled to productively use previously taught vocabulary). Based on these findings, the students also identified this weakness in their previous English studies.

Table 5.12 shows the findings concerning the various strategies used by the learners for studying vocabulary. Vocabulary notebooks were the most common strategy used by the students (84.3 percent), while writing translations was also common (about 70 percent). Other strategies were used by between 42 percent and 53 percent of the students.

The open-ended questionnaire item elicited mostly responses that could be classified as being positive or negative. After categorizing the responses, several patterns emerged from the data.

Table 5.13 presents the learners' responses that were classified as being positive. I believe six themes could be extracted from this data:

Table 5.13 Positive responses about experiences studying vocabulary

Category	Subcategory	Example from the data
Learners' responses about techniques used to introduce vocabulary	Pronunciation for the target vocabulary	Remembering the pronunciation makes vocabulary easy.
	New vocabulary through readings	Memorizing words from a reading passage is easier because we can learn how to use the words.
	New vocabulary through listening	Looking at vocabulary as I listen is effective.
	Memory	I like to memorize.
	Quantity	Not having to memorize too many new words. If the number of words is small, it's easy. When I think it seems easy, it's easy to get started.
Learners' responses about techniques for reviewing previously taught vocabulary	Vocabulary cards	Vocabulary cards are a good way to study.
	Vocabulary books	Studying vocabulary notebooks every day is helpful.
	Repetitive exposure	Trying to use the vocabulary over and over again helps me remember.
Learners' responses about activities that help students acquire targeted vocabulary	Dictionary	It is easy to remember as I look up words in the dictionary.
	Use	I like easy to use vocabulary. We can use the word straightaway.
Learners' responses about what vocabulary should be targeted	Type of word	Learning familiar words for our daily life and nouns and verbs is good.
	Short words	Short words and common words in long sentences are easy to remember.
	Common words	Daily English is good for studying.
	L1	Comparing English words with Japanese is helpful. For example, "My mother is angry with me" and "My mother is occurred with me." (It doesn't make sense, but angry and occur both mean OKORU in Japanese.)

1. The way new words were presented was important in the students' view.
2. Students preferred to learn new words extracted from a reading or listening text. Alternatively, they liked to learn a new word's pronunciation along with its meaning.

Table 5.14 Negative responses about experiences studying vocabulary

Category	Subcategory	An examples from the data
Learners' responses about aspects of studying vocabulary that are problematic	Use targeted vocabulary	I had trouble when I had to figure out how I can use the words in a particular situation.
	Words that have many meanings	If the vocabulary has many meanings, it's difficult.
	Differences from their L1	It's difficult to remember the vocabulary that we don't use in Japanese.
Learners' responses about aspects of vocabulary instruction that they did not enjoy	Studying uncommon words	I want to improve my English skill, so I'll try to answer in English. I like studying vocabulary, but it is often difficult for me. The reason is some words are not useful in daily conversation. Actually, some Japanese students learn English only for passing entrance exam or getting high scores, so many students dislike studying vocabulary I think.
	Dictionary	I dislike having to look up new words in a dictionary every time.
	Memory and quantity	Learning too many new words is not fun.

3. Targeting too many words at one time could be counterproductive in their opinion. One student responded that between ten and twenty new vocabulary items is a suitable number.
4. The students also felt repeated exposure to new vocabulary was necessary for acquisition.
5. Vocabulary cards were the most effective strategy for studying vocabulary in the students' opinion. The students explained that by using vocabulary cards, they were repeatedly exposed to the targeted vocabulary.
6. Targeted vocabulary should be common and/or useful for daily life. The low-proficiency students in this study likely preferred vocabulary that was at their level.

The students often responded that using the targeted vocabulary productively was crucial for acquisition.

The negative responses can be seen in Table 5.14. The learners commonly responded about two problematic aspects of studying vocabulary.

1. The students did not like to study words that they identified as being uncommon or not useful. This pattern is similar to the students' positive feelings about common vocabulary, but could indicate the students would lose motivation when asked to learn words that they characterize as not being useful.

2. The students felt words that have several meanings are especially difficult. Though not mentioned specifically, it was likely some students were referring to delexicalized verbs. Delexicalized verbs are common enough that the students would have been exposed to them several times, but they also have meanings that vary depending on the collocates with which they are used.

The findings from this questionnaire were evidence that the initial area of concern for this study was also viewed by the students as a weakness in their previous vocabulary study. The responses also impressed me by the level of awareness shown by the students. They commonly identified characteristics such as "repetition of targeted vocabulary," "using new words productively," and "selection of targeted vocabulary" as being important aspects of vocabulary instruction. In addition, I was surprised by the number of students who identified "words with many meanings" as being problematic. If I am correct in assuming delexicalized verbs are included in this category of words, my choice to target these structures in this reflective cycle was appropriate. I felt these findings provided insight into procedures that were effective in the students' view and thus likely to improve student motivation. Furthermore, these findings supported the original area of concern for this study and choice of targeted vocabulary.

Quantitative results for reflective cycle 2

Tables 5.15 to 5.22 show the results for the questions from the survey. A total of sixty-seven students from group A and sixty-eight students from group B completed the survey. The students indicated the degree to which they agreed with the statements listed below. A Likert scale was used for Tables 5.15–5.21, and, as in cycle 1, a point value was assigned to each response (strongly agree – 5 points; agree – 4 points; neutral – 3 points; disagree – 2 points; strongly disagree – 1 point). The eight questions are:

1. Studying collocations has been useful.
2. I am able to use the collocations we studied in conversations.
3. Studying collocations is more helpful than studying individual words.

Table 5.15 Students' responses about studying collocations

Question (n = 135)	Likert		Positive responses		Neutral responses	Negative responses	
1	Mean	SD	5	4	3	2	1
Group A	3.70	0.92	11 (16%)	33 (49%)	17 (25%)	4 (6%)	2 (3%)
Group B	4.04	0.68	17 (25%)	37 (54%)	14 (21%)	0 (0%)	0 (0%)
Total	3.87	0.82	28 (21%)	70 (52%)	31 (23%)	4 (3%)	2 (1%)

Table 5.16 Students' responses about their ability to use collocations in conversations

Question (n = 135)	Likert		Positive responses		Neutral responses	Negative responses	
2	Mean	SD	5	4	3	2	1
Group A	3.25	1.03	7 (10%)	23 (34%)	19 (28%)	16 (24%)	2 (3%)
Group B	3.16	0.80	4 (6%)	16 (24%)	35 (51%)	13 (19%)	0 (0%)
Total	3.21	0.92	11 (8%)	39 (29%)	54 (40%)	29 (21%)	2 (1%)

4. For group A students only: Reading the definitions and example sentences has been useful.
5. For group A students only: Answering questions about the sentences has been useful.
6. For group B students only: Reading the definitions and example sentences has been useful.
7. For group B students only: Doing the "Fill in the blank" questions has been useful.
8. Each week we studied twelve collocations. That was . . .

Table 5.15 shows the results for the first questionnaire item.

Both groups of learners had an overall positive impression of studying collocations. However, the productive group had a higher average response compared to the receptive group (4.04 compared to 3.70 for the receptive group).

The receptive group and the productive group had a similar average response in regard to their ability to use collocations in conversations. The receptive group has a 3.25 average, while the productive group has a 3.16 average.

The productive group had a higher average response when comparing studying collocations to studying individual words. The productive group had an average response of 3.81, while the receptive group had an average response of 3.52.

Table 5.17 Students' responses comparing studying collocations to individual words

Question (n = 135)	Likert		Positive responses		Neutral responses	Negative responses	
3	Mean	SD	5	4	3	2	1
Group A	3.52	1.01	12 (18%)	23 (34%)	21 (31%)	10 (15%)	1 (1%)
Group B	3.81	0.80	11 (16%)	37 (54%)	17 (25%)	2 (3%)	1 (1%)
Total	3.67	0.91	23 (17%)	60 (44%)	38 (28%)	12 (9%)	2 (1%)

Table 5.18 Group A students' responses about reading the definitions and example sentences

Question (n = 69)*	Likert		Positive responses		Neutral responses	Negative responses	
4	Mean	SD	5	4	3	2	1
	3.77	0.79	11 (16%)	35 (51%)	19 (28%)	4 (6%)	0 (0%)

*69 responses (two group B students answered this question by mistake).

Table 5.19 Group A students' responses about the receptive task of answering questions about the sentences

Question (n = 69)*	Likert		Positive responses		Neutral responses	Negative responses	
5	Mean	SD	5	4	3	2	1
	3.67	0.83	11 (16%)	29 (42%)	24 (35%)	5 (7%)	0 (0%)

*69 responses (two group B students answered this question by mistake)

The receptive group had a positive impression about reading the definitions and example sentences in the collocation activities. The average response was 3.77.

The receptive group also responded positively to the receptive activity if answering questions during the collocation tasks. The average response was 3.67.

The productive group had a positive impression about reading the definitions and example sentences in the collocation activities. The average response was 3.95.

The productive group had a positive impression about the cloze activity in the collocation activities. The average response was 4.00.

Table 5.20 Group B students' responses about reading the definitions and example sentences

Question (n = 62)*	Likert		Positive responses		Neutral responses	Negative responses	
6	Mean	SD	5	4	3	2	1
	3.95	0.71	12 (19%)	37 (60%)	11 (18%)	2 (3%)	0 (0%)

*62 responses (six group B students did not answer this question)

Table 5.21 Group B students' responses about the cloze task (productive task)

Question (n = 62)*	Likert		Positive responses		Neutral responses	Negative responses	
7	Mean	SD	5	4	3	2	1
	4.00	0.68	14 (23%)	34 (55%)	14 (23%)	0	0

*62 responses (6 group B students did not answer this question)

Table 5.22 Students' responses in regard to the number of collocations covered each class

Question (n = 135)	Negative responses		Positive responses	Negative responses	
8	Way too many	Too many	Just about right	Not enough	Not nearly enough
Group A	0 (0%)	14 (21%)	47 (70%)	5 (7%)	1 (1%)
Group B	1 (1%)	5 (7%)	59 (87%)	1 (1%)	2 (3%)
Total	1 (1%)	19 (14%)	106 (79%)	6 (4%)	3 (2%)

Given the tasks and time required to complete them, 12 collocations was perceived to be an appropriate number per week in the students' opinion. The productive group had a higher percentage of students who responded (87 percent) that twelve collocations was "just about right" compared to the receptive group (70 percent).

The audio-recordings were assessed blind for fluency by three judges. The means and standard deviations are shown in Table 5.23. The blind judges used a seven-point scale to judge fluency: a score of 1 was extremely dysfluent and a score of 7 was extremely fluent. Prior to the assessment, the blind judges undertook a benchmark identification session to minimize the chance of inconsistent

Table 5.23 Mean, standard deviation, and *t*-value for spoken fluency assessment

	Group A (receptive)			Group B (productive)		
	Pre-intervention	Post-intervention	Difference	Pre-intervention	Post-intervention	Difference
M	2.81	3.09	0.28	2.84	3.56	0.72
SD	1.53	1.17		1.39	1.50	
t	1.6048			2.9112		

judgment. The voice recordings used during this session were not part of the later assessment process. A Fleiss' kappa test was conducted to measure inter-rater reliability. The observed agreement was measured at 0.375.

Both the receptive group and the productive group had higher scores on their post-intervention spoken fluency assessment. The receptive group's post-intervention score (a seven-point scale) was 0.28 higher than their pre-intervention score. The productive group's post-intervention score was 0.72 higher than their pre-intervention score. A two-tailed dependent *t*-test was performed on the results for the productive and receptive groups. There was not a significant effect for the receptive group, $t(31) = 1.60$, $p < 0.05$. There was a significant effect, however, for the productive group, $t(31) = 2.91$, $p < 0.05$, with the students receiving a higher score on the post-intervention spoken fluency assessment.

The quantitative results are discussed in greater detail in Section 5.3. These results are also compared with the qualitative results from the open-ended questionnaire item. Overall, these quantitative responses indicate the collocation intervention was worthwhile in the learners' opinion, and there is evidence the productive group improved their spoken fluency. Several transcripts of the narrative retells are presented in the following section.

Transcriptions of the narrative retells used for the fluency assessment

The following is a random sampling of the narrative retells. The narrative retell task can be seen in Appendix 9, and a description of the procedures used to implement this assessment are given in Section 5.3. The students' identification numbers for this study are followed by both transcripts of their pre-intervention and post-intervention spoken assessments. Within each transcript, pauses are indicated by brackets with the number within the bracket indicating the duration of the pause in seconds. The students' use of a Japanese word or expression is indicated by (J), and (?) represents an utterance that I could not identify. After each transcript, the expert judges' scores for fluency are given. The scale for this assessment ranges from a score of 1 for an extremely dysfluent speech sample to a score of 7 for an extremely fluent speech sample.

Receptive group (group A)

19201000130A—male (first retell)

wake up seven o'clock (2.2) at (12.2) (J) (5.7) at eat breakfast and (5.8) clean. In the afternoon, (1.7) stretch (1.0) at (1.6) to study (4.2) after (8.2) (J) (4.7) goodnight. Sorry. At night, (3.6) cooking at night (1.2) after watch TV. Last, (2.8) bed in.

Fluency score: 1

1920100013JA (second retell)

get up bed and dress. After breakfast, eat eat breakfast. After, (2.9) (J) (2.4) clean. In the afternoon, (2.8) in the afternoon (1.8) stretch, after (3.0) study study. After sleep. At night, cooking. After, watch TV and (1.5) go to bed.

Fluency score: 2

Here, the student's initial attempt to complete the narrative picture sequence consists of many lengthy hesitations and some use of Japanese when the English word was unknown. The second attempt is slightly better, but there are still lengthy pauses and some repetition. For the second picture in the sequence, the student was able to use the word "dress" in the second retell; in the first retell the student could not articulate this part of the retell at all. The collocation "get dressed" was a targeted collocation from list 2. In the second attempt, he also used another targeted collocation "go to bed," whereas in the first retell the unnatural expression "bed in" was used.

19301100930A—male (first retell)

wake up at seven. And I (2.3) I (2.3) take (2.5) take off my clothes and taking my clothes. I eat and I eat breakfast and I (1.4) wash my (1.8) clothes. In the afternoon, I (2.0) I play sports and I (1.4) study (2.2) I study studied. And (2.7) I (1.6) and I (2.3) I slept (2.0) slept (0.9) on the sofa with cat.

Fluency score: 2

1930110093JA (second retell)

got up seven at seven. I (3.1) (J) I changed clothes (1.9) I have breakfast (1.7) and I (2.6) I (2.4) do do laundry. In the afternoon, I (1.8) I exercise (1.1) I play exercise and I (2.7) studies (1.7) I study. And I (0.9) and I sleep. At night, I make dinner and I watch TV and I go to bed.

Fluency score: 3

The student reduced both the total number of pauses and their total duration in the second retell. Furthermore, the second retell contains several natural collocations such as "changed clothes," "have breakfast," "make dinner," "do laundry," and "go to bed" (the final two collocations listed here are from list 2). In the first retell, he also uses some collocations, but these collocations are accompanied by repetition (I eat and I eat breakfast), mistakes in meaning and accuracy (take off my clothes and taking my clothes), or pauses within the chunk of language (wash my (1.8) clothes).

1910110004OA—male (first retell)

get up and (3.2) wear the (1.9) clothes and eat breakfast. (8.5) and (4.2) wash the clothes. In the afternoon, (2.3) training and study (6.0) and (2.2). At night, cook the dinner and watch the TV (1.9) and go to bed.

Fluency score: 2

1910110004JA (second retell)

get up (1.1) and (2.9) wear the clothes. After, eat breakfast. After, wash the clothes. In the afternoon, (3.2) training, (1.3) and (2.0) studying and (1.3) sleeping. At night, (3.4) cooking dinner. After, watch the TV. After, go to bed.

Fluency score: 2

The student was able to reduce the duration of the pauses for the second retell, but both retells contain several unnatural collocations such as "wear the clothes," "cook the dinner," and "watch the TV."

1910110115OA—female (first retell)

get up (1.1) seven and change my clothes. And take breakfast and (1.2) wash (1.4) (?) clothes. In the afternoon, (1.8) I stretches and study (6.8) and sleep (0.8) on the sofa. At night, I cooked and watching TV, at last sleep.

Fluency score: 2

1910110115JA (second retell)

get up (1.0) at seven and changed (1.0) clothing (1.0) change clothes and (2.2) have breakfast and (2.8) cleaning (2.6) clothes. In the afternoon, I (2.3) usually exercise(0.5)ing exercise and do my homework and sleep on the sofa. At night, (0.9) I cooking for dinner and watching TV and sleep and go to bed.

Fluency score: 3

Both retells contained several pauses, but the second retell finished with a relatively long section of mostly uninterrupted speech. The first retell also had a long pause within the collocation "wash clothes" that likely indicated dysfluency to the judge.

1910110117OA—female (first retell)

get up (0.7) seven and wear clotha and eating (0.6) breakfast (1.7) and (3.5) washing (1.2) clothes. In the afternoon, (7.5) stretch, and (4.5) do my homework (2.5) and (4.3) sleep. At night, cooking (1.0) dinner, watch TV (4.6) go to bed.

Fluency score: 2

1910110117JA (second retell)

get up after (2.1) wear (1.4) wear my clothes. After, (2.1) eat breakfast. After, (1.6) washing (1.8) clothes. In the afternoon, (4.0) exercise. After, (1.9) do my homework after (3.2) have a nap. At night, (1.7) cook cook the dinner, after, watch TV, after, go to bed.

Fluency score: 3

Both retells contained several lengthy pauses, but the first retell was marked with three occasions of pauses occurring within a collocation: "eating (0.6) breakfast," "washing (1.2) clothes," and "cooking (1.0) dinner." The second retell only had one instance of this dysfluency marker. Another noticeable difference in the second retell was the increased use of the simple present, which was the correct verb tense for this narrative description. She also used the collocation "have a nap," which better describes that part of the retell as opposed to "sleep," which was used in the first retell.

Productive group (group B)

1910110018OB—female (productive group—first retell)

get up at seven and (2.6) warm clothes and have a breakfast and do laundry. In the afternoon, (1.2) I (3.2) training and (1.4) study and go to (0.6) bed. At night, (2.2) cook dinner and watch (1.1) TV and (1.2) go to (0.6) bed.

Fluency score: 3

1910110018JB (productive group—second retell)

wake up and clothes (4.1) clothes and have a breakfast and do laundry. In the afternoon, (1.9) I (1.6) I do exercise and (1.5) do homework and (1.1) sleep (0.9) in the bed. At night, (1.7) do cooking do cook and watch TV (1.0) and go to bed.

Fluency score: 3

Both retells are similar in the number of pauses and their duration. Furthermore, mostly the same collocations and words were used to describe the narrative picture sequence. In the second retell she used "do exercise" (as opposed to "training"), which was likely the result of the collocation "do some exercise" being taught during the intervention. However, she also used an unnatural collocation "do cook" as opposed to the more natural expression "cook dinner," which was used in the first retell.

1910110119OB—male (first retell)

get up at seven. (3.5) I take off my pajama. (3.6) I (5.3) I eat breakfast. (4.3) clean clean my clothes clothes. In the afternoon, (8.6) exercise (1.2) work hard. (4.3) sleep. At night, (5.8) cook (0.8) cook dinner, watching TV, go to bed.

Fluency score: 2

1910110119JB (second retell)

get up early. (3.5) I usually (1.2) wear my clothes, having (3.6) have a breakfast, (2.3) washing (1.4) wash my clothes. In the afternoon, (3.2) training, studying hard, (4.7) have a nap. At night, (5.2) cook a dinner, watch a TV, (5.9) go to bed.

Fluency score: 2

The student was able to convey each picture from the sequence; however, in both retells there are frequent and lengthy pauses that indicate dysfluency.

1930110090OB—female (first retell)

woke up at 8 (1.3) and (1.4) change the clothes. After that, eat breakfast (1.4) and (4.0) (?) (6.3). In the afternoon, (3.4) do exercise and (5.7) (?) homework. After that, (2.3) (?) sleep.

Fluency score: 2

1930110090JB (second retell)

get up at eight and (2.2) dressed up (1.9) and eat breakfast. After that, do laundry. In the afternoon, do some exercise and study (1.2) and have a nap. At night, make dinner and watch TV. After that, go to bed.

Fluency score: 5

The most noticeable difference between the two retells is the absence of pauses within the second attempt. The second attempt also contained several targeted collocations from list 2 such as "do laundry," "do some exercise," "have a nap," "make dinner," and "go to bed." In the first retell, she was either unable to articulate these parts of the picture sequence or used an unnatural word or expression.

19101101210B—female (first retell)

get up and (1.7) take clothes and eat breakfast and (1.5) clean clothes. In the afternoon, (5.4) training, and (3.4) study and (2.0) sleep. At night, (2.5) I usually (1.9) cook (2.3) for dinner and watch TV and go to bed.

Fluency score: 2

1910110121JB (second retell)

get up and change (1.4) my clothes and (5.2) have breakfast and (5.3) washing (2.6) clothes. In the afternoon, (1.0) I usually (1.8) stretch and (3.3) do my homework and (5.5) sleep. At night, I usually (3.4) cooking cook dinner and watch TV and go to bed.

Fluency score: 4

Both retells contained several lengthy pauses. In the second retell, she used the collocation "change my clothes," which is a suitable description for this part of the picture sequence as opposed to "take clothes." She also self-corrected and was able to produce "cook dinner" whereas in the first retell she produced "cook for dinner."

19201100600B—male (first retell)

get up at (2.8) ten (3.6) and I (4.6) I take I put (1.4) on (0.9) clothes and I eat breakfast (3.1) and wash (1.9) my clothes. In the afternoon, (4.2) I (1.9) exercise (2.0) and (0.8) study (2.2) and sleep. At night, (3.3) I cooked (1.3) I cook (3.6) dinner and watch TV (1.3) and (2.6) go to bed at eleven.

Fluency score: 3

1920110060JB (second retell)

wake up (1.5) wake at (4.3) get up at seven. (4.0) and put on (3.9) clothes (2.7) eat (1.4) breakfast (2.0). Then (2.0) I wash (1.3) clothes. In the afternoon, (2.5) I (2.9) I have exercise (1.8) and (1.9) study my homework. (3.2) and sleepy (1.3) on sofa. At night, (1.9) I cook dinner and watch TV. Finally, I go to bed.

Fluency score: 2

Both retells have many pauses. However, the student was able to correctly articulate each picture in the sequence in the first retell. In the second retell, his fluency score was likely lowered because he used three unnatural collocations: "have exercise," "study my homework," and "sleepy on the sofa."

In these segments of the students' narrative retells, several themes emerged. In instances where the students were able to improve their fluency scores, there was one or more of the following qualities:

* avoiding pauses within collocations,
* decreasing the number of pauses and their total duration,
* using more natural expressions, and
* having longer uninterrupted utterances.

Several of the second retells transcribed above contain one or more of the targeted collocations from the intervention. In some instances, the student used the targeted collocation in the second retell whereas they used an equally appropriate expression in the first retell to describe that part of the picture sequence. For example, 19101101115OA used the word "study" in her first retell and "do my homework" in her second retell; both of these choices adequately convey the meaning of this part of the narrative retell. In other instances, such as with 1930110090JB, the student used a targeted collocation from list 2 in their second retell to articulate a part of the picture sequence that they were unable to describe in their first attempt.

As described in Section 3.4, for this study the focus was on perceived fluency, which Lennon (1990a) defines thus, "Fluency is an impression on the listener's part that the psycholinguistic process of speech planning and speech production are functioning easily and efficiently" (p. 391). The blind judges could take all aspects of the speech sample into account such as speed, pauses, repairs, conveying meaning, accuracy, intonation and pronunciation. The transcriptions are presented here to provide a more thorough account of the assessment process; however, they do not convey all aspects of the speech samples that could have potentially influenced the fluency assessment.

Qualitative results for reflective cycle 2

The open-ended item on questionnaire two together with my field notes provided useful qualitative data. While the student responses were generally short, and my field notes only provided insight into the procedures, several patterns emerged during the analysis that are presented below. The student responses commonly emphasized the value of studying collocations and the problematic nature of delexicalized verbs. Many responses focused on the level of the material and how useful the targeted collocations were in their opinion. A final group of responses critiqued the procedures used during the intervention. Within this group, there was a pattern of support for productive tasks.

During my analysis of this data set, I made every effort to be objective, drawing extensively on the words of the students to convey the patterns I noticed within their responses. In analyzing these patterns, it was important not to select data to support my preconceived notions as a teacher researcher or to use them selectively to support the outcomes I wanted to achieve. In Table 5.24, the qualitative data has been categorized to convey the themes that emerged during the analysis of the data. The full set of data can be seen in Table A.3 in the Appendices. The main themes that emerged through the qualitative analysis focused on the value of studying collocations, the problematic nature of delexicalized verbs, and the suitability of the materials and procedures used during the intervention. In addition, the students made recommendations for techniques, which in their opinion would help in the acquisition of collocations.

Discussion for reflective cycle 2

The data collected during this reflective cycle proved useful to me in addressing the research questions shown in Section 5.3. Each research question is discussed individually to show what findings were made and what implications I could draw then out for further investigation.

The first research question asked about the students' responses to studying collocations. As in reflective cycle 1, the students formed a positive impression of the exercises that they undertook. This finding was also supported by the qualitative data collected. Many students responded in the open-ended question that they felt studying collocations was worthwhile and useful. In my field notes, I wrote "the students are engaged and seem to enjoy the tasks." These findings support the incorporation of collocation activities into low-proficiency English classes due to the students' positive impression of these tasks. However, the collocation activities were a new approach to vocabulary study for the students, and there was a possibility that the students would become less enthusiastic about this approach over time.

As with the first reflective cycle, the students also indicated that in their opinion studying collocations was more beneficial than studying individual words. Several open-ended questionnaire responses also mentioned that collocations

Table 5.24 Cycle 2: Qualitative data

Category	Subcategory	Examples from the receptive group data	Examples from the productive group data
Value of studying collocations	Important part of vocabulary learning	I'm really glad I learned collocation. I'm in group A. I read the questions and answer. I got many new vocabulary from it	Studying collocation makes my English improve
	Comparison with individual word study	I don't like studying individual words, but this was collocations and I studied it so enjoy	It was difficult to put verb and noun together before
	Productive challenges of collocations		It is really tough to study collocation for me
Delexicalized verbs	Variations in verb meanings	It is difficult because the verbs like "have," "take," etc., are used the same but the meaning is different.	It was difficult to remember the meaning of the collocation
	Productive challenges	It is easy to mix up the arrangement for verbs like have and get	It was difficult to figure out that I should use "take," "have," or "make"
	Level appropriateness	There were some familiar vocabulary. It was good there are many easy vocabulary in the sentences	The vocabulary was easy and good. It was really useful to study that vocabulary
Materials used in the intervention	Level	That was the perfect amount of work and level. Vocabulary in the class is useful for ordinary conversation	The collocation dictionary was good. The level was perfect for me
	Learner need	It was easy to understand and useful for future.	Studying collocation is useful

Procedures used	Exercises	The exercises made me remember the vocabulary. I liked I could use the words that I memorized	The filling up the gap was just like a game and fun!
	Dictionary	It was easy to study because of I could look up difficult vocabulary in the dictionary	I think we should look up the collocations in the dictionary by ourselves to memorize vocabulary. Because of we can fill up the gap after we look up the dictionary
	Memory	It was easy to remember the collocations	It was enjoyable to memorize vocabulary
Learner responses regarding exercises that should be used	Value of productive tasks	It was good to learn vocabulary and arrange the sentence to future one and past one. But speaking is difficult	It is difficult using the words in conversation

were more helpful than individual words. As mentioned in Chapter 1, the initial area of concern for this study was the students' inability to use the targeted items from the GSL. The hope was that by teaching a verb + noun collocation, which represents a larger portion of an utterance, the students would be more able to use the collocations productively. One possible explanation for these results is that the students made the same assumption that collocations were easier to use while speaking.

The average score for the first and third questionnaire items was higher in reflective cycle 2 than in the first reflective cycle. I believe that this difference is largely the result of the students preferring the tasks in the second reflective cycle. I base this opinion on the number of positive responses about the procedure from the open-ended item on questionnaire two.

The second questionnaire item addressed the second research question. In comparison to reflective cycle 1, the students had a slightly more positive belief in their ability to use the targeted collocations while speaking (3.21 compared to 2.90). However, if the overall goal of this study was to be reached, this number needs to be higher. The lack of productive ability was also commonly mentioned in the qualitative data collected. It was clear that in the next reflective cycle, the tasks need to be designed with the goal of increasing the students' confidence in their productive abilities.

Research question 3 concerns the students' development of competence in using collocations from the teacher's perspective. I believed that explicit instruction of delexicalized verb collocations is beneficial for low-proficiency students. The exercises used helped the students identify a problematic area within their English knowledge and also provided a support system for them to gradually improve their productive abilities. The students answered favorably to the questionnaire items regarding the specific tasks used during the intervention (Tables 5.18 to Table 5.21). This impression was reinforced through the qualitative data that largely endorsed the procedures used during reflective cycle 2. In particular, the students felt the dictionary and cloze activity were useful and effective. However, the low-proficiency students in this study identified delexicalized verbs as being especially problematic. Furthermore, they are not confident in their ability to use the targeted collocations in conversations. From my perspective as their teacher, I concurred with the students' self-assessment. It is my opinion that these structures should be explicitly taught to low-proficiency students who do not receive a great deal of exposure to English outside of the classroom.

I also considered "level" when answering research question 3. Both the quantitative data and qualitative data indicated the collocations targeted for this study were of a suitable level for my students. The Likert scale questionnaire items (quantitative data) showed a positive response for studying collocations and a more neutral response for the ability to use the collocations in conversations in the students' opinion. Many student responses to the open-ended questionnaire item focused on level, specifically classifying the individual words as "easy," but using this adjective in a positive way. By "positive way," I am referring to the fact that, despite the words being "easy," they mostly thought they were a suitable choice for this class (not too easy). I believe that over the course of the intervention, the students became aware that the targeted collocations were in fact problematic, especially in regard to their productive ability.

The fourth and fifth research questions were addressed through the spoken assessments. Both the productive and receptive group improved their spoken fluency as assessed by expert blind judges. However, only the improvement of the productive group was significant. While these results are somewhat disappointing considering the initial goal of this study, they did provide information that was used in subsequent reflective cycles.

The final research question concerns the number of collocations targeted each week. In reflective cycle 1, each week fifteen collocations were targeted and the students felt this was "just about right" (85.4 percent). In the second reflective cycle, each week twelve collocations were targeted and 79 percent of the students classified this number as being "just about right." However, there was a considerable difference between the receptive students (70 percent) and the productive students (87 percent) who chose this answer. It was not clear to me what caused this difference given that in my field notes I mentioned that both groups of students took about the same amount of time to complete the weekly tasks.

The data collected over the course of this reflective cycle was helpful in addressing the research questions. The students' responses and quantitative findings also influenced the procedures used in the next reflective cycle.

Changes in procedure implemented for reflective cycle 3

Based on the qualitative and quantitative results for reflective cycle 2, I decided to make several procedural changes for the next reflective cycle. These changes are made with the goal of finding the most efficient and effective method for teaching delexicalized verb collocations to low-proficiency students. I defined efficient in regard to the total time required to complete the exercises. I place more value on class time as opposed to homework time. Effective refers to improvements in the students' spoken fluency.

The first change was a switch from the Toyo 2 group of participants to the HUE 1 group. The data for this AR study was collected over three consecutive university years. However, I started working at a new university during this period, so this move necessitated the change in participants. I believed the HUE 1 group was of a similar level to the Toyo 2 group; I based this assumption on the fact I taught both groups communicative English classes using the same material with approximately the same amount of student comprehension. Unfortunately, this belief could not be strengthened by comparing the results from a standardized test, such as TOEIC, due to the small number of students who had completed such a test. I did not believe this change in participants hindered the data collection in any way. Aside from the fourth reflective cycle, the collocation exercises were presented as an alternative form of vocabulary study.

The other changes made between these two reflective cycles involve procedure. I decided to have the students do the initial collocation exercise as homework. Based on my field notes, I did not think there is much advantage in having the students complete these exercises in class. In addition, I decided not to use the receptive exercises (see Appendix 10 for an example of the receptive exercises). The students still used the collocation dictionary (a receptive task), but they did not answer the receptive questions like the group A students in the second reflective cycle. Based on the qualitative and quantitative data, I felt there was evidence indicating that productive tasks were superior to receptive tasks for improving productive ability with students of this level.

The final change is that I used the final 15 minutes of each class to engage the students in productively demanding tasks using the previous week's collocations. For the purposes of clarity, these tasks are referred to as "productive+" tasks. These tasks are explained in greater detail in the procedure section for reflective cycle 3. A summary of these changes can be seen in Table 5.25.

5.4 Conclusion

The two reflective cycles presented in this chapter produced valuable insight into how low-proficiency students develop productive ability in using delexicalized verb collocations. The data collected during the first reflective cycle supported the belief that low-proficiency Japanese university students could benefit from a collocation focus. Furthermore, this reflective cycle was the first step in the process of developing a set of procedures to introduce collocations to the low-proficiency students. A third important finding was the problematic nature of

Table 5.25 Procedural changes made between reflective cycles 2 and 3

	Reflective cycle 2	Reflective cycle 3
Participants	Toyo 2 group	HUE 1 group
Number of collocations targeted each week	12	12
Collocation dictionary	Yes	Yes
Homework	No collocation homework	Productive collocation exercises (Appendix 11)
Number of groups	2 (receptive and productive)	1 (productive+)
Intervention activities	Receptive group – answering questions Productive group – cloze activity	Productive+ tasks (explained in Section 6.2)
Initial questionnaire about previous vocabulary experience	Yes. Contained both closed and open-ended questions	No
Post-intervention questionnaire	Yes. Contained closed and open-ended questions	Yes. Contained closed and open-ended questions
Spoken assessments	Yes. An initial and post-intervention assessment	Yes. An initial and post-intervention assessment

delexicalized verbs that motivated me to continue my focus on these structures for the next reflective cycle.

The second reflective cycle was enlightening in regard to productive and receptive tasks. The data collected were evidence that productive exercises are superior to receptive exercises for fluency development. In addition, the procedures used for the collocation instruction were further refined, and this development can be seen in the next reflective cycle described in Chapter 6.

Over the course of this study, each reflective cycle produced data that aided in addressing the specific research questions. The results also helped shape the subsequent reflective cycle in terms of the procedures used and the overall goals for the study. The final two reflective cycles are presented in Chapter 6.

The Third and Fourth Reflective Cycles

6.1 Introduction

Along with Chapter 5, this chapter presents the findings from this study, as well as shows the findings from the third and fourth reflective cycles. As mentioned earlier, this sequence of chapters was chosen because it presents the findings in a logical and chronological manner.

6.2 The third reflective cycle

The third reflective cycle built on the findings of reflective cycle 2. The focus was on productive tasks, and this cycle was carried out with a different group of participants (HUE 1). The procedures were further refined based on the findings of previous cycles. However, the research focus was still on finding an effective way to improve the students' productive abilities in using the targeted collocations.

Research questions for reflective cycle 3

The same research questions from reflective cycle 2 were used for reflective cycle 3. In addition, research question 4 compares the groups from reflective cycle 2 with the group from this reflective cycle. This repetition of questions allowed me to compare the students' responses for the productive+ tasks (tasks, described in the procedure section of this chapter, that had greater productive demands than the tasks from reflective cycle 2) with the students' responses for the tasks from reflective cycle 2. A different group of students participated in this reflective cycle as explained in Section 4.5.

1. What are the low-proficiency Japanese university students' responses to studying collocations?
2. In the students' opinion, do they feel capable of using the collocations in conversation?
3. What characterizes the students' development of competence in using collocations as assessed by the teacher throughout the course?
4. What differences in the learners' responses can be seen for the productive+ group compared to the receptive and productive groups from reflective cycle 2?
5. What differences can be seen in the students' spoken fluency between an initial and a summative spoken assessment task?
6. From the students' perspective, how many collocations should be targeted each week?

Procedures for reflective cycle 3

This reflective cycle was carried out at my new university (HUE) from April to July 2013, the following year from reflective cycle 2. This period represents one university semester, and it was the students' first semester at university. The intervention was presented to the students as part of their normal course work. The participants for this reflective cycle, the HUE 1 group, are described in Section 4.5. In total, forty-three students chose to partake in this reflective cycle; however, only twenty-one students completed the final questionnaire. In previous reflective cycles, I was able to remind the students a second time to complete the online questionnaire. However, at my new university I did not have the opportunity to see the students after I first instructed them to complete the questionnaire. This lack of a reminder likely contributed to the small number of students who completed this questionnaire.

During the second class, the students completed an initial spoken assessment task. The procedure used to administer this spoken assessment task was the same procedure used in reflective cycle 2 (described in Section 5.3). After the audio-recordings were completed, I explained the term collocation in a similar manner as in reflective cycle 2. I also gave the students the web address where I posted the weekly collocations and homework assignments.

For the weekly homework exercises, the students were given a set of twelve collocations and instructed to use the collocation dictionary to search for the meanings. The second part of the exercise was a cloze task using the targeted collocations. This exercise is identical to the exercise used with group B in reflective cycle 2 and can be seen in Appendix 11.

In the final 10–15 minutes of the following class, I used these targeted collocations in productively challenging tasks. Several researchers have stated the benefits of using productive tasks for vocabulary instruction (Lewis, 2008; Nation, 2001, 2008; Nattinger & DeCarrico, 1992). Brown (2003) encourages the use of productive tasks that give students more control and allow for uninterrupted communication, so fluency can progress. Griffin and Harley (1996) conducted a study with students in their first year of French study that showed productive tasks to be superior for improving productive abilities. They state that "for production, learning in the direction of English-French is the more effective, since the forward association of English-French will be used at recall" (p. 453). However, the productive tasks for the Griffin and Harley study were translation tasks that did not have the spoken requirement as the tasks used in this reflective cycle. In this reflective cycle, the productively challenging tasks required the students to attend to the form, meaning and use of the targeted collocations during a spoken exercise.

The productive tasks for reflective cycle 3 once more exposed the students to the targeted collocations adding further repetition to the overall procedure, which Nation (2001, 2008) believes aids in vocabulary acquisition. For the purposes of this book, henceforth I refer to these classroom exercises as productive+ tasks. The productive+ tasks were designed to be more productively challenging than cloze tasks. By more productively challenging, I required that the tasks had the students say the targeted collocation out loud as part of a larger discourse while also including the productive challenges associated with cloze exercises. In total I used five different productive+ tasks:

1. *Translate and make a sentence* – I (the teacher) placed twelve cards around the classroom. Each card had one of the English collocations from the previous week's homework assignment written on the back and the Japanese translation on the top. The students worked with a partner, and each pair of students started at one of the cards. The first student in each pair read the Japanese translation and said the corresponding English collocation. The second student in the pair then used the English collocation in a sentence. If both students agreed that the sentence was suitable, they moved to another card. If they were unsure, they raised their hands and I provided help. The students could also check the English translation on the back of the card.

2. *Half a crossword* – I created two crossword grids. On grid "A," I wrote half of the previous week's collocations as the across answers. On grid "B," I wrote the other half of the previous week's collocations as the down answers. There were no clues provided on either crossword. The students worked in pairs: one student had crossword grid "A" and the other student had "B." One student asked for a hint from their partner by saying "what is number 2?" Their partner had to provide a "hint." A hint could be a Japanese translation, a cloze sentence, or a description of the targeted collocation. The students continued asking for and giving hints until both crossword grids were complete.

3. *Create a conversation* – Each student worked with a partner. I gave each pair of students one of the previous week's collocations. The students worked together and wrote a short two-person four-line conversation that included the targeted collocation. As the students were working, I walked around the class and corrected their English. The most common problem was the students' creation of an unnatural use for the targeted collocation. After most of the pairs of students had finished, they posted their completed short conversations on the wall. The students then walked around the class with their partner reading out loud each other's conversations.

4. *Conversation cloze* – This activity was similar to "create a conversation"; however, in this activity I wrote all of the short two-person four-line conversations myself. The conversation was a cloze activity with the targeted collocation removed and written on the back of the card, so the students could check their answers. One student was "A" and read the first line of the conversation. The other student was "B" and read the second line. This continued until the conversation was completed. When one of the students encountered the blank space, they had to fill it in with the correct collocation in the correct verb tense for the given situation. All of the collocations were from the previous week's list. The students continued around the classroom until all twelve conversations had been completed.

5. *Partner quiz* – Each student worked with a partner. On the projector, I showed the twelve English collocations from the previous week's homework. The students would alternate quizzing each other. The students could ask for a Japanese translation, for an English translation, or for a sentence using one of the collocations. If the students were unsure about a sentence, they raised their hands and I offered assistance.

Each week, I prepared one of the activities for the class. All five of these activities could be done within 15 minutes of class time if the students had completed the homework. These productive+ tasks are critiqued in the discussion section on this reflective cycle (Section 6.2).

In the eighth class, the students completed a test covering the first five sets of collocations. A test covering collocation sets six through ten was administered in the fourteenth class. Each of these tests constituted 15 percent of the students' final grade. The tests were the same ones as used for reflective cycle 2. An example can be seen in Appendix 12. Since the focus of this study was spoken fluency, the test results were not used as evidence of the students' increased ability to use the collocations productively.

In the last class, the students used the voice recorders for the post-intervention spoken assessment. The assessment was administered in exactly the same way as it was done in the second class and as it was done in reflective cycle 2. The two audio-recordings did not influence the students' final grade. The students were encouraged to do their best. In addition, I instructed the students to complete the post-intervention questionnaire that was posted on the same website as the homework assignments. A summary of the procedures used in reflective cycle 3 can be seen in Table 6.1.

Data collection for reflective cycle 3

I used three data collection tools during this reflective cycle. At the beginning and end of the intervention, I collected audio-recordings from the students. The procedure used to collect these recordings was the same as reflective cycle 2 and is described in Section 5.3. Both sets of recordings were assessed for fluency.

The second data collection tool was a questionnaire. The questionnaire was administered at the end of the intervention. It contained closed items posed as Likert scale questions and an open-ended question. The questionnaire provided both qualitative and quantitative data. Despite forty-three students participating in this reflective cycle, only twenty-one completed this questionnaire (see Section 6.2 for an explanation).

The final data collection tool was the field notes I wrote during the intervention. The field notes were primarily produced during time the students completed the productive+ tasks. These notes provided qualitative data.

Quantitative findings for reflective cycle 3

The quantitative data for reflective cycle 3 was gathered through the use of closed questionnaire items and the assessment of the voice recordings. Each

Table 6.1 Summary of procedure for reflective cycle 3

Week	In-class collocation work	Class time required in minutes	Homework
1	There were no collocation exercises done during the first class.		
2	Pre-intervention voice recordings. Explain the term collocation. Explained homework exercises.	15	Complete the collocation exercises for set 1.
3	Productive+ task for collocation set 1.	15	Complete the collocation exercises for set 2.
4	Productive+ task for collocation set 2.	15	Complete the collocation exercises for set 3.
5	Productive+ task for collocation set 3.	15	Complete the collocation exercises for set 4.
6	Productive+ task for collocation set 4.	15	Complete the collocation exercises for set 5.
7	Productive+ task for collocation set 5.	15	Study for the test.
8	Collocation test for set 1, 2, 3, 4, and 5.	30	Complete the collocation exercises for set 6.
9	Productive+ task for collocation set 6.	15	Complete the collocation exercises for set 7.
10	Productive+ task for collocation set 7.	15	Complete the collocation exercises for set 8.
11	Productive+ task for collocation set 8.	15	Complete the collocation exercises for set 9.
12	Productive+ task for collocation set 9.	15	Complete the collocation exercises for set 10.
13	Productive+ task for collocation set 10.	15	Study for the test.
14	Collocation test for set 6, 7, 8, 9, and 10.	30	
15	Post-intervention voice recordings. Post-intervention questionnaire (completed outside of class).	12	

questionnaire item was designed to provide insight into a specific research question for this reflective cycle. Several of the questionnaire items were the same as the ones used for previous reflective cycles to allow for comparison. This overlap allowed me to determine if the change in intervention procedure differently affected the students' responses for specific aspects of studying collocations. The questionnaire used in this reflective cycle can be seen in Appendix 15.

Table 6.2 shows the results for the questionnaire item "studying collocations has been useful."

Approximately 71 percent of the students agreed or strongly agreed with the questionnaire statement. The mean for this statement was 3.85.

The learners' responses to the questionnaire item "I am able to use the collocations we studied in conversations" are shown in Table 6.3.

Of the students who completed this questionnaire, twelve gave a neutral or negative response about their productive ability. The mean is 3.33 for this questionnaire item.

The students were asked to indicate their level of agreement with the statement "studying collocations is more helpful than studying individual words." The results for this item are presented in Table 6.4.

For this item, 86 percent of the responses agreed or strongly agreed with the statement. The mean was 4.14.

Tables 6.5 to 6.7 show the learners' responses for the specific activities used during the intervention. Table 6.5 shows the learners' responses for the statement "reading the definitions and example sentences has been useful." This statement references the first part of the collocation homework (Appendix 11).

Table 6.2 Students' responses about studying collocations

Question (n = 21)	Likert		Positive responses		Neutral responses	Negative responses	
	Mean	SD	5	4	3	2	1
	3.85	0.79	4 (19%)	11 (52%)	5 (24%)	1 (5%)	0 (0%)

Table 6.3 Students' responses about their ability to use collocations in conversations

Question (n = 21)	Likert		Positive responses		Neutral responses	Negative responses	
	Mean	SD	5	4	3	2	1
	3.33	0.80	1 (5%)	8 (38%)	9 (43%)	3 (14%)	0 (0%)

Table 6.4 Students' responses comparing studying collocations to individual words

Question (n = 21)	Likert		Positive responses		Neutral responses	Negative responses	
	Mean	SD	5	4	3	2	1
	4.14	0.65	6 (29%)	12 (57%)	3 (14%)	0 (0%)	0 (0%)

Table 6.5 Students' responses about reading the definitions and example sentences

Question (n = 21)	Likert		Positive responses		Neutral responses	Negative responses	
	Mean	SD	5	4	3	2	1
	3.71	0.78	3 (14%)	10 (48%)	7 (33%)	1 (5%)	0 (0%)

Table 6.6 Students' responses about the cloze task (productive task)

Question (n = 21)	Likert		Positive responses		Neutral responses	Negative responses	
	Mean	SD	5	4	3	2	1
	4.00	0.63	4 (19%)	13 (62%)	4 (19%)	0 (0%)	0 (0%)

Table 6.7 Students' responses about the productive+ tasks

Question (n = 21)	Likert		Positive responses		Neutral responses	Negative responses	
	Mean	SD	5	4	3	2	1
	3.81	0.87	4 (19%)	11 (52%)	4 (19%)	2 (10%)	0 (0%)

The mean is 3.71 for this statement. Thirteen of the twenty-one responses either agreed or strongly agreed with this questionnaire item.

The students were asked to assess the usefulness of the cloze task. The results for the item "doing the fill in the blank questions has been useful" are seen in Table 6.6.

The percentage of positive responses for this questionnaire item is 81 percent. The mean score is 4.00.

The final questionnaire item specifically enquiring about the exercises used during the intervention asked the students to assess their level of agreement for

Table 6.8 Students' responses in regard to the number of collocations covered each class

Question (n = 21)	Negative responses		Positive responses	Negative responses	
	Way too many	Too many	Just about right	Not enough	Not nearly enough
	0 (0%)	0 (0%)	20 (95%)	1 (5%)	0 (0%)

Table 6.9 Mean, standard deviation, and *t*-value for spoken fluency assessment

	Productive+ group		
	Pre-intervention	Post-intervention	Difference
M	2.81	4.14	1.33
SD	0.91	1.17	
t	8.54694		

the statement about the usefulness of the productive+ tasks. The results shown in Table 6.7 refer to the questionnaire item "doing the speaking and crossword questions at the end of class has been useful."

This questionnaire item elicited a positive response rate of 71 percent. The mean is 3.81.

As with the other questionnaire, the students were asked about the number of collocations targeted each week. The results for the questionnaire item "each week we studied twelve collocations. That was . . ." are seen in Table 6.8.

Of the twenty-one students who completed this questionnaire, twenty responded that twelve collocations per week was "just about right."

Table 6.9 shows the mean, standard deviation, and *t*-value or the spoken assessment. The pre-intervention and post-intervention scores represent the average student fluency on a scale of one to seven as assessed by a blind judge.

The productive+ group had higher scores on their post-intervention spoken fluency assessment. Fluency was measured on a seven-point scale. A score of one was extremely dysfluent and a score of seven was extremely fluent. The productive+ group's post-intervention score was 1.33 higher than their pre-intervention score. A two-tailed dependent *t*-test was performed on the results for the productive+ group. There was a significant effect for the productive+ group, $t(42) = 8.54$, $p < 0.05$, with the students receiving a higher score on the post-intervention spoken fluency assessment. A random sampling of transcripts from the spoken assessment for this reflective cycle can be seen in Section 6.2.

The quantitative finds are also discussed in greater detail in Section 6.2. These findings are juxtaposed with the qualitative findings from the open-ended questionnaire item and field notes. Overall, these quantitative responses indicate the collocation intervention was worthwhile in the learners' opinion, and there is evidence the productive+ group improved their spoken fluency.

Transcripts from spoken assessment for reflective cycle 3

The following transcriptions were randomly taken from the audio-recordings of the pre-intervention and post-intervention speaking task. The speaking task was a narrative retell, the same as was used in reflective cycle 2 and can be seen in Appendix 9. The same procedures as reflective cycle 2 were used to implement this assessment (Section 5.3). For both the first and second retells, the same spoken task was used; however, there was a gap of approximately four months between the administration of each of these assessments, so the effects of task repetition were believed to be minimal.

The transcripts below are introduced by the student's identification number for this study and the student's gender. Pauses within a retell are indicated by brackets with the number within the bracket indicating the duration of the pause in seconds. A (J) indicates that the student used a Japanese word or expression during this part of the retell. The expert judge's scores for fluency are given after each transcript and range from a score of 1 for an extremely dysfluent speech sample to a score of 7 for an extremely fluent speech sample.

A132046 – female (first retell)

get up as the seven o'clock and then change my clothes and eat breakfast. Then wash my clothes. In the afternoon, I do the training and then (1.3) I do that (0.6) I do the study and I study English or I do my homework and then I have a slept a little bit. At night, I cook (0.9) the dinner and watch TV. After that, I go to bed.

Fluency score: 4

J132046 – (second retell)

got up in the morning and then change my clothes (0.6) and have a breakfast. After that, (0.6) wash my clothes. In the afternoon, I usually do some exercise, studied, and have a nap. At night, I make a dinner. Then watch TV and fall asleep.

Fluency score: 5

Both retells have a few short pauses, but these pauses likely did not hinder the student's fluency to a great degree. In the second retell, she used two targeted collocations (do some exercise, have a nap) that better described these parts of the narrative retell than the word choices used in her first retell (do the training, have a slept a little bit). In both retells, she was able to convey all parts of the picture sequence with only a few minor mistakes.

A133004 – female (first retell)

get up (3.2) seven o'clock (1.7) and (7.1) wear (5.2) change and eat breakfast (1.5) and (2.2) wash (7.2) wear. In the afternoon, (4.2) stretch and study. After that, (4.5) go bed.

Fluency score: 2

J133004 (second retell)

get up seven o'clock. After that, I changed clothes and eat breakfast. (9.3) After breakfast, I wash my clothes (5.4) I do laundry. In the afternoon, (2.4) I stretched and studies English (2.7) and (0.9) have a nap. At night, I cook I make dinner (6.9) and (1.2) after eat dinner I watch TV (4.7) and I go to bed.

Fluency score: 3

Both retells have frequent lengthy pauses. However, in the second retell, the student had longer utterances that conveyed the meaning of the corresponding pictures in the narrative retell. The second retell also has the targeted collocations "do laundry," "have a nap," "make dinner," and "go to bed." In the first retell, she either did not articulate this part of the picture sequence or used an inappropriate word combination (wash wear).

A133005 – male (first retell)

get morning get (2.6) get up and wear the T-shirts (1.7) and (2.7) I eat breakfast then(2.5) I wash the T-shirts. In the afternoon, (1.9) I sports and (2.2) study (2.2) so I very I am very tired. Then I go to sleep go to bed. At night, (6.0) I cooking I am cooking (1.1) after I am cooking and watching TV. (2.2) Then I go to bed.

Fluency score: 2

J133005 – (second retell)

get up morning and wear T-shirts. (2.6) In morning, I eat breakfast and after (1.2) washing up my shirts. In the afternoon, I was I (1.7) I training and study training and study (5.3) and go to bed (6.0) take a break. At night, I make dinner and after the dinner I after dinner I watching TV and go to bed sleep.

Fluency score: 3

The second retell had fewer pauses than the first, but both retells had several unnatural expressions and verb tense mistakes. However, despite these mistakes, the student was able to articulate each picture in the sequence.

A133010 – female (first retell)

get up and (1.4)(J) I usually get up and (4.5) (J) wear the clothes and eat breakfast then (1.9) wash a lot of (1.7) clothes. In the afternoon, I training and study and have a nap. At night, (2.7) I at night, I cook (1.3) I cooking and watch TV then I go to the bed.

Fluency score: 3

J133010 – (second retell)

got up early and (2.8) (J) got up early and (5.8) change clothes and eat breakfast and do laundry. In the afternoon, (1.4) (J) I I do some exercise, and study and have a nap. At night, I eat I cook dinner and watch TV and go to bed.

Fluency score: 5

Both retells were hindered by the use of Japanese and at least one lengthy pause. However, the student was able to express each part of the narrative sequence in both retells. The main difference between the two retells was the use of natural expressions such as "change clothes," "do laundry," and "do some exercise" in the second retell where in the first retell these same parts of the narrative picture sequence were expressed using awkward word combinations such as "wear the clothes," "wash a lot of (1.7) clothes," and "I training."

A133022 – male (first retell)

get up (2.9) and (3.4) change the clothes. Next, I (1.0) have a breakfast and wash (1.0) all (0.6) clothes. In the afternoon, (5.8) I (1.5) play (7.7) stretch. Next, I study (0.9) English and (4.0) I take a nap. At night, (2.0) I cooking cook (1.8) dinner and watch the TV and go to bed.

Fluency score: 3

J 133022 – (second retell)

get up and (3.3) I change clothes. Next, next I have a breakfast and (2.4) (J) (4.0) (J) wash laundry. In the afternoon, (4.6) I stretched (3.4) my body and next I do a homework and I take a nap. At night, (4.3) I make a dinner and (3.3) I watch (1.2) the TV. In the end, I go to the bed.

Fluency score: 3

Both retells have frequent lengthy pauses. Each picture in the sequence is articulated in both the first and second retells; however, each retell contains several awkward expressions and grammatical mistakes.

The transcripts presented above are included in this section to provide additional information about the spoken assessment. Similar to the transcripts from reflective cycle 2, several themes emerged. Pauses within a retell adversely affected the students' fluency; however, in instances in which the pause was short and/ or between a clause boundary, it appeared the students' fluency score was only slightly lowered. In several retells, the students were able to convey the meaning of all the pictures in the narrative sequence despite using unnatural expressions and utterances with grammatical errors. Finally, many of the targeted collocations from the intervention were used in the second retell to help the students articulate a section of the picture sequence that they were unable to accurately express in their first attempt. The judge likely considered other aspects of the speech samples, but these themes appear to be particularly influential.

Qualitative findings for reflective cycle 3

The qualitative data for this reflective cycle was compiled through the use of an open-ended question on the post-intervention questionnaire and from my field notes. Compared to reflective cycle 2, only a small number of students completed the questionnaire. However, I noticed several patterns in the data that provided insight into:

- the learners' responses in regard to the speaking exercises using the targeted collocations,
- the value of the collocation dictionary,
- the advantages of studying collocations as opposed to exclusively studying individual words,
- the usefulness and suitability of the material used during the intervention, and
- the effectiveness of the productive+ tasks used during the intervention.

The students' responses are categorized in Table 6.10. All examples from the data are actual quotations from the students elicited by the open-ended questionnaire item.

Table 6.10 Qualitative findings from reflective cycle 3

Category	Sub-category	Example from the data
Procedures used for collocation instruction	Speaking aspect of the productive+ exercises	I think speaking makes our English improve. Just studying vocabulary doesn't help me. I feel I improve my English when I use new vocabulary in conversation. I think studying collocations is good for speaking English because we use collocations when we speak English. It was tough to memorize the collocations but I could use them in the conversation. That was good.
	Productive+ tasks as a whole	I like the exercise at the end of each class. There are 4 reasons. First, we can study collocations with classmates. Second, we can stand up, walk around and move our body. Third, collocations consist of words that we have already know, so it is not too difficult but also it is not too easy. Fourth, it is useful studying about collocations. Japanese students haven't studied about collocations enough because we don't need them to pass an university entrance examination, but we need them when we try to write an essay.
Materials used for collocation instruction	Dictionary	That was good to make example sentences. It was easy to remember collocation with some pictures. I feel happy when I understand the meaning with it. It was sometimes difficult to understand the pictures but if I knew collocation I could understand it.
	Usefulness and level	When I can make just simple English sentences. I'm not sure I achieved goal of the class. It was difficult to memorize collocation but it was useful. It's very useful. It is confusing to use verb such as take a bus and get a train.
Comparison to studying individual words		Learning collocation is more fun than just memorize vocabulary. It was difficult figure out put "a" or nothing. ex.) visit a website? visit website. Collocation is better than just memorize vocabulary. It's easy to remember. It was difficult to remember on and for (preposition).

Discussion for reflective cycle 3

The data collected during reflective cycle 3 was useful in addressing the research questions from Section 6.2. The research questions are discussed individually to show what findings were made and the aspects of the findings that were further investigated.

The first research question focused on the students' perception of their experiences of studying collocations. As with the first two reflective cycles, the students' impression of this experience was positive. The mean score for the first questionnaire item, as seen in Table 6.2, was 3.85, which indicated the students thought the collocation instruction was useful. In addition, Table 6.4 shows the findings from the questionnaire item comparing studying collocations to studying individual words. The mean score of 4.14 indicates the students believed a focus on collocations is more helpful than studying individual words. The qualitative data also supported this positive response. The following quotes taken from Table 6.10 show the students find collocation study to be useful and more effective than addressing vocabulary instruction by targeting individual words:

> It was difficult to memorize collocation but it was useful.

> Collocation is better than just memorize vocabulary. It's easy to remember. It was difficult to remember on and for (preposition).

These findings are consistent with the findings from the first two reflective cycles.

The second questionnaire item, which had the students assess their productive ability in using the targeted collocations, addressed research question 2. The mean score for this item was 3.33 (Table 6.3) with nine students (43 percent) agreeing or strongly agreeing that they are capable of using the targeted collocations in conversations compared to three students who disagreed with the statement. Since a lack of productive ability using previously taught vocabulary was the initial area of concern for this study (described in Chapter 1), this finding is encouraging, especially when considered with the findings for the fifth research question described below. The qualitative data also supported the notion that the students felt they were making progress in regard to their spoken proficiency as seen in the following responses:

> I feel I improve my English when I use new vocabulary in conversation.

> I think studying collocations is good for speaking English because we use collocations when we speak English.

> It was tough to memorize the collocations but I could use them in the conversation. That was good.

The following two quotes taken from my field notes also address the students' ability to use the targeted collocations in conversations:

> The students who did not do the homework, had a lot of trouble in the speaking exercises.

> The students enjoyed the speaking exercises.

These responses and excerpts from my field notes show the students had a favorable impression of the speaking exercises, but it is not clear that this enjoyment is synonymous with an improvement in productive ability. However, it should be noted that my impression during the intervention was that the students needed the homework exercise to prepare them for the productively challenging tasks used at the end of the class. Each of the productive tasks described in Section 6.2 is discussed in greater detail at the end of the section.

The third research question focuses on the students' development of competence in using collocations throughout the intervention. This question is best answered by examining the students' performance during the productive tasks because during this portion of the class the students demonstrated their ability (or lack of ability) in using the targeted collocations. The following quotation taken from my field notes provides insight:

> It was clear that many students did not do the homework, perhaps as many as 30%. I can easily tell the students who did the homework from those who didn't, especially by monitoring the students at one of the cloze conversations. The students who had done the homework would fill in the blank correctly or make a mistake that still indicated they had an idea about the answer (used an incorrect delexicalized verb, used a different collocation from the homework, were able to provide one half of the collocation). If I suspected a student of not having done the homework, I would ask them directly. Most of these students admitted they did not do the homework. The students who did not do the homework had very little chance of doing the exercises successfully.

The quotation above underscores the importance of repetition in acquiring collocation competence. To efficiently enable students to use a collocation productively, it appears necessary to progress through a series of stages where students are initially exposed to the targeted structures, are required to compete exercises involving the collocations, and then engage in productively challenging tasks. The majority of my students had to prepare themselves for the speaking exercises by completing the homework, and the students who did not prepare performed at a much lower level than the other students, so they were easily identified. Other researchers (Lewis, 2008; Schmitt, 2000; Ur, 1991) have also stressed the positive influence of repetition on vocabulary acquisition.

The fourth research question compared the findings from this reflective cycle to reflective cycle 2. The purpose of this question was to gauge the learners' responses for the productive+ tasks used in this intervention to the receptive and productive tasks from reflective cycle 2. The students had a positive impression of the usefulness of the tasks from this cycle as seen in the following mean scores taken from Table 6.5, 6.6, and 6.7: reading definitions and example sentences (3.71); cloze tasks (4.00); productive+ tasks (3.81). In reflective cycle 2 (Tables 5.18 to 5.21), the learners' responses about the usefulness of the receptive tasks had the following mean scores: reading definitions and sentences (3.77); answering questions about the sentences (3.67). The learners' responses about the productive tasks from reflective cycle 2 had the following mean scores: reading definitions and example sentences (3.95); cloze tasks (4.00). While each group of students had a positive impression of their tasks, the mean scores for the productive and productive+ tasks were higher. As mentioned in the procedures section for reflective cycle 3, researchers have stated the effectiveness of productive tasks (Lewis, 2008; Nation, 2001, 2008; Nattinger & DeCarrico, 1992). The qualitative data also supported the notion that the learners preferred tasks that were productively demanding as seen in the following quotes:

> I think speaking makes our English improve. Just studying vocabulary doesn't help me.

> I feel I improve my English when I use new vocabulary in conversation.

In reflective cycle 2, the qualitative data (Section 5.3) also indicated the students preferred tasks that were productively demanding.

To address the fifth research question, a comparison of an initial (preintervention) and summative spoken assessment was conducted. As seen in Table 6.9, the mean score for the students' spoken fluency increased by 1.33 as measured blind by an expert judge on a seven-point scale (see Section 5.3 for a description of this procedure). This difference was statistically significant and is evidence the productive+ tasks lead to an improvement in the learners' speaking ability.

The final research question focused on the number of collocations targeted each week. In this reflective cycle, 95 percent of the students responded that twelve collocations per week was "just about right." This is consistent with the previous two reflective cycles in which the students also responded positively about targeting twelve or fifteen collocations on a weekly basis.

While this was not an original research question, the qualitative data also included quotes that I used to evaluate the productive+ tasks used during this reflective cycle. The following quotes concerning the procedures used were taken from my field notes. I have organized this data in Table 6.11 according to the specific productive+ task to which it refers.

With the exception of "translate and make a sentence," all of the tasks were worthwhile in my opinion as the teacher. However, it was difficult to verify if the language produced by the students was accurate as seen in the following quote from my field notes:

> All of the productive+ tasks were difficult to monitor.

Overall, I believe the productive aspects of these tasks were well received by the students as evidenced by the questionnaire responses discussed above and effective for improving the students' spoken abilities as corroborated by the improvement in the spoken assessment.

Changes in procedure implemented for reflective cycle 4

Reflective cycle 3 not only provided data that addressed the research questions for this cycle, but it also brought to light other aspects of an increased collocation focus in classrooms, such as exposure to the targeted structures and task design, which were investigated in the fourth and final reflective cycle for this study. Specifically, the findings from the third reflective cycle supported the claims of other researchers (Lewis, 2008; Schmitt, 2008; Ur, 1991) that an instructional procedure that incorporates repetition of targeted structures and requires use of these structures is effective for improving the students' productive abilities. Between previous cycles, it was necessary to make changes in procedures to specifically address the research questions for the next reflective cycle. This need was also present between the third and fourth cycles. The most notable change in procedure was the shift in focus from delexicalized verb collocations to frequent adjective + noun collocations. Table 6.12 presents the changes in procedures that were implemented.

Table 6.11 Data taken from field notes concerning productive+ tasks

Productive+ task	Examples from data
Translate and make a sentence	The students did not put much effort into this exercise. This exercise was difficult to monitor. Students progress through this exercise much faster than I anticipated. When I join a group to offer assistance, it takes much longer to complete the translation and sentence. Either the students are not making sentences when I am not present or they misunderstood what to do.
Half a crossword	Crosswords were very enjoyable for the students. Many Ss would stick to the simple translation hints.
Create a conversation	The writing of a conversation using a collocation was okay, but I had to check the students' usage of the collocation. Many groups used the collocations in unnatural ways. Every group that had the collocation "get comfortable" misused this collocation. They understood the meaning after I showed them the picture from the dictionary. Having the students go around and read the other collocation conversations was enjoyable for them.
Conversation cloze	Spoken cloze activity was my favorite, but it was also the most difficult to monitor. Ss really tried to understand the situation of the conversation. The simple act of moving around seems to keep the students interested/motivated. The students seem to like the challenge of filling in the blanks. The first few times they would make verb tense mistakes, but they would reduce these mistakes in later conversations.
Partner quiz	The partner quiz was very difficult to monitor. However, I did not notice many mistakes. The students would sometimes discuss if the sentence was okay in partners. Occasionally, some students would ask me for help but not as much as I would have liked. Some students might have assumed their partner created a good sentence and did not ask for confirmation from me. Most of the corrections I made were when I listened in as opposed to being asked for help.

It should be noted that for the fourth reflective cycle a collocation dictionary was not used. This decision was made because I felt the adjective + noun collocations were more challenging than the delexicalized verb collocations from the previous two reflective cycles. I believed the task of matching the English collocations with their Japanese translations would increase the likelihood of acquiring the targeted collocations.

Table 6.12 Procedural changes made between reflective cycles 3 and 4

	Reflective cycle 3	**Reflective cycle 4**
Participants	HUE 1 group	HUE 1 group
Number of collocations targeted each week	12	15
Collocation dictionary	Yes	No
Homework	Productive collocation exercises (Appendix 11)	Productive collocation exercises (Appendix 17)
Number of groups	1 (productive+)	1 (productive+)
Intervention activities	Productive+ tasks (explained in Section 6.2)	Productive+ tasks (explained in Section 6.2)
Collocations targeted	Delexicalized verb + noun collocations	Frequent adjective + noun collocations
Post-intervention questionnaire	Yes. Contained closed and open-ended questions	Yes. Contained closed and open-ended questions
Spoken assessments	Yes. An initial and post-intervention assessment	No

A second change in procedure was using collocation sets containing 15 structures as opposed to 12. This modification was made because there was a possibility one class during the semester would be cancelled. Having eight sets as opposed to ten, created a degree of flexibility that ultimately was not needed.

6.3 The fourth reflective cycle

This reflective cycle was the final data collection period for this study. As with previous cycles, its purpose was to address issues or questions that arose through the research process that had been undertaken to date.

The goals for this reflective cycle were similar to the previous cycles in that there was a focus on the students' responses. However, there were two procedural changes made in order to address the specific questions for this cycle. The first change was targeting frequent adjective + noun collocations as opposed to the delexicalized verb collocations from reflective cycles 2 and 3. This change was implemented to investigate whether the data collected to date was a direct result of the language targeted as opposed to the procedures used. The second change was the use of the same group of participants from reflective cycle 3. The previous reflective cycles all used a different group of participants. This cycle was the first opportunity to collect data from a group of students who had previously studied collocations.

Research questions for reflective cycle 4

As mentioned above, the research questions for this cycle focused on the learners' responses and were influenced by the two procedural changes described in Section 6.3. As with other reflective cycles, there was an overlap between questions for this cycle and questions from previous cycles. This repetition was included to allow for a comparison of learners' responses.

1. What are the low-proficiency Japanese university students' responses to studying collocations?
2. Will the students feel capable of using the collocations in conversation?
3. What characterizes the students' development of competence in using collocations as assessed by the teacher throughout the course?
4. What differences did the students identify between studying the adjective + noun collocations this semester as compared to the delexicalized verb collocations from the previous semester?
5. From the students' perspective, how many collocations should be targeted each week?

Procedures for reflective cycle 4

This reflective cycle was carried out over the participants' second university semester, which was from October through January. This semester immediately followed the data collection period from reflective cycle 3 and the same group of participants were used (the HUE 1 group described in Section 4.5). The intervention procedure was presented to the students as part of their normal course work. For this cycle, forty-three students agreed to participate, but only thirty-eight students completed the final questionnaire. I am unsure of the reason the five students did not complete this final questionnaire.

During the second class, I briefly explained that the target language would be frequent adjective + noun collocations. Since these students undertook the exercises from reflective cycle 3, I am confident they understood the term collocation. I explained that each week they were required to complete the exercises for one set of collocations, and that these exercises could be found on a website I created. Each exercise presented a list of fifteen collocations in "part A" in the form of a matching task: the students had to match the English collocation with its Japanese translation. Morgan and Rinvolucri (2004) have stated that fifteen vocabulary items is a suitable number for each session. As with the previous reflective cycles, the fifteen collocations for each set were randomly compiled from the collocation lists. The second part (part B) of the exercise was a cloze task using the fifteen targeted collocations from "part A." After completing the exercise, the students could check their answers that were also posted on the website. The use of L1 for introducing vocabulary has been endorsed by researchers (Lewis, 2008; Morgan & Rinvolucri, 2004; Nation, 2008, 2004; Ur, 1991) because "translation is . . . an instinctive part of the way the mind approaches learning a second language" (Lewis, 2008, p. 60). The inclusion of cloze tasks is also recommended for vocabulary instruction (Nation, 2001; Ur, 1991).

During the final ten to fifteen minutes of the following class, the previous week's collocations were used in a productive task in order to maximize the likelihood of acquisition by repeatedly exposing the students to the targeted vocabulary (Lewis, 2008; Schmitt, 2008; Ur, 1991) and by requiring the students to use the words in spoken discourse (Lewis, 2008; Nation, 2001, 2008; Nattinger & DeCarrico, 1992). Nation (2001) states that "repetition thus adds to the quality of knowledge and also to the quantity or strength of this knowledge" (p. 76).

The productive tasks were the same tasks used in the third reflective cycle and are described in detail and critiqued in Section 6.2. The only difference from the previous reflective cycle was that I did not use the "translate and make a sentence" task due to the difficulties I had with this task also described in Section 6.2. Each of these tasks could be completed in the allotted time despite the use of a different type of collocation (adjective + noun).

In the seventh class, the students completed a short review exercise. I used the same "partner quiz" task with the only difference being the students could quiz their partner on any collocation from sets one through four. A second review exercise was conducted in the thirteenth class for sets five through eight.

In the eighth class, the students completed a test covering the first four sets of collocations. A test covering collocation sets five through eight was administered in the fourteenth class. Each of these tests constituted 15 percent of the students' final grade. The tests were in a similar format to the tests used in reflective cycles 2 and 3. An example can be seen in Appendix 18.

In the last class, I instructed the students to complete the post-intervention questionnaire, which was posted on the same website as the homework assignments. A summary of the procedures used in reflective cycle 4 can be seen in Table 6.13.

Table 6.13 Summary of procedure for reflective cycle 4

Week	In-class collocation work	Class time required in minutes	Homework
1	There were no collocation exercises done during the first class.		
2	Explain the term collocation. Explain homework exercises.	5	Complete the collocation exercises for set 1.
3	Productive+ task for collocation set 1.	15	Complete the collocation exercises for set 2.
4	Productive+ task for collocation set 2.	15	Complete the collocation exercises for set 3.
5	Productive+ task for collocation set 3.	15	Complete the collocation exercises for set 4.
6	Productive+ task for collocation set 4.	15	No homework.
7	Review for collocation sets 1, 2, 3, and 4.	15	Study for the test.
8	Collocation test for sets 1, 2, 3, and 4.	30	Complete the collocation exercises for set 5.
9	Productive+ task for collocation set 5.	15	Complete the collocation exercises for set 6.
10	Productive+ task for collocation set 6.	15	Complete the collocation exercises for set 7.
11	Productive+ task for collocation set 7.	15	Complete the collocation exercises for set 8.
12	Productive+ task for collocation set 8.	15	No homework.
13	Review for collocation sets 5, 6, 7, and 8.	15	Study for the test.
14	Collocation test for set 5, 6, 7, and 8.	30	
15	Post-intervention questionnaire (completed outside of class).	5	

Data collection for reflective cycle 4

For this reflective cycle, two data collection tools were used. The first tool was field notes that were taken during the last 15 minutes of each class while the students were completing the speaking tasks. My goal was to assess how engaged the students were during these exercises and to determine if the students were using the target language correctly.

The second data collection tool used during reflective cycle 4 was a post-intervention questionnaire. During the fifteenth week, the students were instructed to complete the questionnaire sometime after class. The questionnaire elicited both quantitative and qualitative data.

Quantitative findings for reflective cycle 4

The quantitative data for the fourth reflective cycle was collected through the use of closed questionnaire items. Each item provided insight into a specific research question for this reflective cycle. As with the post-intervention questionnaire used in reflective cycle 3, several of the items were the same as items from previous cycles. This overlap allowed me to determine if the change from delexicalized verb collocations to frequent adjective + noun collocations affected the students' responses for specific aspects of the intervention. The questionnaire used in this reflective cycle can be seen in Appendix 16.

As with the quantitative data from the three previous cycles, a Likert scale was used and the responses were assigned a value, so the mean and standard deviation could be calculated. Table 6.14 shows the results for the questionnaire item "studying collocations has been useful."

Approximately 69 percent of the students agreed or strongly agreed with the questionnaire statement. The mean for this statement was 3.79.

The students' responses shown in Table 6.15 refer to the questionnaire item "I am able to use the collocations we studied when I am having a conversation."

Table 6.14 Students' responses about studying collocations

Question (n = 38)	Likert		Positive responses		Neutral responses	Negative responses	
	Mean	SD	5	4	3	2	1
	3.79	0.62	4 (11%)	22 (58%)	12 (32%)	0 (0%)	0 (0%)

Table 6.15 Students' responses about their ability to use collocations in conversations

Question (n = 38)	Likert		Positive responses		Neutral responses	Negative responses	
	Mean	SD	5	4	3	2	1
	3.58	0.83	5 (13%)	15 (39%)	15 (39%)	3 (8%)	0 (0%)

Table 6.16 Students' responses comparing studying collocations to individual words

Question (n = 38)	Likert		Positive responses		Neutral responses	Negative responses	
	Mean	SD	5	4	3	2	1
	3.89	0.92	12 (32%)	12 (32%)	12 (32%)	2 (5%)	0 (0%)

Table 6.17 Students' responses about the level of difficulty of this semester's collocation work compared to the previous semester

Question (n = 38)	Likert		Positive responses		Neutral responses	Negative responses	
	Mean	SD	5	4	3	2	1
	3.23	0.94	4 (11%)	10 (26%)	15 (39%)	9 (24%)	0 (0%)

Of the students who completed this questionnaire, eighteen gave a neutral or negative response about their productive ability. The mean is 3.58 for this questionnaire item.

The students were asked to indicate their level of agreement with the statement "studying collocations is more useful than studying individual words." The results for this item are presented in Table 6.16.

For this item, 64 percent of the responses agreed or strongly agreed with the statement. The mean was 3.89.

Table 6.17 shows the students' responses for the statement about the level of difficulty of this semester's collocation work to the previous semester's. The statement was "studying the adjective + noun collocations this semester was easier than studying the verb + noun collocations last semester."

The mean is 3.23 for this statement. Of the thirty-eight students who responded, fourteen agreed or strongly agreed that the collocation study this semester was easier than last semester.

Table 6.18 Students' responses in regard to the number of collocations covered each class

Question (n = 38)	Negative responses		Positive responses	Negative responses	
	Way too many	Too many	Just about right	Not enough	Not nearly enough
	0 (0%)	4 (11%)	32 (84%)	1 (3%)	1 (3%)

As with the other questionnaire, the students were asked about the number of collocations targeted each week. The results for the questionnaire item "each week we studied fifteen collocations. That was . . ." are seen in Table 6.18.

Of the thirty-eight students who completed this questionnaire, thirty-two responded that fifteen collocations per week was "just about right." As mentioned earlier, reflective cycles 1 and four targeted fifteen collocations per week while the second and third cycles targeted twelve collocations per week.

Qualitative findings for reflective cycle 4

The qualitative data was elicited through the use of an open-ended item administered at the end of the intervention. The students' responses were organized based on the patterns that emerged through analysis and provided insight into the following themes:

- The value of studying collocations.
- The level of the material used.
- The procedures used during the intervention.

Table 6.19 presents the students' responses from this reflective cycle.

As in the previous reflective cycles, the students indicated through the open-ended item on the questionnaire that they thought an increased focus on collocations was worthwhile. They also identified the targeted collocations in this reflective cycle as being problematic due to the similarities in several of the collocates' meanings. The high frequency of the targeted collocations and their problematic nature appeared to justify the explicit instruction used during the intervention. However, my field notes that were taken during the speaking exercises indicated that the students had trouble productively using the collocations as seen in the following quotations:

Table 6.19 Qualitative findings from reflective cycle 4

Category	Sub-category	Example from data
Value of studying collocations	Collocations in general	I don't like that in Japanese classes, English is taught according to a fixed rule with words, and it makes the meaning. I thought that it was very beneficial as a person using English that the relationship of real English was able to be studied from Mr. Joshua who is an English native and understands such points. Thank you. By repeating the study of collocations, many English words could be memorized and it was useful. Since the opportunity to come into contact with English was increased by studying collocations compared to high school, I think that collocation activity was good. I think studying collocations is very useful to learn English effectively. I wanna learn more collocations.
	The adjective + noun collocations from reflective cycle 4	It was difficult to learn the native ways of using properly words, such as Current and Present. I thought that the collocation learned in the class was very practical, and helpful for the future. There were many words that were alike rather than the first half, and although it was easy to memorize, proper use of the fine meaning was difficult. Although the words were not difficult and there was no problem in particular, since many words that are the same or were alike were used, it was hard to memorize. I thought that it was difficult because combinations of adjective + noun, which used different words had the same meaning. However, various expressions can be studied.
Level	Comparison with collocations from reflective cycle 3	The material of the verb plus noun felt easy. A verb plus noun was easier to understand, even if the adjective plus noun collocation has an example and it has scene-setting. At the point, I think that the collocations of the second half had a less clear meaning than the first half. Since the verbs in the first half was known, I thought that it was easier.
	Collocations from reflective cycle 4	Since the adjective and nouns were easy and contained mostly in daily conversation, it was easy to memorize.

Category	Sub-category	Example from data
Procedures used	Speaking activities	I think that it was good we needed to make a text from the learned collocation although it is difficult.
		It was easy to translate into Japanese but it was difficult to make an English sentence.
		I think that I was able to learn grammar and daily conversation in relation to the collocations.
		Crossword puzzle was interesting.
	Initial collocation exercises	I can also check the homework myself and I think that it was good.
		The material and exercises were helpful in order to memorize vocabulary.

The speaking exercises are more challenging than last semester.

The students often misuse the collocations.

The students also commented on the relative difficulty of the collocations targeted in this reflective cycle compared with cycle 2:

At the point, I think that the collocations of the second half had a less clear meaning than the first half.

Since the verbs in the first half was known, I thought that it was easier.

The students' responses indicate that while the targeted structures were useful, they were more challenging than the previous semester's collocations.

The qualitative data also indicated that the delexicalized verb collocations from reflective cycle 3 were easier than the adjective + noun collocations for this cycle. The students mentioned that the collocations last semester were familiar and their meaning was easier to understand. While frequency of the collocations and the individual collocates was a criterion for inclusion on this semester's collocation list, delexicalized verbs are still much more frequent and likely more familiar to the students. In addition, the noun components of collocation list three were specifically chosen because their meaning varies depending on the adjective with which they are used.

The final group of responses focused on the procedures used during the intervention. Similar to the qualitative data from previous reflective cycles, the students' responses indicated they endorsed the use of productively demanding tasks. These tasks were difficult as seen in the quotations from my field notes above and the example responses from the data in Table 6.19; however, the students felt it was necessary to use the targeted structures productively if acquisition was to occur.

In the following section, I discuss the findings of reflective cycle 4. I juxtapose the quantitative and qualitative data in order to address each research question.

Discussion for reflective cycle 4

The research questions are now discussed individually in reference to the quantitative and qualitative data that were collected over the course of the intervention for reflective cycle 4. The first research question was addressed through both the quantitative and qualitative data. The students' responses to the open-ended questionnaire item indicated that they valued the collocation instruction during both this semester and the previous semester. The students felt that studying collocations was an effective way to improve their English abilities. This finding was also supported by the quantitative data presented in Section 6.3. The Likert scale questionnaire item "studying collocations is useful" elicited a mean score of 3.79 with 69 percent of the students agreeing or strongly agreeing with this statement. Furthermore, 64 percent of the learners agreed or strongly agreed that studying collocations is more useful than studying individual words. The mean score for this questionnaire item was 3.89 with only 5 percent of the learners disagreeing to the statement.

The second research question asked if the students felt capable of using the targeted collocations in conversations. While the qualitative data suggests the students felt the speaking tasks were beneficial, only twenty of the thirty-eight students agreed or strongly agreed that they felt confident in their productive ability to use the targeted structures. However, the mean score of 3.58 for this statement was higher than the 3.33 mean for the same statement in reflective cycle 3.

My field notes were useful in addressing research question three. As seen in Section 6.3, I noted that the students struggled with using the collocations during the speaking tasks. The students' responses in Table 6.19 indicated that the speaking tasks were challenging because many of the collocates were similar in meaning. I believe that the students were able to do the initial computer exercises for each set of collocations because these tasks were less productively demanding. However, as the productive demands increased, the students were less able to complete the tasks. While explicit instruction is useful to expose students to problematic collocations, language instructors must create tasks in which the students must repeatedly use the targeted structures for acquisition to occur. This finding is similar to Nation's (2001) belief that

> It is possible and helpful to approach the learning of word forms, for example, through explicit learning, but that essentially the most effective knowledge for this aspect of vocabulary is implicit and there must be suitable repeated opportunities for this kind of learning to occur. (p. 34)

The fourth research question can be addressed by comparing the third and fourth reflective cycles. The responses for both cycles indicated the students felt the targeted collocations to be useful for their future English language needs and a worthwhile focus of study. However, the qualitative and quantitative data are contradictory in regard to a comparison of level for the two reflective cycles. The quantitative data suggests the students felt the material for reflective cycle 4 was easier than for reflective cycle 3. However, the qualitative data suggests collocation list three to be more difficult. My field notes indicated that the students had trouble completing the speaking tasks for both collocation lists two and three. I believe the data supports the choice of these collocations for instruction based on the students' productive difficulties and the high frequency of these structures.

The final research question can be addressed through the quantitative data seen in Table 6.18. In regard to the number of collocations targeted each week, 84 percent of the students felt that fifteen collocations was "just about right." This result is similar to the three previous reflective cycles in which the students indicated that twelve or fifteen collocations per week was suitable.

6.4 Conclusion

This chapter presented the findings from the final two reflective cycles for this study. These two cycles presented the opportunity to use the same group of participants with two different types of targeted collocations: delexicalized verb collocations for reflective cycle 3 and frequent adjective + noun collocations for reflective cycle 4. The findings indicated that despite the type of collocation targeted, students felt a collocation focus was useful. Furthermore, tasks that required learners to use the structures were seen as being beneficial for language acquisition. The collocations included in lists 2 and 3 were chosen because they were thought to be problematic for low-proficiency English language learners.

This belief was supported through the findings as many students indicated that these structures were difficult to use productively.

The fourth reflective cycle was the final data collection period for this study. The following chapter discusses all four reflective cycles through an overview and comparison of the findings.

Discussion and Conclusion

7.1 Introduction

This chapter focuses on the implications of the findings and methodological choices beyond the scope of this paper. The findings are interpreted from the perspective of the field of vocabulary acquisition as a whole as opposed to specifically looking at the teaching of collocations.

7.2 Limitations of this research

In this section, I discuss several limitations of this study. Over the course of the four reflective cycles, several procedural changes were made to better suit the needs of my students. However, by making these procedural changes, the comparisons I made between intervention groups are subject to debate. In the discussion that follows I discuss the possible limitations in the findings that were made, the data analysis that was used, and the procedures that were implemented in the intervention stage of this study.

Limitations of the findings

While this study had four reflective cycles using three different groups of participants, all of the students who took part in this investigation were of the same (low) English proficiency level and from the same country (Japan). The decision to focus on low-proficiency students was made to address the disparity in collocation research that to date has largely focused on advanced students (Eyckmans, 2009; Jiang, 2009; Nesselhauf, 2003; Revier, 2009). However, by only focusing on low-proficiency students, the findings may not be applicable to students at a higher English proficiency level.

Another possible limitation of the findings is the fact that over the course of this study only two specific types of collocations (delexicalized verb collocations and frequent adjective + noun collocations) were investigated. These two types represent only a small portion of the total number of collocations used in English, and the findings from this study might have been different if various types of collocations were investigated.

As seen in the findings presented in Chapters 5 and 6, the students had a positive impression of studying collocations. However, the student responses were elicited after only one semester (reflective cycles 1, 2, and 3) or two semesters (reflective cycle 4) of explicit collocation instruction. It is possible that the positive responses are partially the result of the novelty of a different approach to vocabulary acquisition. It is unknown if the students would still have a positive impression of studying collocations over a longer period of time. Furthermore, the questionnaire included the word "useful," which might have indicated a preferred response to the students.

The post-intervention questionnaire findings for reflective cycle 3 can also be questioned. Of the forty-three participants who took part in this reflective cycle, only twenty-one completed the final questionnaire. It is possible that the more motivated students were the ones to complete this questionnaire, and that these findings are not representative of the total group of participants.

Limitations in the data analysis

In regard to the data analysis, there are three possible limitations. The first limitation concerns the students' responses elicited through the four questionnaires that had open-ended items. Many of these responses were written in Japanese by the students and then translated to English by an experienced Japanese university instructor with a high level of English proficiency. However, the responses were not back translated to ensure accuracy.

The statistical analysis from reflective cycles 2 and 3 can also be brought into question. A matched pair t-test was used to analyze the difference in a pre-intervention and post-intervention spoken fluency assessment. For reflective cycle 2 especially, a valid argument can be made that the ANOVA would have been a more suitable statistical measurement given the fact that there were two intervention groups (receptive and productive). Furthermore, the Fleiss' kappa test that was conducted to measure inter-rater reliability only had an observed agreement of 0.375.

The spoken assessment (see Sections 5.3 and 6.2 for excerpts) was an elicited monologue in which the students described a series of pictures. While this procedure provided a measure of consistency in the assessment between students, it can be argued that a monologue is not the most representative speech sample for measuring fluency. A speech sample taken from a conversation might be a more accurate indicator of a student's fluency.

Limitations in the procedures used

Several aspects of the procedures used during the various reflective cycles can also be questioned. In this chapter, I compared findings from the second and third reflective cycles. While these two cycles used the same collocation list (list 2), reflective cycle 3 included a homework assignment, but reflective cycle 2 did not.

Another potential weakness in the procedures used during this study concerns the spoken assessment task. To elicit the speech sample, I used a series of pictures depicting daily routine activities. Collocation list 2, which was used for the two cycles in which a speech sample was taken, contained several delexicalized verb collocations that could be used to describe these activities. Specifically, eight of the 120 collocations (6.7 percent) from list two could have been used during the spoken assessment, and the excerpts seen in Sections 5.3 and 6.2 show that several targeted collocations were used. Therefore, the improvements in spoken fluency might only relate to the students' ability to use the targeted collocations as opposed to their overall fluency capabilities.

Finally, between the second and third reflective cycles, I started working at a different university. As a result, the participants used during these two cycles were also different, yet I compared the findings from the two cycles in this chapter. Specifically, I proposed that the productive+ tasks from reflective cycle 3 were superior for improving fluency to the receptive and productive tasks from cycle 2. The fluency improvement seen in the findings could have been a result of using a different group of students as opposed to the change in procedure. However, this change did provide a measure of triangulation to my findings.

7.3 Revisiting the original purpose of the study

Before conducting this study, I targeted individual words from the General Service List (GSL) and designed classroom activities around these individual lexical items. I included an aspect of vocabulary instruction within my curriculum, and I specifically allotted class time each week to teach targeted structures in my low-proficiency university communication classes. However, at that time my students were not effectively improving their spoken abilities with the targeted words despite my efforts.

A review of the literature suggested a focus on collocations might address this shortcoming in my teaching practice. However, the literature contained mostly proposals for the benefits of a collocation focus with little empirical evidence provided as support. Furthermore, the majority of studies that had been conducted tended to use intermediate or advanced level language learners. Despite these studies using participants with a different proficiency from those in this study, the research designs did provide a framework for my own investigation. I decided initially to investigate the students' impressions of a classroom focus on collocations as opposed to individual words. I wanted to learn how the students would respond to this new form of instruction and gain insight into effective ways to teach collocations.

I recognized these two aims were vague and consequently it was inefficacious to strictly define the direction the research would take. However, I postulated that by framing research questions around student responses I would gain the knowledge necessary to advance my research in both design and desired outcome.

While I was initially unsure of how I would arrive at my goal, the desired outcome of my study was never in doubt: the improved productive abilities of my students in using targeted language. I wanted to produce a procedure, based in theory and supported by evidence, for how language instructors can efficiently approach vocabulary instruction within the constraints of their classes. The findings should be viewed from this pedagogical perspective and the importance of this investigation should be determined by its value to second language instructors.

The exploratory and pedagogical nature of this study can be seen in the research questions from the first reflective cycle through to the final cycle. Initially, the research questions focused on students' perceptions, specifically their impression of the alternative form of vocabulary instruction, their self-assessment of their productive abilities with the targeted structures, and their perception of the procedure used during the treatment. The second reflective cycle's research questions overlapped and evolved from the questions in the first cycle. The students' perceptions of the value of a classroom collocation focus and their impressions of the procedures used within the intervention were addressed. The research questions for the third reflective cycle were similar to the second cycle with the exception that one of these questions focused on the procedural differences employed in these two cycles. This inclusion illustrates how the intervention procedures evolved as the study progressed and how the focus remained on pedagogy. To address the final set of research questions I elicited the students' perceptions as I had in the previous three cycles. However, in this cycle the targeted structures had been changed from delexicalized verb collocations to frequent adjective plus noun collocations. The goal of this cycle was to add a level of robustness to the findings by using the most effective procedure from the previous cycles to target a different type of collocation. The evolution of the research questions shows how the findings influenced procedural changes in subsequent reflective cycles, while the research focus remained on producing practical classroom knowledge.

7.4 How the findings relate to form-focused instruction

While form-focused instruction was not an area that was copiously presented in the literature review of this book aside from Section 3.5, the findings from this study support the belief that this type of instruction is beneficial in second language classrooms (Brown, 2007; Ellis, 2001, 2006; Williams, 2005). Spada (1997) describes form-focused instruction as "any pedagogical effort which is used to draw the learners' attention to language form either implicitly or explicitly" (p. 73). Brown (2007) similarly explains that within form-focused instruction, there are many possibilities for how language content can be presented to the students ranging from consciousness raising activities to explicit instruction of target language depending on the learning context and purpose. The value of form-focused instruction is seen in the growing evidence that language learning is aided by the deliberate teaching and learning of language items (Nation, 2001).

Of particular relevance to this study, is the approach used to teach vocabulary. During the early years of communicative language teaching, form-focused vocabulary instruction was not prioritized (Brown, 2007). However, researchers (Hulstijn, 2001; Laufer & Paribakht, 1998; Nation, 2008; Read, 2004) believe that explicit vocabulary focus is more effective for vocabulary acquisition than relying on incidental exposure alone. Brown (2007) states that "learners can be guided in specific ways to internalize these important building blocks of language" (p. 436). Nation (2001) contends that explicit vocabulary instruction should constitute a substantial portion of a language course. He states that "a course should involve the direct teaching of vocabulary and the direct learning and study of vocabulary" (2001, p. 2). Other researchers (Durrant & Schmitt,

2010; Nesselhauf, 2003; Webb & Kagimoto, 2009) have specifically endorsed the use of explicit instruction for the teaching of collocations. In this study, the students received this form of direct vocabulary instruction, and they showed improvement in spoken fluency between an initial and post- intervention spoken assessment.

7.5 Implications for the teaching of vocabulary

The focus of this study was collocations; however, the evidence discovered over the course of the investigation can also be used to scrutinize other aspects of vocabulary instruction. These findings provide insight into the choice of language to target, the techniques used to introduce new vocabulary to students, the importance of "use" within exercises, and the need for repetition for acquiring new words.

The choice of targeted vocabulary is important in terms of both level and usefulness. The students' responses indicate that the length, meaning and frequency of a given word contribute to its level of difficulty. The students expressed that long words are problematic while shorter words are easier to acquire. In addition, the meaning of a word also influences the effort required to acquire it. For example, words with one concrete meaning and/or a direct L1 equivalent are easier to learn than words with multiple meanings or words that do not have an identical L1 counterpart. Nation (2008) makes a similar claim when he compares the meaning for the word "free" in Thai and English to illustrate the difficulties students encounter when learning words with multiple meanings. In Thai, "free" has only one meaning of not needing to be paid for, but in English it has other additional meanings. A word's frequency also influences how difficult it is to acquire in the students' opinion. This belief of the students is consistent with Milton (2009) who states that frequency is influential in when a word is acquired by a language learner. Words that are frequent in the L2 are seen as being easier based on the fact that the number of exposures is likely to be higher for these words. While these characteristics contribute to an individual lexical item's level, it is also important to consider the number of new vocabulary items to which teachers expose their students (Milton, 2009; Schmitt, 2008). The learners indicated that targeting too many words at one time is counterproductive and harmful to student motivation. A word's usefulness is determined by how common it is in the L2 and the students' ability to productively use the new structure. Words that are common and/or used to express ubiquitous concepts, such as daily routines are easier to acquire in the students' opinion. Schmitt (2008) also endorses the targeting of these words as they provide a solid basis for more advanced study. Similarly, if a new word can be immediately used in a productive situation, it is seen as being easier to learn. To summarize, instructors should consider the criteria described above and their students' English proficiency when choosing new vocabulary to target. In addition, to maximize the chance of acquisition, they should focus on words that can be immediately used in speaking tasks.

Another aspect of target vocabulary selection requires the instructor to identify categories of language that are suitable for explicit instruction. These categories of language likely consist of structures that are difficult to acquire through exposure alone. During this study, I identified two such categories: delexicalized verb collocations and frequent adjective + noun collocations. Delexicalized verb collocations are unlikely to be learnt through exposure alone because the word combinations are often arbitrary and students might not consider the complete collocation when they encounter these chunks of language. The finding that this collocation structure is problematic for English language learners is consistent with previous researchers' (Chan & Liou, 2005; Nation, 2001; Nesselhauf, 2005) statements about the challenges students have with delexicalized verbs. Specifically, Chi, Wong, and Wong (1994) state that the delexicalized verb loses its original meaning depending on the words with which it is used making these collocations especially difficult to acquire.

In the second group, the nouns from the frequent adjective + noun collocations have meanings that are largely dependent on the adjectives with which they are used. For example, the meaning of the noun "way" has a different meaning in the collocation "best way" from its meaning in the collocation "long way." It is logical to assume that "way" would be more difficult to acquire through exposure alone than nouns with a concrete meaning. However, by focusing on the complete collocation, these structures become less problematic. While exposing students to large quantities of comprehensible input is an effective approach to English language instruction, the findings from this study indicated that this approach should be supplemented with explicit teaching of structures such as the two previously described. This approach is consistent with researchers such as Nation (2008) and Schmitt (2008) who also endorse the selective use of explicit instruction for vocabulary instruction. Furthermore, it dovetails with the recommendations of researchers (Bahns & Eldaw, 1993; Conzett, 2000; Handl, 2009; Hill, 2000; Jiang, 2009; M. Lewis, 1994; Reppen, 2010; Wray, 2008) about the benefits of collocation instruction.

Over the course of this investigation, I continually refined the procedure for introducing and reviewing the targeted collocations. In the third and fourth reflective cycles, I assigned homework containing receptive tasks with L1 translations and cloze exercises to introduce the collocations to the students. I feel this approach is also suitable for teaching individual lexical items as it does not require class time and it prepares the students for productively challenging tasks in the following class.

The findings from this study show evidence that vocabulary tasks are most effective when there is a requirement to use the targeted language productively. The students in the third reflective cycle made significant improvements in spoken fluency after a semester of productively challenging speaking exercises. Other researchers (Milton, 2009; Nation, 2000; Schmitt, 2008) have also stated the benefits of productive exercises for vocabulary acquisition, and Fan (2009) specifically mentions use as being important for the students if they are to acquire collocations. Furthermore, the learners' responses indicate that they value these exercises and that they feel their previous vocabulary instruction did not adequately prepare them to use new words in productive situations. Having an aspect of "use" in vocabulary exercises also has a consciousness raising effect by making the students aware that despite their receptive knowledge of the new words, they lack the productive ability needed to articulate the new language.

Lastly, repetition was identified as being a consequential element in vocabulary instruction similar to the proposals made by other researchers (Durrant & Schmitt, 2010; Nation, 2008; Schmitt, 2008). Fan (2009) and Wood (2010) have stated that repetition, along with use, is critical for improving a student's productive ability. By repeatedly exposing the students to previously introduced vocabulary through both receptive and productive tasks, the likelihood of acquisition increases. This finding is supported by the learner responses concerning previously studied vocabulary, my field notes taken during the third and fourth reflective cycles, and the students' improvement on a summative spoken assessment from the third reflective cycle in which repetition was an influential aspect of the procedure used.

To summarize, the findings from this study are applicable to the larger field of vocabulary teaching. Specifically, instructors should deliberately select the new target words, introduce these words through tasks that do not consume class time, and incorporate "use" and repetition into follow-up classroom exercises.

7.6 The relevance of the study for teacher education

The findings from this study are also applicable to the larger field of teacher education. Teacher education programs should make prospective teachers aware of collocations and the importance collocations have on a learner's productive abilities. Teachers should also be conscious of aspects of language that are suitable for explicit instruction. In addition, a well-designed language program should expose students to the target language repeatedly.

While new teachers are likely mindful of the importance of vocabulary, they need to be made aware of the depth of knowledge required to gain command over a given word. Receptive ability of a lexical item is only one aspect of the knowledge required before a word is fully acquired by a language learner. Learners need to be aware of a lexical item's form, meaning and use. Form includes aspects such as a word's pronunciation, spelling, and how it can be conjugated. Meaning can be represented by an L1 translation, but it also involves the meaning a word carries in the L2 given the context in which it is used. "Use" includes aspects of knowledge such as the formality a word has, its register, and also the words with which it is commonly used (a word's collocates). Collocation knowledge is another way to refer to this last aspect of "use." Instructors can improve a learner's knowledge of collocations in a variety of ways such as explicitly teaching collocations as chunks of language as I did in this study. Another approach is to simply raise awareness, so students can notice collocations within the input they receive. Henriksen and Stenius Stoehr (2009) state that language instructors have not paid enough attention to collocations due to several reasons such as a lack of comprehension problems despite collocation errors, a lack of collocation awareness in both the teacher and student, and a lack of understanding of the importance of improving the depth of vocabulary knowledge for a given word. Collocation knowledge influences a learner's productive ability more so than their receptive ability. A language learner might be able to comprehend an utterance without having knowledge of the specific collocations that were used. The learner might not be aware that they are incapable of using a lexical item because they do not know the words that are commonly used with the lexical item. By expanding a student's knowledge of words that they are already familiar with, as opposed to continually teaching unknown individual lexical items, an instructor can attend to a language learner's productive ability in a more effective manner.

Language instructors would become more efficient if they differentiated aspects of vocabulary that are more suitable for explicit instruction. As mentioned previously, two such areas were identified and targeted over the course of this investigation, and researchers (Handl, 2009; Shin & Nation, 2008; Wood, 2010; Wray, 2008) have stated the importance of identifying suitable collocations for instruction. I use one criterion for identifying these categories of language: a problematic nature for acquisition through exposure alone. For example, the adjective + noun collocations from the fourth reflective cycle are structures that would be difficult to acquire through exposure alone because the noun collocate has a meaning that is dependent on the adjective with which it is used (see the previous section for an example). However, if the entire collocation is treated as a chunk of language, the different meanings associated with the one lexical item can be acquired. To illustrate with the previous example, if a student learns that the noun "way" has a meaning similar to "method" they would likely understand and be able to produce the collocations "easy way" and "best way." However, if they encountered the collocation "long way" they might be able to understand its meaning given the context, but they would be less likely to be able to use this collocation in a conversation. They might produce a chunk of language like "long distance" instead of "long way" to describe this concept. On the other hand, if they learn these collocations as chunks of language, this productive problem is avoided. In addition to determining if an aspect of vocabulary is opaque for language learners, instructors should consider their students' needs and level along with the teachability and frequency of the target structures when identifying groups of words more suitable for explicit instruction. While I only employed two such aspects of vocabulary during this study, it is likely that for each different English proficiency level many more categories of words exist, which would be suitable for explicit instruction. Language teachers should view vocabulary from this perspective when determining the content and approach for their classes.

The third finding that has relevance to the larger field of teacher education is the importance of repetition within a language course. The nature of the teaching/learning situation influences how much conscious thought an instructor needs to spend trying to incorporate repetition of targeted vocabulary into their curriculum. The more exposure a language learner has to the target language, the less important repetition becomes. For example, learners studying at an intensive language school in an L2 speaking country are exposed to a large amount of input and the repetition of targeted vocabulary is an organic process. However, in an EFL setting in which the students only receive a small amount of exposure to the target language (similar to this study), instructors need to be deliberate in incorporating repetition into their classes. The students supported this belief through their responses on the previous vocabulary experiences questionnaire. While they were specifically addressing vocabulary instruction when they endorsed repetition, this concept likely applies to all aspects of English. Furthermore, the students in this study made the greatest improvements in the third reflective cycle, which had the most repetition of the delexicalized verbs. However, it is not possible to quantify the impact repetition had on the students' performance compared to previous reflective cycles, given that this cycle also used a homework assignment and speaking activities while reflective cycle 2 did not. In spite of that, the repetition of the delexicalized verb collocations throughout the intervention likely contributed to the students' improved performance on the summative spoken assessment. Language classes would become more effective if instructors design several activities that elicit the targeted vocabulary and spread these activities over several classes.

This study had a specific focus on two types of collocations, but the findings yielded insight into the larger field of vocabulary acquisition. This study produced evidence that explicit instruction is an effective way to teach certain groups of vocabulary, that students benefit from a focus on collocations, and that repeatedly exposing students to the target language aids in its acquisition. Education programs should include these three concepts when instructing future teachers on how to design vocabulary components within a well-balanced language curriculum.

7.7 Action research as a methodology

The choice of AR as a methodology was made with consideration of the research goals, the teaching context, and the expected outcome of this study. The research goals for this investigation were pedagogical in that each goal was related to how vocabulary can be effectively taught, so that students can productively use newly acquired words. The teaching context allowed for a longitudinal study, but it also narrowed the possibilities for the research design. At the conclusion of this study, I expected to have produced practical knowledge that would be beneficial for teachers in their approach to vocabulary instruction. The methodology of AR proved to have strengths and weaknesses in regard to the original aims, the teaching/learning situation, and the expected results.

This original motivation for this study started when I noticed a weakness in my teaching practice: my students' inability to use previously taught individual lexical items productively. Each research goal for this study focused on one aspect or perspective of this classroom problem. Consequently, AR was a sound choice of methodology because of its close connection to the classroom. The findings from an AR study are generated through a monitored intervention in procedure, which in the case of this study was a new approach to vocabulary instruction. The methodology of AR allowed me to elicit student responses concerning the new approach and then make procedural changes based on the newly acquired knowledge in subsequent reflective cycles. Each change in procedure was justified by my and the students' observations of the activities using collocations, and was thus closely connected to pedagogy. However, while other language instructors might empathize with the original weakness in my teaching practice, the findings from this AR study might not be relevant to another teaching/learning situation.

This investigation was conducted at two Japanese universities over the course of four semesters. Using AR in this teaching/learning situation offered both advantages and disadvantages. First, the demands of conducting an AR study dovetail well with the normal responsibilities of a university language instructor. The methodology of AR is flexible in research design and accommodating of newly acquired knowledge. Consequently, AR studies can be aligned with the specific teaching environment and appropriately altered after data analysis. As described in Chapter 4, a university language classroom provides a suitable environment to carry out AR as AR produces practical knowledge through an intervention in one's teaching practice. Interventions can involve changes in classroom procedure and data collection can be done during classes and/or through actual assessments. However, in my experience the ongoing nature of AR studies can be difficult to manage. For example, at the beginning of this study, I did not anticipate conducting four reflective cycles, and consequently had to adjust the research goals throughout the process. Furthermore, when a study extends over a longer than anticipated time frame, the likelihood of a change in working situations also increases. This change could necessitate a substantive adjustment in research design and goals.

Finally, by conducting research within a pedagogical setting the findings are likely to be of practical value because aspects of the study, such as the procedure, data collection and data analysis are influenced by the constraints of language instruction within a classroom. The research goals for this study were made with the aim of both understanding and improving an aspect of my practice, which

I identified as a weakness. However, I was limited by constraints such as the number of students in my class, the amount of class time I could earmark for the intervention, and the English proficiency of the students. As the research process progressed, I was able to adapt and extend the study as necessary in order to realize the original goals, but each change was still restricted by the characteristics of the classroom previously described. While these restrictions presented challenges throughout the AR process, they also increased the probability of the results being of practical value to language instructors. Given the ongoing nature and pedagogical influences of an AR investigation, the culmination of a study has a high likelihood of addressing the original area of concern.

The overall process of conducting an AR study was rewarding, but it also presented several challenges that had to be overcome. The study's aims, context, and expected outcome should be considered when deciding on AR as a methodology.

7.8 Research agenda

Throughout this AR process, I became aware of several areas of collocation instruction that need further investigation but were not addressed in this study. I therefore make the following four proposals for extending the research of this study and for furthering other avenues of collocation research.

1. Experimental study using a different fluency assessment. The procedures used throughout this investigation could also be used in a quantitative study to produce findings that could be generalized to other teaching/ learning situations. A study of this nature could employ two groups: a control group that focuses on individual lexical items and a treatment group that focuses on collocations. The fluency assessment could be completed using audio-recordings and software similar to what was used in Wood's (2010) study. By controlling the variables and using a research design that is replicable, the findings would likely be of greater value to the second language acquisition community.

2. Case study using low-proficiency students and general collocation instruction. This study used several large groups of low-proficiency students and two specific types of collocations. However, a greater depth of knowledge might be gained by using a research design similar to Jiang's (2009) consciousness-raising study but with a case study of a small group

of low-proficiency students. Instead of the specific focus on delexicalized verb collocations and frequent adjective plus noun collocations seen in this study, an investigation of a consciousness-raising approach to all kinds of collocations might provide evidence of the potential benefits of collocation instruction for low-proficiency students. The case study approach would allow the researcher to examine how low-proficiency students acquire collocational knowledge in a greater depth than was possible in this investigation.

3. Investigation of different types of collocations and aspects of English suitable for explicit instruction. As mentioned in the previous proposal, this study focused on two specific types of collocations. However, it is unknown if the students would have had a similar amount of success if a different kind of collocations were targeted. Furthermore, other aspects of English, aside from the collocation lists used in this investigation, are likely best taught through explicit instruction as opposed to relying on exposure alone. The identification of these categories of the English language would help instructors target problematic language. However, when compiling these lists, researchers should use some empirical evidence to support their selection as opposed to only using intuition.

4. Collocation instruction and written fluency. This investigation focused on spoken fluency; however, it is not clear if the findings have any relationship with written fluency. The procedure used for a study on writing and collocations could use a similar approach but with a fluency assessment of student writing.

While I tried to be as comprehensive as possible over the course of this study, it became clear the field of collocation research has many avenues in need of further investigation.

7.9 Conclusion

Considering the initial goals for this study, I believe the time and effort spent have been worthwhile. Originally, I wanted to produce practical knowledge that would be of use to other language teachers, to help my students with their spoken fluency, and to ultimately become a better language teacher. The findings from this study are useful for teachers whose students struggle with their spoken abilities. Furthermore, the students who took part in this study on average improved their spoken fluency. I have also improved my abilities as a language teacher by engaging in reflective practice and by learning more about how to effectively teach vocabulary.

Aside from the original goals, this study also shed light on other aspects of vocabulary instruction. This study is new in extending a focus on phraseological collocations to lower proficiency learners, in investigating a range of pedagogic tasks through which such learners can be engaged, and in developing their awareness of phraseological collocations as a concept. Furthermore, over the course of the four reflective cycles, I identified two types of collocation suitable for explicit instruction. Through a form-focused instructional approach, these structures can be more easily acquired by English language learners. Furthermore, the procedures used for this explicit instruction provide a template for how targeted vocabulary can be introduced to the students and elicited in spoken tasks.

The process of conducting an AR study was also challenging and rewarding. I found the ongoing nature of my study to be formidable, but through this form of trial and error investigation I was able to ultimately end on a satisfactory result. I strongly believe there is a need for more AR studies in second language classes as they connect the research to pedagogy.

My initial thoughts for how this study would progress were quickly dismissed as data were collected and analyzed. I did not foresee the extended nature this study would ultimately take or how often I would need to adjust my research design to best serve the needs of my students. The original goal was to produce practical knowledge that would be of value to language instructors while also being supported by empirical evidence. Considering the original area of concern and the progress made by the students in the final two reflective cycles, I feel I have achieved this goal.

Appendices

Appendix 1: Collocation List

Apply for a job
Arrange flowers
Attract tourists
Be in a good mood
Be in a queue
Board a plane
Break a promise
Break a record
Break the rules
Call a taxi
Call an ambulance
Call friends
Catch a ball
Catch a cold
Catch a plane
Catch fire
Catch fish
Cause damage
Change trains
Check email
Climb a mountain
Come early
Come to a decision
Cross the road
Depart from an airport
Do a search
Do business
Do housework

Do nothing
Do someone a favor
Do the washing-up
Fall in love
Feed your pet
Feel lonely
Feel sick
Follow the road
Get a job
Get divorced
Get dressed
Get drunk
Get in touch
Get into a car
Get lost
Get married
Get out of bed
Get ready
Get upset
Get worried
Give someone a lift
Go bad
Go bald
Go by sea
Go on foot
Go online
Go out for dinner
Go out with friends
Go overseas
Grow flowers
Hand in your work
Have a drink
Have a headache
Have a problem
Have children
Have lunch
Hire a car
Install software

Keep a promise
Keep an appointment
Keep calm
Keep quiet
Leave the light on
Live on your own
Live together
Look for a job
Look in a drawer
Make a mess
Make a noise
Make friends
Make furniture
Make money
Make progress
Make someone laugh
Make time for
Miss a bus
Owe money
Park a car
Pay attention
Pay bills
Pay by credit card
Pay off a loan
Pay someone a compliment
Pay someone a visit
Plant crops
Ride a bike
Run out of time
Save a document
Save electricity
Save energy
Save money
Save someone a seat
Save someone's life
Save something on a computer
Save time
Set the alarm

Set the table
Set up a business
Slip on the ice
Spend some time
Stay at someone's house
Stay in touch
Take a break
Take a chance
Take a rest
Take a taxi
Throw a party
Tidy your room
Use the stairs
Wait for a bus
Waste time
Work in the garden

Appendix 2: Collocation List 2

(Node words are in bold.)

Apply or a job
Be in a good mood
Call an ambulance
Carry out experiments
Catch a cold
Catch a plane
Catch fire
Cause damage
Check email
Come early
Come late
Come on time
Come prepared
Come right back
Come to a decision
Delete a file
Do a search
Do housework
Do laundry
Do nothing
Do some exercise
Do someone a favor
Do the cooking
Do the washing up
Do your best
Do your hair
Do your homework

Fall asleep
Fall in love
Feel sick
Find a partner
Forward an email
Get a haircut
Get a job
Get a loan
Get a train
Get angry
Get comfortable
Get divorced
Get dressed
Get drunk
Get home
Get lost
Get married
Get ready
Get wet
Get worried
Give someone a lift
Go abroad
Go bad
Go fishing
Go online
Go out for dinner
Go out of business
Go out with friends
Go overseas
Go to bed
Hand in your work
Have a baby
Have a bath
Have a conversation
Have a drink
Have a good time
Have a headache
Have a holiday

Have a nap

Have a problem

Have a rest

Have an argument

Have children

Have fun

Have lunch

Have time

Install software

Keep calm

Keep in touch

Keep quiet

Live on your own

Live together

Look for a job

Make a difference

Make a mistake

Make a noise

Make a reservation

Make an appointment

Make dinner

Make money

Make someone angry

Make someone laugh

Make the bed

Open an attachment

Pay attention

Pay someone a visit

Pay the rent

Pay well

Restart a computer

Save a document

Save electricity

Save energy

Save money

Save something on a computer

Save time

Spend some time

Take a break
Take a bus
Take a class
Take a look
Take a message
Take a photo
Take a seat
Take a taxi
Take an exam
Take medicine
Take notes
Take someone's temperature
Take your time
Visit a website
Waste time
Write a prescription
Write an essay

Appendix 3: Collocation List 3

(Node words are in bold.)

Account **balance**
Bad **behavior**
Best **performance**
Best **way**
Better **idea**
Better **position**
Better **use**
Big **difference**
Clear **idea**
Clear **view**
Close **relationship**
Complete **change**
Conscious **decision**
Current **account**
Current **position**
Current **situation**
Current **state**
Detailed **account**
Different **story**
Different **view**
Different **way**
Difficult **decision**
Difficult **question**
Difficult **situation**
Direct **effect**
Direct **result**
Easy **way**

Effective **use**
Effective **way**
Full **account**
Full **use**
Further **action**
Further **discussion**
Further **information**
General **view**
Good **behavior**
Good **condition**
Good **effect**
Good **idea**/great **idea**
Good **performance**
Good **question**
Good **reason**
Good **relationship**
Good **resul**t
Good **use**
Good **view**
Good **way**
Good **work**
Great **interest**
Hard **work**
High **interest**
High **performance**
Human **behavior**
Immediate **action**
Immediate **effect**
Important **difference**
Important **question**
Long **story**
Long **way**
Main **argument**
Main **difference**
Main **problem**
Main **reason**
Necessary **condition**
New **idea**

New i**nformation**
New **plan**
New **position**
New **system**
New **way**
Only **answer**
Only **difference**
Only **problem**
Only **reason**
Only **way**
Open **question**
Other **information**
Other **reason**
Other **way**
Other **work**
Particular **interest**
Particular **problem**
Particular **situation**
Particular **way**
Political **decision**
Political **situation**
Political **system**
Poor **condition**
Poor **performance**
Present **position**
Present **situation**
Present **state**
Present **system**
Private **information**
Public **interest**
Real **problem**
Real **reason**
Recent **work**
Right **answer**
Right **decision**
Right **way**
Serious **problem**
Short **answer**

Short **stories**
Simple **answer**
Small **change**
Social **action**
Social **behavior**
Social **change**
Social **system**
Special **relationship**
Strong **argument**
Strong **position**
Sudden **change**
True **story**
Whole **question**
Whole **story**
Whole **system**
Wrong **way**
(5) Year **plan**

Appendix 4: Post-Treatment Questionnaire Used During Reflective Cycle 1

Studying collocations (verb + noun word units) – 配置(動詞+名詞単語ユニット)を研究してます。

The purpose of this questionnaire is to learn about students' attitudes toward studying collocations (verb + noun word units, e.g., "check email"). Please answer the questions honestly. There are no right or wrong answers. The results will be kept confidential and anonymous. Thank you for taking the time to complete this questionnaire.

このアンケートの目的は、配置(動詞+名詞単語ユニット: 例えば、"check email")を学生がどういう気持ちで勉強しているかという事について研究する為です。

正直に質問に答えてください。 その答えに正しいとか間違いなどということは一切ありません。 結果は、秘密厳守かつ匿名となります。

お忙しいところ、このアンケートにご協力下さってありがとうございます。

Please check the most appropriate answer.

最も適切な答えをチェックしてください。

1. Studying collocations has been useful. 配置を研究するのは役に立っている。

   Strongly agree 非常にそう思う

   Agree そう思う

   Neutral ふつう

   Disagree そう思わない

   Strongly disagree 全くそう思わない

2. I am able to use the collocations we studied when I am having a conversation. 会話の中で、私は勉強した配置を使用することが出来る。
   Strongly agree 非常にそう思う
   Agree そう思う
   Neutral ふつう
   Disagree そう思わない
   Strongly disagree 全くそう思わない

3. Studying collocations is more useful than studying individual words. 配置を勉強することは個々の単語を研究するより役に立つ。
   Strongly agree 非常にそう思う
   Agree そう思う
   Neutral ふつう
   Disagree そう思わない
   Strongly disagree 全くそう思わない

4. Writing sentences using the collocations was helpful. 配置を使用することで文を書くのに役立った。
   Strongly agree 非常にそう思う
   Agree そう思う
   Neutral ふつう
   Disagree そう思わない
   Strongly disagree 全くそう思わない

5. Each week we studied 15 collocations. That was . . . 毎週、私たちは15の配置を勉強しました。それは。。。
   Way too many 非常に多すぎた
   Too many 多すぎた
   Just about right ちょうど良かった
   Not enough 十分でなかった
   Not nearly enough 全然十分ではなかった

If you would like to see the results of this questionnaire, please leave your email address and I will send you a copy. Thanks again for taking the time to do this questionnaire.

このアンケートの結果を見たい方は、Eメールアドレスを残してください。そうしましたらコピーを送ります。

アンケートに協力して下さりましてありがとうございました。

Appendix 5: First Test Used During Reflective Cycle 1

Vocabulary test #1

Name: _____

Student #: _____

Class: _____

Score: _____/30

Part 1: Match the words /5

Feel Forward Direct Run Restart Keep Break Make Do Pay

1. _____ sick
2. _____ a movie
3. _____ business
4. _____ a computer
5. _____ cash
6. _____ out of time
7. _____ someone's heart
8. _____ progress
9. _____ an email
10. _____ a promise

Part 2: Complete the story using some of the phrases from the box. You might have to change the verb tense (go→went) /10

Last Sunday, I had a relaxing day. I woke up early and _____ to the store
to buy some eggs, bread, and potatoes. I didn't have any cash so I _____
. I came home and cooked a big breakfast for my wife. She usually _____

but I wanted to help her. I _____ because she was still sleeping. After she woke up, we ate breakfast, and then I cleaned the house. I _____, _____, and washed the windows. In the afternoon, we _____ together. We sat on the sofa and talked about many things. We _____ about our next vacation: we will go to Hawaii!!! In the evening, we opened a bottle of wine and _____ outside our house. It was a nice evening. Before bed, I _____ and brushed my teeth. I love Sundays!

Have a drink   Take a taxi   Have a bath   Come to a decision   Pay by credit card   Keep quiet   Make the bed   Do the cooking   Do the washing up   Spend some time

---

Part 3: Choose five of the following phrases and write a sentence. You must show you understand the phrase. Longer sentences are better /15

Apply for a job	Do a favor	Take a photo
Go bad	Save electricity	Have a holiday

1. _____

    _____

2. _____

    _____

3. _____

    _____

4. _____

    _____

5. _____

    _____

Appendix 6: Example of a Matching Exercise from Reflective Cycle 1

Collocation set 5: Match the following "verb + noun" collocations with the meaning. After you check the answers write the collocations and the meanings in your vocabulary notebook

Arrange flowers	**Board a plane**	**Clear the table**
Arrive at an airport	Call a taxi	Climb a mountain
Attract tourists	Catch fish	Climb over a fence
Be in a queue	Change the sheets	Cross a river
Be out of petrol	Change trains	Cross the road

Meanings

A. 旅行者を引き付けます	**B.** 電車を乗り換えます	**C.** 川を渡ります
D. ガソリンを使い果たしました	**E.** 列に並ぶ	**F.** 道路を渡ります
G. 花を生けます	**H.** 山に登ります	**I.** シートを変えます
J. 飛行機に乗る	**K.** 垣根を乗り越します	**L.** タクシーを呼ぶつもりです
M. 空港に到着します	**N.** テーブルをきれいにします	**O.** 魚を捕ります

Answers

Arrange flowers – G	**Board a plane – J**	**Clear the table – N**
Arrive at an airport – M	Call a taxi – L	Climb a mountain – H
Attract tourists – A	Catch fish – O	Climb over a fence – K
Be in a queue – E	Change the sheets – I	Cross a river – C
Be out of petrol – D	Change trains – B	Cross the road – F

Appendix 7: Excerpt from the Collocation Dictionary

Delete a file – ファイルを削除する
You can delete the file. I made a copy.

Do a search – 検索する
Use google to do a search for information about Japan.

Do housework – 家事をする
I did housework on Saturday. I cleaned the windows, swept the floor, and washed the sheets.

*Do laundry – 洗濯をする
I do the laundry every Sunday morning.

Do nothing – 何もしない
I was tired so I did nothing all weekend.

Appendix 8: Excerpt from Field Notes Taken During Reflective Cycle 2

Data collection week 3

What happened?

I noticed a student writing translations for all of the collocations in a notebook prior to doing the exercises. I had encouraged the students to initially look up the words in the dictionary that was provided to them. Some students seem to be finishing the exercises quite quickly. I had to "quiz" a student who completed the task in 10 minutes (allotted time was 20 minutes). It turned out he did not have a good grasp on the collocations. Hopefully, he will spend more time on them next class.

General observations for receptive and productive groups

Not much value to doing these exercises in class. Can easily be done outside of class.

Ss are not using the collocation dictionary enough. Do they really understand the collocations or just think they do? Overconfident. This is the same for both treatment groups. Perfect example of this is "catch fire." Ss all seem to believe it means "to light a cigarette." I catch fire a cigarette. I do not notice any difference in regard to level of engagement or time spent completing the activity depending on the treatment group. Will questionnaire 2 support this? Having the Ss do the exercises on the computer seems to have increased the level of interest as opposed to last RC.

Appendix 9: Spoken Assessment Task

On Sundays, I usually . . .

In the afternoon . . .

At night . . .

Appendix 10: Example of Receptive Task for Reflective Cycle 2

Set 3 group A

Part A: Use your collocation dictionary for these

Do some exercise	Get angry	Look for a job
Call an ambulance	Get drunk	Pay well
Come prepared	Go out of business	Save a document
Do nothing	Have an argument	Take a/an (English) class

Part B: Read the following sentences

1. I need money. I will <u>look for a job</u> this weekend. I want a job that <u>pays well</u> and is not difficult.
2. Tom <u>does some exercise</u> every day. He goes to the gym or he rides his bike for 30 minutes.
3. Next year Anna will <u>take an English class</u>. She wants to work for an international company after university.
4. I <u>saved the document</u> on the desktop. You can copy it.
5. The man <u>got drunk</u> at a bar and drove his car home. He hit another car and hurt his head. A woman <u>called an ambulance</u> from a pay phone at 7–11.
6. Hiro and Akiko <u>had an argument</u> about money. Hiro <u>got angry</u> because Akiko bought a new car.
7. I was lazy last weekend. I <u>did nothing</u> on Saturday and I just did a little homework on Sunday.
8. The restaurant <u>went out of business</u> because it was too expensive.
9. <u>Come prepared</u> to class tomorrow. Please bring your notebook, textbook, and your homework.

Part C: Answer the following questions

1. Where did I save the document?
2. What did the man do after he got drunk?
3. Who called an ambulance? From where?
4. When will I look for a job?
5. Do I want a job that does not pay well?
6. How does Tom do some exercise?
7. Why did the restaurant go out of business?
8. When did I do nothing?
9. What did Hiro and Akiko have an argument about?
10. Why did Hiro get angry?
11. The students need to come prepared to class tomorrow. What will they bring?
12. What class will Anna take next year?

Appendix 11: Example of Productive Task for Reflective Cycle 2

Set 3 group B

Use your collocation dictionary for these

Do some exercise	Get angry	Look for a job
Call an ambulance	Get drunk	Pay well
Come prepared	Go out of business	Save a document
Do nothing	Have an argument	Take a/an (English) class

Read the following sentences and fill in the blanks using the collocations above.

1. I need money. I will this weekend. I want a job that _____ and is not difficult.
2. Tom _____ every day. He goes to the gym or he rides his bike for 30 minutes.
3. Next year Anna will. She wants to work for an international company after university.
4. I _____ on the desktop. You can copy it.
5. The man _____ at a bar and drove his car home. He hit another car and hurt his head. A woman _____ from a pay phone at 7–11.
6. Hiro and Akiko _____ about money. Hiro because Akiko bought a new car.
7. I was lazy last weekend. I _____ on Saturday and I just did a little homework on Sunday.
8. The restaurant _____ because it was too expensive.
9. to class tomorrow. Please bring your notebook, textbook, and your homework.

Appendix 12: Collocation Test from Reflective Cycle 2

Collocation test 2

Name: _____

Student number: _____

Score: _____/100

Part 1: Write the English translation

	Answers
1. 静かにしている	1.
2. 試験を受ける	2.
3. 時間を節約する	3.
4. 写真を撮る	4.
5. ウェブサイトにいく	5.
6. メールを転送する	6.
7. お風呂に入る	7.
8. 席をとる	8.
9. 夕食をつくる	9.
10. 冷静をたもつ	10.
11. 薬を飲む	11.
12. 昼寝をする	12.
13. 話	13.
14. お金を稼ぐ	14.
15. 恋に落ちる	15.
	/30

Part 2: Fill in the blanks. You might have to change the verb tense

Take a break have lunch fall asleep catch a plane hand in your work waste time take a seat have time get a job come early get ready	Answers
Student A: Did you _____ (1) _____ yet?	1.
Student B: No, not yet. Let's go to the cafeteria. I'm hungry.	2.
Student A: Did you _____ (2) _____ for English class?	3.
Student B: Yes. I gave it to the teacher this morning. I _____	4.
(3) _____ and finished it in the library this morning.	5.
Student A: Why didn't you finish it last night?	6.
Student B: I didn't _____ (4) _____. I have been really	7.
busy. I _____ (5) _____ at 7–11 last month and I work	8.
every Sunday night.	
Student A: Did you _____ (6) _____?	
Student B: Yes. From 9:30 until 10:00 pm. I didn't study or do	
homework. I just _____ (7) _____ and read a magazine.	
What did you do last night?	
Student A: Nothing. I was really tired. I _____ (8) _____	
_ at 9 p.m.	

/16

Part 3: Read the story and answer the questions

I will go to bed early tonight because tomorrow I am going to Hawaii. I saved money for three months so I could pay for this trip. I am catching a plane from Haneda airport at 5 am in the morning. My friend is giving me a lift to the airport because the buses and trains start at 6 am. I don't want to take a taxi because they are expensive. I have already gotten ready. I prepared my passport and packed my bags this morning. I am going to go fishing in the ocean and have fun on the beach.

	Answers
1. What time am I catching a plane?	1.
2. When did I get ready for this trip?	2.
3. Why will I go to bed early tonight?	3.
4. Will I give my friend a lift to the airport?	4.
5. How long did I save money for?	5.
6. Is taking a taxi expensive?	6.
7. Where will I go fishing?	7.
8. Where will I have fun?	8.

/8

Part 4: Fix the mistakes in the following sentences. If there are no mistakes, write "okay"

	Answers
1. The students made a search on the Internet for information about Japan.	1.
2. Mike and Sally have a baby last year. It was a girl.	2.
3. I will make a reservation at the new restaurant.	3.
4. The milk went bad because I didn't put it in the fridge.	4.
5. The doctor made a prescription for me. I had a cold.	5.
6. We will had a good time at the park tomorrow.	6.
7. John is making a nap on the sofa. He is tired.	7.
	/14

Part 5: Fill in the blanks. Complete the sentences using collocations from the homework /32

1. Akiko _____ _____ _____ for the dentist. She will go there on Friday at 2 pm.
2. Jane _____ _____ _____ for the test. She studied for 2 hours every night the week before the test. She got an "A."
3. The building _____ _____ last night at 1 am. It was burning until 3 am. No one was hurt but the building is destroyed.
4. After university, I _____ _____ _____ _____ in a small apartment in Toronto. It was an old apartment but I liked it.
5. Jane and Bill are a great couple. Bill _____ _____ _____ ___ with his jokes and he is a lot of fun. Jane is more serious but she is very nice.
6. I will _____ _____ next year. I want to go to Australia or Canada.
7. I _____ _____ on my computer last weekend. I now have Microsoft Word, Excel and PowerPoint.
8. Sally _____ _____. She went to a yakiniku restaurant for lunch and she ate too much. She will take some medicine.
9. The students _____ _____ teacher _____ in class today. They were talking during class and did not pay attention to the teacher. She was really upset.

10. Mike will _____ _____ tomorrow. He has a dentist appointment in the morning.

11. I _____ _____ _____ on my computer and on my memory stick. I can email you a copy.

12. I _____ _____ _____ at the barber shop in Sapporo station. It was really cheap and quick.

13. You can _____ a lot of _____ working for Google.

14. I _____ _____ _____ and the baby woke up. My mother was upset and told me to be quiet.

15. The best way to get from the airport to the city is to _____ ___ _____ _____. The buses are about the same cost and not as convenient.

16. There's John! He is walking to school today. We should _____ ___ _____ _____ _____. It looks like it might rain, and he has that big bag.

Appendix 13: Post-Intervention Questionnaire Used in Reflective Cycle 2

Studying collocations (multiword units) – 配置(動詞＋名詞単語ユニット)を研究してます　例. check email))。

I am a PhD student conducting research about vocabulary. The purpose of this questionnaire is to learn about your attitudes toward studying collocations (multiword units, e.g., check email). There are no right or wrong answers. Please answer the questions honestly. The results will be kept confidential and anonymous. Thank you for taking the time to complete this questionnaire.

　私は博士号の学生で配置について研究しています。

　このアンケートの目的はあなたの（動詞＋名詞単語ユニット　例. check email))の学習意欲について学ぶためです。

　答えに間違いや正しいといったことは一切ありません。質問に正直に答えて下さい。

　結果は、秘密厳守かつ匿名となります。

　お忙し中アンケートにご協力下さりましてありがとうございます。

　Please check the most appropriate answer.

　最も適切な答えをチェックしてください。

1. Which group were you in? あなたはどのグループに属しますか。
   - A
   - B
2. Studying collocations has been useful.　配置を学習することは役に立っている。
   - Strongly agree 非常にそう思う
   - Agree そう思う
   - Neutral ふつう
   - Disagree そう思わない
   - Strongly disagree 全くそう思わない

3. I am able to use the collocations we studied in conversations. 会話の中で、私は勉強した配置を活用することが出来る。
   - Strongly agree 非常にそう思う
   - Agree そう思う
   - Neutral ふつう
   - Disagree そう思わない
   - Strongly disagree 全くそう思わない

4. Studying collocations is more helpful than studying individual words. 配置を勉強することは個々の単語を学習するより役に立つ
   - Strongly agree 非常にそう思う
   - Agree そう思う
   - Neutral ふつう
   - Disagree そう思わない
   - Strongly disagree 全くそう思わない

5. Each week we studied 12 collocations. That was . . . 毎週、私たちは12の配置を勉強しました。それは。。。
   - Way too many 非常に多すぎた
   - Too many 多すぎた
   - Just about right ちょうど良かった
   - Not enough 十分でなかった
   - Not nearly enough 全然十分ではなかった

6. For group A students only: Reading the definitions and example sentences has been useful. グループAの学生の方へ。リーディングの定義と例文は役立った。
   - Strongly agree 非常にそう思う
   - Agree そう思う
   - Neutral ふつう
   - Disagree そう思わない
   - Strongly disagree 全くそう思わない

7. For group A students only: Answering questions about the sentences has been useful. グループAの学生の方へ。文についての質疑応答は役立った。
   - Strongly agree 非常にそう思う
   - Agree そう思う
   - Neutral ふつう
   - Disagree そう思わない
   - Strongly disagree 全くそう思わない

8. For group B students only: Reading the definitions and example sentences has been useful. グループBの学生の方へ。 リーディングの定義と例文は役立った。
   - Strongly agree 非常にそう思う
   - Agree そう思う
   - Neutral ふつう
   - Disagree そう思わない
   - Strongly disagree 全くそう思わない
9. For group B students only: Doing the "Fill in the blank" questions has been useful. グループBの学生の方へ。 穴埋め問題をすることは役立った。
   - Strongly agree 非常にそう思う
   - Agree そう思う
   - Neutral ふつう
   - Disagree そう思わない
   - Strongly disagree 全くそう思わない
10. Please comment on your feelings about studying collocations (the exercises we did at the end of each class). For example, what did you like? What did you find easy? What did you dislike? What did you find difficult? You can answer in Japanese.　コロケーションの学習（毎回クラスの最後に行った練習）について、あたなの考えを書いてください。 例えば、何が好きか、何が簡単だと感じるか、何が嫌か、何が難しいと感じるか、など。日本語で回答しても構いません

If you would like to see the results of this questionnaire, please leave your email address and I will send you a copy. Thanks again for taking the time to do this questionnaire.　このアンケートの結果をご覧になられたい方は、Eメールアドレスを書いておいてください。コピーの方を送らさせて頂きます。　アンケートに協力して下さりましてありがとうございました。

Email address: _____

Appendix 14: Initial Vocabulary Questionnaire for Reflective Cycle 2

Studying collocations (multiword units) – 配置(動詞+名詞単語ユニット)を研究してます。

I am a PhD student conducting research about vocabulary. The purpose of this questionnaire is to learn about your attitudes toward studying vocabulary. There are no right or wrong answers. Please answer the questions honestly. The results will be kept confidential and anonymous. Thank you for taking the time to complete this questionnaire.

私は博士号の学生でボキャブラリーについて研究しています。

このアンケートの目的はあなたのボキャブラリーの学習意欲について学ぶためです。

答えに間違いや正しいといったことは一切ありません。質問に正直に答えて下さい。

結果は、秘密厳守かつ匿名となります。

お忙し中アンケートにご協力下さりましてありがとうございます。

Please check the most appropriate answer.

最も適切な答えをチェックしてください。

How motivated are you about studying English? あなたは英語を勉強することに対するやる気はどうですか?*

- Very motivated 非常にやる気がある
- Motivated やる気がある
- Neutral ふつう
- Not too motivated あまりやる気がない
- Not motivated at all 全くやる気がない

1. Have you studied vocabulary words before (word lists, word cards, memorized words from a text book, memorized words from a reading passage, etc.)? あなたは以前にボキャブラリーワードを学習したことがありますか。（ワードリスト、単語帳、テキストブックから単語を記憶する、長文の中で単語を記憶する等）*
   - Yes
   - No

2. I can usually understand the words I studied when I hear or read them. それらを聞いたり読んだりしたときに、たいていその単語を理解出来る。*
   - Strongly agree 非常にそう思う
   - Agree そう思う
   - Neutral ふつう
   - Disagree そう思わない
   - Strongly disagree 全くそう思わない
   - NA

3. I can usually use the words I studied when speaking or writing. 話したり書いたりするときに、その単語をたいてい使うことが出来る。*
   - Strongly agree 非常にそう思う
   - Agree そう思う
   - Neutral ふつう
   - Disagree そう思わない
   - Strongly disagree 全くそう思わない
   - NA

4. *After several weeks, I can still understand the words I studied when I read or hear them. 何週間かたった後でも、このボキャブラリーを読んだり聞いたりしたときに理解出来る。
   - Strongly agree 非常にそう思う
   - Agree そう思う
   - Neutral ふつう
   - Disagree そう思わない
   - Strongly disagree 全くそう思わない
   - NA

5. *After several weeks, I can still use the words I studied when speaking or writing. 何週間かたった後でも、学習した単語を話したり書いたりしたときに使いこなすことが出来る。
   - Strongly agree 非常にそう思う
   - Agree そう思う
   - Neutral ふつう

- Disagree そう思わない
- Strongly disagree 全くそう思わない
- NA

6. *Studying individual words in my previous classes has been useful. それぞれの単語を授業の前に予習しておくことは役立った。
   - Strongly agree 非常にそう思う
   - Agree そう思う
   - Neutral ふつう
   - Disagree そう思わない
   - Strongly disagree 全くそう思わない
   - NA

7. I have used the following methods for studying vocabulary (please check all that apply).以下の方式でボキャブラリーの学習をしたことがある。あてはまる全てのものにチェックして下さい。
   - Word cards　単語カード
   - Vocabulary notebooks　単語帳
   - Memorizing word lists　　単語リストで記憶した
   - Writing sentences　文を書き出す
   - Fill in the blank exercises　穴埋め問題
   - Writing translations from a dictionary　辞書を使って翻訳する
   - Memorizing words from reading passages　長文を使って単語を覚える

8. Please comment on your feelings about studying vocabulary. For example, What do you like? What do you find easy? What do you dislike? What do you find difficult? You can answer in Japanese. 語彙を学習することについて、あたなの考えを書いてください。例えば、何が好きか、何が簡単だと感じるか、何が嫌か、何が難しいと感じるか、など。日本語で回答しても構いません。

If you would like to see the results of this questionnaire, please leave your email address and I will send you a copy. Thanks again for taking the time to do this questionnaire.　このアンケートの結果をご覧になられたい方は、Eメールアドレスを書いておいてください。コピーの方を送らさせて頂きます。　アンケートに協力して下さりましてありがとうございました。

Email address: _____

Appendix 15: Post-Intervention Questionnaire for Reflective Cycle 3

Studying collocations (multiword units) – 配置(動詞＋名詞単語ユニット)を研究してます　例. check email))。

I am a PhD student conducting research about vocabulary. The purpose of this questionnaire is to learn about your attitudes toward studying collocations (multiword units, e.g., check email). There are no right or wrong answers. Please answer the questions honestly. The results will be kept confidential and anonymous. Thank you for taking the time to complete this questionnaire.

　私は博士号の学生で配置について研究しています。

　このアンケートの目的はあなたの（動詞＋名詞単語ユニット　例. check email)）の学習意欲について学ぶためです。

　答えに間違いや正しいといったことは一切ありません。質問に正直に答えて下さい。

　結果は、秘密厳守かつ匿名となります。

　お忙し中アンケートにご協力下さりましてありがとうございます。

Please check the most appropriate answer.

　最も適切な答えをチェックしてください。

　*=Required

1. *How motivated are you about studying English?　あなたは英語を勉強することに対するやる気はどうですか?
   * Very motivated 非常にやる気がある
   * Motivated やる気がある
   * Neutral ふつう
   * Not too motivated あまりやる気がない
   * Not motivated at all 全くやる気がない

2. *Studying collocations has been useful.　配置を学習することは役に立っている。
   - Strongly agree 非常にそう思う
   - Agree そう思う
   - Neutral ふつう
   - Disagree そう思わない
   - Strongly disagree 全くそう思わない

3. *I am able to use the collocations we studied in conversations.　会話の中で、私は勉強した配置を活用することが出来る。
   - Strongly agree 非常にそう思う
   - Agree そう思う
   - Neutral ふつう
   - Disagree そう思わない
   - Strongly disagree 全くそう思わない

4. *Studying collocations is more helpful than studying individual words. 配置を勉強することは個々の単語を学習するより役に立つ
   - Strongly agree 非常にそう思う
   - Agree そう思う
   - Neutral ふつう
   - Disagree そう思わない
   - Strongly disagree 全くそう思わない

5. *Reading the definitions and example sentences has been useful. リーディングの定義と例文は役立った。
   - Strongly agree 非常にそう思う
   - Agree そう思う
   - Neutral ふつう
   - Disagree そう思わない
   - Strongly disagree 全くそう思わない

6. *Doing the "Fill in the blank" questions has been useful. 穴埋め問題をすることは役立った。
   - Strongly agree 非常にそう思う
   - Agree そう思う
   - Neutral ふつう
   - Disagree そう思わない
   - Strongly disagree 全くそう思わない

7. *Doing the speaking and crossword questions at the end of class has been useful.　クロスワード問題をすることは役立った。
   - Strongly agree 非常にそう思う
   - Agree そう思う
   - Neutral ふつう
   - Disagree そう思わない
   - Strongly disagree 全くそう思わない

8. *How long did it take to finish the computer activities each week?　毎週コンピューターアクティブティを終えるのにどのくらいかかりましたか。
   - Less than 10 minutes. 10分未満
   - 10 to 15 minutes 10–15分
   - 15 to 20 minutes 15–20分
   - 20 to 25 minutes 20–25分
   - More than 25 minutes. 25分以上

9. Each week we studied 12 collocations. That was . . . 毎週、私たちは12の配置を勉強しました。それは。。。 *
   - Way too many 非常に多すぎた
   - Too many 多すぎた
   - Just about right ちょうど良かった
   - Not enough 十分でなかった
   - Not nearly enough 全然十分ではなかった

10. Please comment on your feelings about studying collocations (the exercises we did at the end of each class). For example, What did you like? What did you find easy? What did you dislike? What did you find difficult? You can answer in Japanese.　コロケーションの学習（毎回クラスの最後に行った練習）について、あたなの考えを書いてください。例えば、何が好きか、何が簡単だと感じるか、何が嫌か、何が難しいと感じるか、など。日本語で回答しても構いません

If you would like to see the results of this questionnaire, please leave your email address and I will send you a copy. Thanks again for taking the time to do this questionnaire.　このアンケートの結果をご覧になられたい方は、Ｅメールアドレスを書いておいてください。コピーの方を送らさせて頂きます。　アンケートに協力して下さりましてありがとうございました。

Email address: _____

Appendix 16: Post-Intervention Questionnaire Used During Reflective Cycle 4

Studying collocations (verb + noun word units) – 配置(動詞+名詞単語ユニット)を研究してます。

The purpose of this questionnaire is to learn about students' attitudes toward studying collocations (adjective + noun word units, e.g., "hard work"). Please answer the questions honestly. There are no right or wrong answers. The results will be kept confidential and anonymous. Thank you for taking the time to complete this questionnaire. このアンケートの目的は、配置(動詞+名詞単語ユニット: 例えば、"check email")を学生がどういう気持ちで勉強しているかという事について研究する為です。正直に質問に答えてください。 その答えに正しいとか間違いなどということは一切ありません。結果は、秘密厳守かつ匿名となります。お忙しいところ、このアンケートにご協力下さってありがとうございます。

Please check the most appropriate answer. 最も適切な答えをチェックしてください。

1. Studying collocations has been useful.
   配置を研究するのは役に立っている。
   • Strongly agree 非常にそう思う
   • Agree そう思う
   • Neutral ふつう
   • Disagree そう思わない
   • Strongly disagree 全くそう思わない
2. I am able to use the collocations we studied when I am having a conversation. 会話の中で、私は勉強した配置を使用することが出来る。
   • Strongly agree 非常にそう思う
   • Agree そう思う
   • Neutral ふつう

- Disagree そう思わない
- Strongly disagree 全くそう思わない

3. Studying collocations is more useful than studying individual words.
配置を勉強することは個々の単語を研究するより役に立つ。
- Strongly agree 非常にそう思う
- Agree そう思う
- Neutral ふつう
- Disagree そう思わない
- Strongly disagree 全くそう思わない

4. Studying the adjective + noun collocations this semester was easier than studying the verb + noun collocations last semester.
今学期の「形容詞＋名詞」配置の学習は、前学期の「動詞＋名詞」配置を学習することより簡単でしたか。
- Strongly agree 非常にそう思う
- Agree そう思う
- Neutral ふつう
- Disagree そう思わない
- Strongly disagree 全くそう思わない

5. Each week we studied 15 collocations. That was . . .
毎週、私たちは15の配置を勉強しました。それは。。。
- Way too many 非常に多すぎた
- Too many 多すぎた
- Just about right ちょうど良かった
- Not enough 十分でなかった
- Not nearly enough 全然十分ではなかった

6. Please comment on your feelings about studying collocations (the exercises we did at the end of each class). For example, What did you like? What did you find easy? What did you dislike? What did you find difficult? You can compare studying collocations this semester (adjective + noun) to studying collocations last semester (verb + noun). You can answer in Japanese. コロケーションの学習（毎回クラスの最後に行った練習）について、あたなの考えを書いてください。例えば、何が好きか、何が簡単だと感じるか、何が嫌か、何が難しいと感じるか、など。今学期学習したこと（形容詞＋名詞）と前学期に学習したこと（動詞＋名詞）とを比較しても構いません。日本語で回答しても構いません。

If you would like to see the results of this questionnaire, please leave your email address and I will send you a copy. Thanks again for taking the time to do this questionnaire. このアンケートの結果を見たい方は、Eメールアドレスを残してください。そうしましたらコピーを送ります。アンケートに協力して下さりましてありがとうございました。

Appendix 17: Example Homework Assignment from Reflective Cycle 4

List 8 adjective + noun collocations

Part 1: Match the English collocation with its Japanese translation

1. Different story	新しい配属
2. Political situation	政治状況
3. Other reason	最近の作品、最近の仕事
4. (Account) balance	まるで話が違う
5. Recent work	良いアイディア
6. Good way	その唯一の違い
7. Particular problem	全く変わる
8. New position	他の理由
9. Particular interest	バランス
10. Good view	良い方法
11. Good use	激しい言い争い
12. Strong argument	十分利用する
13. Complete change	個人の問題
14. Only difference	良く見える、良い眺め
15. Good idea	特に関心

Part 2: Fill in the gaps with the collocations from above

1. He made a _____, but I still disagreed with him.
2. The house I so different. It looks so good. It is a _____.
3. The _____ between the two apartments is that this one has a slightly bigger kitchen.
4. That's a _____! Let's go to the new Italian restaurant.
5. He has a _____ in African art.
6. She liked her _____, but she missed her children.
7. This _____ is very common among the elderly.

8. We don't know why the car wouldn't start. Maybe the battery died or there might be some _____.
9. The _____ in South Africa is much better than it was twenty years ago.
10. There were green fields as far as the eye could see. But inside the house it was a _____; there wasn't much space at all.
11. She put her university degree to _____ by getting a good job at a large company.
12. It was a nice apartment with a _____ of the river.
13. The job is very difficult and doesn't pay well. It is not a _____ to earn money.
14. His _____ is quite different from what he did in the past.
15. I checked my _____ at the ATM.

Appendix 18: First Test from Reflective Cycle 4

Collocation test 1

Name: _____

Student number: _____

Score: _____/130

Part 1: Write the English translation for the following collocations (each translation is worth 2)

---

1. 座の詳細 or 詳細な報告
2. 人間の行動
3. 悪い状態
4. 最終決定
5. 重要な違い
6. 明確なアイディア
7. 不成績、不振
8. 強い立場、堅固な立場
9. 主な問題
10. 問題の全容
11. 良い質問
12. 特別な関係
13. 現状況
14. 現状
15. 長話（話が長い）
16. 政治制度
17. 実際的使用能力
18. 長い道のり
19. 効果的な方法
20. 他の仕事

Part 2: Fill in the blanks with collocations from the homework (each question is worth 3)

1. I really need to find a job soon. My current **a**_____ **b**_____ is only 20000 yen. I need more money before next month.
2. The government took **i**_____ **a**_____ after the earthquake. They quickly sent help to the area.
3. My **m**_____ **a**_____ is that we need more room. This apartment is too small for us. We should move.
4. The students in the grade 4 class are showing **g**_____ **b**_____ this year. Last year, in grade 3, they caused a lot of trouble.
5. I bought a bike from a second hand store yesterday. It is a few years old, but it is in **g**_____ **c**_____. I saved money and still got a nice bike.
6. I want to make the **r**_____ **d**_____, but I am not sure. If I move to Tokyo, I can get a good job. However, if I stay here, I will be close to my family. I don't want to make a mistake.
7. He did his presentation in a very **e**_____ **w**_____. It was easy to understand.
8. The committee has not decided yet. There will be **f**_____ **d**_____ next week.
9. There is a **b**_____ **d**_____ in the size of the 2 apartments. The first one is really big, but the second one is tiny.
10. He had a **b**_____ **i**_____ about the project. We should use PowerPoint instead of making a poster. It will look really good and be easier.
11. You can get **f**_____ **i**_____ about the typhoon at 6 pm on NHK. They will discuss it in more detail.
12. There is **h**_____ **i**_____ in the new exhibit at the museum.
13. She gave such a **g**_____ **p**_____. I really enjoyed the movie. She is a great actress.
14. I moved the plant to a **b**_____ **p**_____ in front of the window. It wasn't getting much sunlight where it was.
15. Sally might get promoted from her **c**_____ **p**_____ as sales clerk. She might become a manager.
16. I have an **i**_____ **q**_____: what should we do if it rains and we cannot go to the park?

17. The students asked the teacher many _ **ff** _ _ **ns**. The teacher did not know all the answers.

18. Bill told me the _ _ **l** _ _ **s** _ _ he is not coming to the party. He isn't sick. He just doesn't want to see his ex-girlfriend.

19. I have a very _ _ **se** _ _ **la** _ _ with my sister. We always talk on the phone and help each other.

20. They got lost in the mountains when they were hiking, but their _ _ **lar s**_ _ was not that bad. They had enough supplies and the weather was good.

21. I am in a real _ _ **cu** _ _ **tu** _ _ . My two best friends are fighting. They both get jealous when I spend time with the other friend.

22. I just read a great book. It was the _ _ **e** _ _ **y** about four friends who got lost in the mountains. They were lost for three days.

23. The school is using a _ _ **w**_ _ **st** _ _ for class registration. It is much easier than before.

24. A day at The Sanctuary in London costs £35 and this includes _ _ **l** _ _ **e** of facilities such as pools, sauna, steam room and jacuzzi.

25. You need to make _ _ **tt** _ _ of your time. You spend too much time playing games and not enough time studying.

26. The _ _ **l** _ _ to get to the airport from the station is by bus. The train does not go there.

27. The _ _ **t** _ _ to clean a coffee maker is to use vinegar.

28. I can show you an _ _ **as**_ _ **w**_ _ to print. Just hit "control" and "p" at the same time.

29. There is _ _ **a**_ _ **e**_ _ in the new English program at the university. Many high school students came to the presentation at open campus.

30. If you want a job as a pizza delivery person, you need a car. That is a _ _ **ss**_ _ **o**_ _ for the job.

Table A.1 Positive responses about experiences studying vocabulary (full data set)

Category	Subcategory	Examples from the data
Learners' responses about techniques used to introduce vocabulary	Pronunciation for the target vocabulary	It is easy when we learn the pronunciation. Learning the accent helps me. We should memorize words with sounds. Remembering the pronunciation makes vocabulary easy. If it's easy to understand the pronunciation, it is easy to remember. Learning the pronunciation is fun. I like reading new words out loud.
	New vocabulary through readings	It is easy to memorize vocabulary as I read a sentence. Remembering words as reading sentences is an easy way to study vocabulary. Learning vocabulary that is in a long passage as I understand the story. I think it's effective way to learn to remember the vocabulary with whole sentences. Memorizing words from a reading passage is easier because we can learn how to use the words. When I learn words in a long story. I can consider the words' meaning. I like when I guess the meaning for the unfamiliar word in the long passage and my guess was correct. I like when we can figure out with an example sentence. If we know vocabulary, we usually can guess the meaning, so I think vocabulary is important.
	New vocabulary through listening	Remembering the spelling and guess the spelling with listening. Looking at vocabulary as I listen is effective.
	Memory	Just memorizing is easy. I like to memorize.
	Quantity	Learning new words in a group of 10 or 20 is good. Not having to memorize too many new words. If the number of words is small, it's easy. When I think it seems easy, it's easy to get started.

Category	Subcategory	Examples from the data
Learners' responses about techniques for reviewing previously taught vocabulary	Vocabulary cards	Trying to check vocabulary cards over again is good. Vocabulary cards are a good way to study. Checking vocabulary cards every day is helpful. Using vocabulary cards every day. Remembering with vocabulary card. Writing some examples with vocabulary words.
	Vocabulary books	Using a vocabulary book is a good way to study. Using a vocabulary book is easy. Studying vocabulary notebooks every day is helpful.
	Repetitive exposure	It was easy to remember words that occur frequently in a long passage. It was easy to remember the word that we use in daily life. Easy to remember words that I have heard before or Japanese English. Trying to use the vocabulary over and over again helps me remember. I feel I can memorize the words when I try it many times.
Learners' responses about activities that help students acquire targeted vocabulary	Dictionary	Looking up new words in a dictionary. It is easy to remember as I look up words in the dictionary. I like looking up the meaning of vocabulary.
	Use	It is important to write, not just read. write speak write speak write speak!!! Writing the vocabulary is useful. Looking up the words in a dictionary and trying to write a lot is good. Filling up the gap exercises are easy. I like learning new words – improving conversation by learning new words. We can improve our English with new vocabulary. I like easy to use vocabulary. We can use the word straightaway. I like using the new vocabulary in conversations. I like using the new vocabulary that I just memorized. I like when I use the vocabulary and remember how to use it in the conversation in English. I'm really glad to increase the number of new words. It makes me study harder. I prefer speaking to reading. If we can increase the number of words, it makes our conversation better.

Category	Subcategory	Examples from the data
Learners' responses about what vocabulary should be targeted	Type of word	Verbs and nouns are easy to remember. It was easy to remember interesting words. It was easy to remember my favorite words. Learning challenging vocabulary. It is more interesting to learn a little difficult vocabulary than easy ones. I like learning new words in sentences or word combinations (multiword units), remembering with sentences and collocation. Learning familiar words for our daily life and nouns and verbs is good.
	Short words	Short words and common words in long sentences are easy to remember. Easy to read words are easy to remember. If the vocabulary is simple to spell, it's easy to remember, so I like them.
	Common words	Daily life vocabulary is easier. Familiar words in Japanese are easier to remember. Daily English is good for studying. It's easy to remember easy words. It's easy to remember verbs and the frequent words. Words with short spellings and frequent ones are easy. The words that have short spellings and are used for daily English. Daily English words are easy. It was easy to remember daily English. It is easy when I try to remember the short spelling and familiar ones. If it's a familiar word, I can just remember. Familiar words that I can use in daily life are the best. Easy vocabulary and useful words are the best. It is good when we learn the word that is useful in our daily life.
	L1	It was easy to remember the words that are Japanese English. It was easy to remember the word such as Japanese English and familiar ones. It is easy when the words have a translation. Comparing English words with Japanese is helpful. For example, "My mother is angry with me" and "My mother Is occurred with me." (It doesn't make sense, but angry and occur both mean OKORU in Japanese.)

Table A.2 Negative responses about experiences studying vocabulary (full data set)

Category	Subcategory	Examples from the data
Learners' responses about aspects of studying vocabulary that are problematic	Use targeted vocabulary	We have to use the proper verb, for instance past, present, and future. Memorizing the spelling and how to use vocabulary is hard. Writing the sentence with the vocabulary can be hard. I had trouble when I had to figure out how I can use the words in a particular situation. It's enjoyable to remember some vocabulary but it's difficult use them in the sentences. It was difficult to remember collocations, idioms and prepositions. It's confusing. Even if I think I already memorized some vocabulary, but it's easy to forget when I don't see the vocabulary for a long time. I realized I memorized new words when the vocabulary came up in my mind right away. Filling up the gap and long sentences are difficult. Filling up the gap is tricky.
	Words that have many meanings	It was difficult to remember vocabulary that has a similar meaning and spelling. Words that are similar to other words are difficult. Remembering vocabulary that has many different meanings is difficult, so I have to try harder. I have trouble with pronunciation and when the word has many meanings. The words that have many meanings are difficult to understand. It's difficult to remember vocabulary that has many meaning and similar spelling ones. Similar spellings and meanings of vocabulary is difficult. If the vocabulary has many meanings, it is hard to learn. Words that have many meanings are difficult. Each word has different meanings, so we have to be flexible to use them. If the vocabulary has many meanings, it's difficult. When I learn similar spelling vocabulary that has many meanings, I have trouble. It should be a familiar word for me but it's confusing if they have another meaning. If the word has many meanings, it is difficult.

Category	Subcategory	Examples from the data
		It was difficult to remember some basic verbs like "take," "make," etc.
		It is hard to remember the vocabulary that has many meanings.
		I have trouble telling the difference between the vocabulary that has many meanings.
		It's difficult to learn difficult pronunciation words and when the vocabulary has many meanings or similar meanings.
		It makes me feel tired when I see the vocabulary has many different meanings.
	Differences from their L1	It's difficult remember the vocabulary that we don't use in Japanese.
		It's easy to remember ordinary words that we also use in Japanese, and I can use them flexibly, but if it's not familiar word, such as we don't use them even in Japanese, it is difficult.
Learners' responses about aspects of vocabulary instruction that they did not enjoy	Studying uncommon words	The vocabulary that we never use in our life is difficult and long spelling ones.
		Unfamiliar vocabulary is hard to learn.
		When I feel the words we study are a waste of time.
		I want to improve my English skill, so I'll try to answer in English. I like studying vocabulary, but it is often difficult for me. The reason is some words are not useful in daily conversation. Actually, some Japanese students learn English only for passing entrance exam or getting high scores, so many students dislike studying vocabulary I think.
		It is difficult when we don't usually use the new words in our life and they don't have any rules about spelling. We have to just memorize. That's why I don't like it.
	Dictionary	I dislike searching in a dictionary.
		I dislike having to look up new words in a dictionary every time.
	Memory and quantity	When we try to just memorize voc, it's boring.
		Learning too many new words is not fun.
		Too many words for memorizing.
		I don't like to just memorize automatically because there isn't any goal.
		Basically, I don't like to memorize vocabulary, but if there are new words in the sentences it's fun to learn.
		It is difficult to memorize long words.

Table A.3 Qualitative data for reflective cycle 2

Category	Subcategory	Examples from the receptive group data	Examples from the productive group data
Value of studying collocations	Important part of vocabulary learning	I think you are good at communicate with students. And you taught vocabulary with collocation. That was good. Your teaching stuff, all of them were really fun! I could remember some familiar idioms that I didn't know before. I could learn new expressions. I'm really glad I learned collocation. I'm in group A. I read the questions and answer. I got many new vocabulary from it.	Studying collocation makes my English improve. It was good to learn many idiom.
	Comparison with individual word study	Your class is more useful than another English class that I took before. I don't like studying individual words, but this was collocations and I studied it so enjoy.	I don't like to learn only one word. It was difficult to put verb and noun together before.
	Productive challenges of collocations		It was difficult to choose article for the collocation. It is really tough to study collocation for me. It was difficult to memorize the collocations.
Delexicalized verbs	Variations in verb meanings	"Make" must be memorized with the word following it since various meanings are accomplished.	It was difficult to remember the meaning of the collocation.

Category	Subcategory	Examples from the receptive group data	Examples from the productive group data
		It is difficult because the verbs like "have," "take," etc. are used the same but the meaning is different. The meaning changes of "have" and "get" when they are used differently. It is difficult to know the difference between "a" or "an," or the difference between "have" and "make." I liked connecting the meaning with the verb.	
	Productive challenges	It is easy to mix up the arrangement for verbs like have and get. It is easy to make a sentence when using have or take. It is difficult when the collocation is different from Japanese (give someone a lift).	It was confusing to use make, take, and have. It was difficult to figure out that I should use "take," "have," or "make"
	Level appropriateness	I think the class was too basic and easy for me. You should let us study more difficult vocabulary. There were words that had already been known. There were some familiar vocabulary. It was good there are many easy vocabulary in the sentences.	The vocabulary was easy and good. It was really useful to study that vocabulary. I liked the collocations that had an easy English word in it. It was good there are many easy vocabulary in the sentences.
Materials used in the intervention	Level	That was perfect for me. It was difficult to memorize the vocabulary.	The collocation dictionary was good. The level was perfect for me.

Category	Subcategory	Examples from the receptive group data	Examples from the productive group data
		The English was simple and easy to understand for me. That was perfect. The amount of work and level. That was the perfect amount of work and level. Vocabulary in the class is useful for ordinary conversation. The questions were too easy for me. I thought it's enjoyable to study easy vocabulary and use it in the class.	
	Learner need	I thought it's really useful for ordinary life. The answers for the English sentence were pretty easy. It was easy to understand and useful for future.	It was useful. Studying collocation is useful. I like studying verbs that are for ordinary life.
Procedures used	Exercises	The exercises made me remember the vocabulary. I love answers the questions after reading. I don't like filling up the gap and memorize idiom. I liked the number of questions. I liked I could use the words that I memorized. I could study productively because of the question sentences are not too long.	The filling up the gap was just like a game and fun! I think that filling the blank is the easiest.

Category	Subcategory	Examples from the receptive group data	Examples from the productive group data
	Dictionary	It was good to have the translation as reading. The sentences are not too long. It was easy to study because of I could look up difficult vocabulary in the dictionary. I liked the dictionary. The picture attached helped me memorize.	I think we should look up the collocations in the dictionary by ourselves to memorize vocabulary. Because of we can fill up the gap after we look up the dictionary. The collocation dictionary is a good idea, but it was a little difficult to look up the vocabulary. And not simple to do that. I hope you change for the better. It is useful to do work and look up the dictionary. Looking up in the dictionary made us improve. I think that searching word's mean is the most difficult. I like to learn with pictures. I didn't use a dictionary because most of the meanings I already knew. The collocation work is very useful. I just want you to translate in Japanese above the vocabulary on the computer.
	Memory	It was easy to remember the collocations.	I liked memorizing vocabulary. It was enjoyable to memorize vocabulary.

Category	Subcategory	Examples from the receptive group data	Examples from the productive group data
Learner responses regarding exercises that should be used	Value of productive tasks	I think you should let students fill up the gap with collocation. Not just let them answer "yes, he does" It was difficult to know how to use collocations It is difficult to have a conversation with the vocabulary I'd like to try to read example sentences in our conversation It was good to learn vocabulary and arrange the sentence to future one and past one. But speaking is difficult	It is difficult using the words in conversation. It is difficult to translate from ordinary Japanese conversation to English one. It's more difficult to speak English than to write English.

Appendix 19: Consent Form – 同意書

Background – バックグラウンド

As a research student, I am conducting a small scale experiment about students' perceptions of studying collocations (verb + noun word units, e.g., check email). In very general terms, my aim is to improve understanding of how students best learn collocations in L2. Using productive ability as a measure (do students retain the collocations and are they able to use the collocations in a productive assessment), I hope to improve our understanding of the effectiveness of productive and receptive tasks. In addition, I will measure student perceptions of the usefulness of studying "verb + noun" collocations.

　研究員として、学生の配置(句動詞ユニット)の認知に関する小規模な実験を行っています。　一般的に、私の研究の目的は、配置(動詞＋名詞　例)check email)についてどうしたら学生が最もわかり易く学べるように改善できるかということです。　測定としてスピーキングとリーディングを用い、(学生が第二言語の中でどう配置を覚えるか、そして、それがスピーキングとリーディンの中において配置を使いこなせるか)スピーキングとリーディングで受容的なタスクの有効性の理解を改良していけることを望んでいます。　さらに、私は'動詞+名詞'配置を研究するにあたりそれが学生にとって効果的なものととらえられているかという事にについても測定するつもりです。

I would like to use the information I have collected from you in class. Your results will be kept confidential and anonymous. You do not need to take part in this study. If you do take part, you can withdraw at any time. Thank you.

　クラスで集めた情報を使用したいと思います。　あなたのテスト結果は秘密かつ匿名で保たれます。この研究に必ず参加しなければならないということはありません。もしこれに参加しても途中でやめる事も出来ます。　宜しくお願いします。

Agreement (協定)

I hereby agree that the work I have been asked to hand in as part of my English class can be used for research purposes conducted by Joshua Antle.

　私は、アンテル　ジョシュアの研究目的に、英語のクラスの一部で提出を求められたものを使用することに同意します。

SIGNED: _____

DATE: _____

NAME: _____

References

Ahulu, S. (1998). Lexical variation in international English. *English Today, 14*(3), 29–34.

Antle, J. B. (2014). Two words at a time: Frequent adjective + noun collocations for intermediate English language learners. In N. Sonda & A. Krause (Eds.), *JALT2013 conference proceedings* (pp. 297–307). Tokyo: JALT.

Avison, D., Lau, F., Myers, M., & Nielsen, P. A. (1999). Action research. *Communications of the ACM, 42*(1), 94–7.

Bachman, L. (2004). *Statistical analyses for language assessment.* Cambridge: Cambridge University Press.

Bahns, J. (1993). Lexical collocations: A contrastive view. *ELT Journal, 47*(1), 56–63.

Bahns, J., & Eldaw, M. (1993). Should we teach EFL students collocations? *System, 21*(1), 101–14. doi:10.1016/0346-251X(93)90010-E.

Barfield, A. (2009a). Exploring productive L2 collocation knowledge. In T. Fitzpatrick & A. Barfield (Eds.), *Lexical processing in second language learners* (pp. 95–110). Bristol: Multilingual Matters.

Barfield, A. (2009b). Following individuals' L2 collocation development over time. In A. Barfield & H. Gyllstad (Eds.), *Researching collocations in another language* (pp. 208–23). New York: Palgrave Macmillan.

Barfield, A., & Gyllstad, H. (2009). Introduction: Researching L2 collocational knowledge and development. In A. Barfield & H. Gyllstad (Eds.), *Researching collocations in another language multiple interpretations* (pp. 1–18). New York: Palgrave Macmillan.

Bartels, N. (2002). Professional preparation and action research: Only for language teachers? *TESOL Quarterly, 36*(1), 71–9.

Baskerville, R. L., & Wood-Harper, A. T. (1996). A critical perspective on action research as a method for information systems research. *Journal of Information Technology, 11*, 235–46.

Bavelas, J. B., Coates, L., & Johnson, T. (2000). Listeners as co-narrators. *Journal of Personality and Social Psychology, 79*(6), 941–52.

Benson, M. (1989). The structure of the collocation dictionary. *International Journal of Lexicography, 2*, 1–14.

Benson, M. J. (1991). Attitudes and motivation towards English: A survey of Japanese freshmen. *RELC Journal, 22*(1), 34–48.

Berwick, R., & Ross, S. (1989). Motivation after matriculation: Are Japanese learners of English still alive after exam hell? *JALT Journal, 11*(2), 193–210.

Boers, F., Eyckmans, J., Kappel, J., Stengers, H., & Demecheleer, M. (2006). Formulaic sequences and perceived oral proficiency: Putting a lexical approach to the test. *Language Teaching Research, 10*(3), 245–61.

Bolander, M. (1989). Prefabs, patterns and rules in interaction? Formulaic speech in adult learners' L2 Sweedish. In K. Hyltenstam & L. K. Obler (Eds.), *Bilingualism across the lifespan: Aspects of acquisition, maturity, and loss* (pp. 73–86). Cambridge: Cambridge University Press.

Bolinger, D. (1975). *Aspects of language* (2nd ed). New York: Harcourt Brace Jovanovich.

Borg, S. (2011). Review of the book *Doing action research in English language teaching: A guide for practitioners*, by A. Burns. *ELT Journal, 65*(4), 485–7.

Braun, V., & Clarke, V. (2006). Using thematic analysis in psychology. *Qualitative Research in Psychology, 3*(2), 77–101.

Brooke, M. (2013). Which research paradigm for TESOL? *Theory and Practice in Language Studies, 3*(3), 430–36.

Brown, H. D. (2007). *Teaching by principles: An interactive approach to language pedagogy*. White Plains, NY: Pearson Longman.

Brown, J. D., & Yamashita, O. S. (1995), English language entrance examinations at Japanese universities: What do we know about them? *JALT Journal, 17*(1), 7–30.

Brown, J. D. (2003). Promoting fluency in EFL classrooms. *Proceedings of the 2003 JALT Pan-SIG Conference*, 1–12.

Brown, J. D., & Rogers, T. S. (2009). *Doing second language research*. Oxford: Oxford University Press.

Browne, C., Culligan, B., & Phillips, J. (2013). A new general service list (1.01). Retrieved from www.newgeneralservicelist.org

Burke Johnson, R., & Onwuegbuzie, A. J. (2004). Mixed methods research: A research paradigm whose time has come. *Educational Researcher, 33*(7), 14–26.

Burke Johnson, R., Onwuegbuzie, A. J., & Turner, L. A. (2007). Toward a definition of mixed methods research. *Journal of Mixed Methods Research, 1*(2), 112–33.

Burns, A. (2005a). *Teaching English from a global perspective. Case studies in TESOL series*. Alexandria: TESOL.

Burns, A. (2005b). State-of-the-art article action research: An evolving paradigm? *Language Teaching, 38*(2), 57–74.

Burns, A. (2007). Action research: Contributions and future directions in ELT. In J. Cummins & C. Davison (Eds.), *International handbook of English language teaching* (pp. 987–1002). New York: Springer.

Burns, A. (2009a). Action research. In J. Heigham & R. Croker (Eds.), *Qualitative research in applied linguistics: A practical introduction* (pp. 112–34). New York: Palgrave Macmillan.

Burns, A. (2009b). Doing action research. In J. Heigham & R. Croker (Eds.), *Qualitative research in applied linguistics: A practical introduction*. New York: Palgrave Macmillan.

Busch, M. (1993). Using Likert scales in L2 research. A researcher comments. *TESOL Quarterly, 27*(4), 733–6.

Carter, R. (1987). *Vocabulary. Applied linguistic perspectives.* London and New York: Routledge.

Celce-Murcia, M. (1991). *Teaching English as a second or foreign language.* Boston: Heinle and Heinle.

Chan, T., & Liou, H.-C. (2005). Effects of web-based concordancing instruction on EFL students' learning of verb–noun collocations. *Computer Assisted Language Learning, 18*(3), 231–51. doi:10.1080/09588220500185769

Chi, A. M., Wong, K. P., & Wong, M. C. (1994). Collocation problems amongst ESL learners: A corpus-based study. In L. Flowerdew and A. K. Tong (Eds.), *Proceedings of the Joint Seminar on Corpus Linguistics and Lexicology* (pp. 157–65). Hong Kong: HKUST.

Collentine, J. (2009). Review of the book *From corpus to classroom: Language use and language teaching*, by A. O'Keefe, M. McCarthy, and R. Carter. *Modern Language Journal, 93*, 453–55.

Conklin, K., & Schmitt, N. (2008). Formulaic sequences: Are they processed more quickly than nonformulaic language by native and nonnative speakers? *Applied Linguistics, 29*(1), 72–89.

Conzett, J. (2000). Integrating collocation into a reading and writing course. In M. Lewis (Ed.), *Teaching collocation: Further developments in the lexical approach* (pp. 70–87). Hove: Language Teaching Publications.

Coomber, R. (2002). Signing your life away? Why Research Ethics Committees (REC) shouldn't always require written confirmation that participants in research have been informed of the aims of a study and their rights—the case of criminal populations. *Sociological Research Online, 7*(1). Retrieved from www.socresonline. org,uk/7/1/coomber.html

Coxhead, A. (2000) A new academic word list. *TESOL Quarterly, 34*(2), 213–38.

Creswell, J. W. (2003). *Research design: Qualitative, quantitative, and mixed methods approaches* (2nd ed.). London: Sage.

Crick, F. (1979). Thinking about the brain. *Scientific American, 9*, 218–32.

Crookes, G. (1993). Action research for second language teachers—Going beyond teacher research. *Applied Linguistics, 14*(2), 130–44.

Crystal, D. (1997). *English as a global language.* Cambridge: Cambridge University Press.

Davis, K. (1995). Qualitative theory and methods in applied linguistics research. *TESOL Quarterly, 29*(3), 427–53.

Davison, R., Martinsons, M., & Ou, C. (2012). The roles of theory in canonical action research. *MIS Quarterly, 36*(3), 763–86.

Dewey, M. (2013). The distinctiveness of English as a lingua franca. *ELT Journal, 67*(3), 346–49.

Dörnyei, Z. (2007). *Research methods in applied linguistics: Quantitative, qualitative, and mixed methodologies.* New York: Oxford University Press.

Dörnyei, Z. (2009). *The psychology of second language acquisition.* Oxford: Oxford University Press.

Durrant, P. (2009). Investigating the viability of a collocation list for students of English for academic purposes. *English for Specific Purposes, 28*(3), 157–69. doi:10.1016/j.esp.2009.02.002

Durrant, P., & Schmitt, N. (2010). Adult learners' retention of collocations from exposure. *Second Language Research, 26*(2), 163–88. doi:10.1177/0267658309349431

Ellis, N. C. (1996). Sequencing in SLA: Phonological memory, chunking, and points of order. *Studies in Second Language Acquisition, 18*, 91–126.

Ellis, N. C. (2002). Reflections on frequency effects in language processing. *Studies in Second Language Acquisition, 24*, 297–339.

Ellis, R. (2001). Investigating form-focused instruction. *Language Learning, 51*(1), 1–46.

Ellis, R. (2006). Current issues in the teaching of grammar: An SLA perspective. *TESOL Quarterly, 40*, 83–107.

Emerson, R. M., Fretz, R. I., & Shaw, L. L. (2011). *Writing ethnographic fieldnotes* (2nd ed.). Chicago: University of Chicago Press.

Eyckmans, J. (2009). Toward an assessment of learners' receptive and productive syntagmatic knowledge. In A. Barfield & H. Gyllstad (Eds.), *Researching collocations in another language* (pp. 139–52). New York: Palgrave Macmillan.

Fan, M. (2009a). An exploratory study of collocational use by ESL students: A task based approach. *System, 37*, 110–23.

Firth, J. R. (1957). Modes of meaning. In J. R. Firth (Ed.), *Papers in linguistics 1934–1951* (pp. 190–215). London: Oxford University Press.

Fletcher, W. (2011). *Phrases in English.* Retrieved from www.phrasesinenglish.org

Foster, P., & Skehan, P. (1999). The influence of source of planning and focus of planning on task-based performance. *Language Teaching Research, 3*(3), 215–47.

Geertz, C. (1973). *The interpretation of cultures.* New York: Basic Books.

Graddol, D. (2010). *English next India: The future of English in India.* London: British Council.

Granger, S. (2009). Commentary on part 1: Learner corpora: A window onto the L2 phrasicon. In A. Barfield & H. Gyllstad (Eds.), *Researching collocations in another language multiple interpretations* (pp. 60–65). New York: Palgrave Macmillan.

Griffin, G. F., & Harley, T. A. (1996). List learning of second language vocabulary. *Applied Psycholinguistics, 17*, 443–60.

Griffiths, R. (1991). Pausological research in an L2 context: A rationale, and review of selected studies. *Applied Linguistics, 12*, 345–64.

Guillot, M. N. (1999). *Fluency and its teaching.* Bristol: Multilingual Matters.

Gyllstad, H. (2009). Designing and evaluating tests of receptive collocation knowledge: COLLEX and COLLMATCH. In A. Barfield & H. Gyllstad (Eds.),

Researching collocations in another language (pp. 153–70). New York: Palgrave Macmillan.

Halliday, M. A. K. (1966). Lexis as a linguistic level. In C. E. Bazell, C. Catford, M. A. K. Halliday, and R. H. Robbins (Eds.), *Memory of J. R. Firth* (pp. 148–62). London: Longman.

Hammersley, M., & Atkinson, P. (1995). *Ethnography: Principles in practice.* New York: Routledge.

Handl, S. (2009). Towards collocational webs for presenting collocations in learners' dictionaries. In A. Barfield & H. Gyllstad (Eds.), *Researching collocations in another language multiple interpretations* (pp. 69–85). New York: Palgrave Macmillan.

Hansen, L., Gardner, J., & Pollard, J. (1998). The measurement of fluency in a second language: Evidence from the acquisition and attrition of Japanese. In B. Visgatis (Ed.), *Proceedings of the JALT 1997 conference on language teaching and learning* (pp. 37–45). Tokyo: Japanese Association of Language Teachers.

Henriksen, B., & Stenius Stoehr, L. (2009). Commentary on part 4: Processes in the development of L2 collocational knowledge – A challenge for language learners, researchers and teachers. In A. Barfield & H. Gyllstad (Eds.), *Researching collocations in another language* (pp. 224–31). New York: Palgrave Macmillan.

Hickey, T. (1993). Identifying formulas in first language acquisition. *Journal of Child Language, 20,* 27–41.

Hill, J. & Lewis, M. (1999). *LTP Dictionary of Selected Collocations.* Hove: Language Teaching Publications.

Hill, J. (2000). Revising priorities: From grammatical failure to collocational success. In M. Lewis (Ed.), *Teaching collocation: Further developments in the lexical approach* (pp. 47–69). Hove: Language Teaching Publications.

Hill, J., Michael, L., & Morgan, L. (2000). Classroom strategies, activities and exercises. In M. Lewis (Ed.), *Teaching collocation: Further developments in the lexical approach* (pp. 88–117). Hove: Language Teaching Publications.

Hoey, M. (2005). *Lexical priming: A new theory of words and language.* London: Routledge.

Horst, M., Cobb, T., & Meara, P. (1998). Beyond a clockwork orange: Acquiring vocabulary in a second language through reading. *Reading in a Foreign Language, 11*(2), 207–23.

Hoshmand, L. T. (2003). Can lessons of history and logical analysis ensure progress in psychological science? *Theory and Psychology, 13,* 39–44.

Howarth, P. (1998). Phraseology and second language proficiency. *Applied Linguistics, 19*(1), 24–44.

Hsu, J. T., & Chiu, C. (2008). Lexical collocations and their relation to speaking proficiency. *Asian EFL Journal, 10*(1), Article 9.

Hulstijn, J. (2001). Intentional and incidental second language vocabulary learning: A reappraisal of elaboration, rehearsal and automaticity. In P. Robinson

(Ed.), *Cognition and second language acquisition instruction* (pp. 258–86). Cambridge: Cambridge University Press.

Jiang, J. (2009). Designing pedagogic materials to improve awareness and productive use of L2 collocations. In A. Barfield & H. Gyllstad (Eds.), *Researching collocations in another language* (pp. 99–113). New York: Palgrave Macmillan.

Jick, T. D. (1979). Mixing qualitative and quantitative methods: triangulation in action. *Administrative Science Quarterly, 24*(4), 602–11.

Johnson, K. (1996). The role of theory in L2 teacher education. *TESOL Quarterly, 30*(4), 765–71.

Karp, I., & Kendall, M. B. (1982) Reflexivity in fieldwork. In P. Second (Ed.), *Explaining human behaviour.* Beverly Hills: Sage.

Kemmis, S. (1993). Action research and social movement: A challenge for policy research. *Education Policy Analysis Archives, 1*(1), 1–8.

Kemmis, S., & McTaggart, R. (2008). Participatory action research: Communicative action and the public sphere. In N. Denzin & Y. Lincoln (Eds.), *Strategies of qualitative inquiry* (3rd ed.) (pp. 271–330). London: Sage.

Kessler, G. (2010). Fluency and anxiety in self-access speaking tasks: The influence of environment. *Computer Assisted Language Learning, 23*(4), 361–75.

Kluge, D. E., & Taylor, M. A. (1999). Outside taping for fluency: A practical system. In A. Barfield, R. Betts, J. Cunningham, N. Dunn, H. Katsura, K. Kobayashi, N. Padden, N. Parry, & M. Watanabe (Eds.), *JALT98 proceedings: Focus on the classroom: Interpretations* (pp. 27–32). Tokyo: JALT.

Komuro, Y. (2009). Japanese learners' collocation dictionary retrieval performance. In A. Barfield & H. Gyllstad (Eds.), *Researching collocations in another language* (pp. 86–98). New York: Palgrave Macmillan.

Krishnamurthy, R. (2006). Collocations. In *Encyclopedia of language & linguistics* (pp. 596–600). Oxford: Elsevier. Retrieved from www.sciencedirect.com/science/article/ B7T84-4M3C3K0-18S/2/ff94af9177a1aee9bd00b95543be9a0d

Kubo, M. (2009). Extensive pair taping for college students in Japan: Action research in confidence and fluency building. *Accents Asia, 3*(1), 36–68.

Kubota, R. (2002) The impact of globalization on language teaching in Japan. In D. Block & D. Cameron (Eds.), *Globalization and language teaching* (pp. 13–28). London: Routledge.

Larson-Hall, J. (2010). *A guide to doing statistics in second language research using SPSS.* New York: Routledge.

Laufer, B., & Hulstijn, J. (2001). Incidental vocabulary acquisition in a second language: The construct of task-induced involvement. *Applied Linguistics, 22*(1), 1–26.

Laufer, B., & Paribakht, T. (1998). The relationship between passive and active vocabularies: Effects of language learning context. *Language Learning, 48*, 365–91.

Lazaraton, A. (1995). Qualitative research in applied linguistics: A progress report. *TESOL Quarterly, 29*(3), 455–72.

Leech, G., Rayson, P., & Wilson, A. (2001). *Word frequencies in written and spoken English: Based on the British National Corpus.* London: Longman.

Lefever, S., Dal, M., & Matthíasdóttir, A. (2006). Online data collection in academic research: Advantages and limitations. *British Journal of Educational Technology, 38*(4), 574–82.

Lennon, P. (1990a). Investigating fluency in EFL: A quantitative approach. *Language Learning, 40*(3), 387–417.

Lennon, P. (1990b). The advanced learner at large in the L2 community: Developments in spoken performance. *International Review of Applied Linguistics in Language Teaching, 28*, 309–21.

Lewis, M. (1994). *The lexical approach. The state of ELT and a way forward.* Boston: Language Teaching Publications.

Lewis, M. (2000). Learning in the lexical approach. In M. Lewis (Ed.), *Teaching collocation: Further developments in the lexical approach* (pp. 155–85). Hove: Language Teaching Publications.

Lewis, M. (2000). There is nothing as practical as a good theory. In M. Lewis (Ed.), *Teaching collocation: Further developments in the lexical approach* (pp. 10–27). Hove: Language Teaching Publications.

Lewis, M. (2008). *Implementing the lexical approach: Putting theory into practice.* London: Heinle/Cengage Learning.

Lin, P. M. S., & Adolphs, S. (2009). Sound evidence: Phraseological units in spoken corpora. In A. Barfield & H. Gyllstad (Eds.), *Researching collocations in another language multiple interpretations* (pp. 34–48). New York: Palgrave Macmillan.

Lindstromberg, S., & Boers, F. (2008). *Teaching chunks of language.* London: Helbling Languages.

Liu, D. (2010). Going beyond patterns: Involving cognitive analysis in the learning of collocations. *TESOL Quarterly, 44*(1), 4–30.

Mackenzie, N., & Knipe, S. (2006). Research dilemmas: Paradigms, methods and methodology. *Issues in Educational Research, 16*, 193–205.

Martyńska, M. (2004). Do English language learners know collocations? *Investigationes Linguisticae, 11*, 1–12.

Matsuura, H., Chiba, R., & Hilderbrandt, P. (2001). Beliefs about learning and teaching communicative English in Japan. *JALT Journal, 23*(1), 67–82.

McCarthy, M. (2010). Spoken fluency revisited. *English Profile Journal, 1*(1), 1–15. doi:10.1017/S2041536210000012

McGregor, S. L. T., & Murnane, J. A. (2010). Paradigm, methodology and method: Intellectual integrity in consumer scholarship. *International Journal of Consumer Studies, 34*(4), 419–27.

McGuire, M. (2009). *Teaching formulaic sequences in the classroom: Effects on spoken fluency.* Presented at the Second Language Research Forum, Michigan State University.

McKay, J., & Marshall, P. (2001). The dual imperatives of action research. *Information Technology & People, 14*(1), 46–59.

Miller, G. A. (1956). The magical number seven, plus or minus two: Some limits on our capacity for processing information. *Psychological Review, 63*, 81–97.

Milton, J. (2009). *Measuring second language vocabulary acquisition.* Clevedon: Multilingual Matters.

Morgan, J., & Rinvolucri, M. (2004). *Vocabulary: Second edition.* Oxford: Oxford University Press.

Myles, F., Hooper, J., & Michell, R. (1998). Rote or rule? Exploring the role of formulaic language in classroom foreign language learning. *Language Learning, 48*(3), 323–63.

Nakata, Y. (2006). *Motivation and experience in foreign language learning.* Bern: Peter Lang.

Nation, I. S. P. (2008). *Teaching vocabulary: Strategies and techniques.* Boston: Heinle Cengage Learning.

Nation, P. (2001). *Learning vocabulary in another language.* Cambridge: Cambridge University Press.

Nattinger, J. R., & DeCarrico, J. S. (1992). *Lexical phrases and language teaching.* Oxford: Oxford University Press.

Nesi, H. (2009). Commentary on part 2: Exploring materials for the study of L2 collocations. In A. Barfield & H. Gyllstad (Eds.), *Researching collocations in another language* (pp. 114–24). New York: Palgrave Macmillan.

Nesselhauf, N. (2003). The use of collocations by advanced learners of English and some implications for teaching. *Applied Linguistics, 24*, 223–42.

Nesselhauf, N. (2005). *Collocations in a learner corpus.* Amsterdam: John Benjamins.

Nunan, D. (1992). *Research methods in language learning.* Cambridge: Cambridge University Press.

O'Dell, F., & McCarthy, M. (2008). *English collocations in use: Advanced.* Cambridge: Cambridge University Press.

O'Keefe, A., McCarthy, M., & Carter, R. (2007). *From corpus to classroom: Language use and language teaching.* Cambridge: Cambridge University Press.

Oxford collocations dictionary: For students of english (2nd ed.). (2009). Oxford: Oxford University Press

Oxford, R. L., & Lee, K. R. (2008). The learner's landscape and journey: A summary. In C. Griffiths (Ed.), *Lessons from good language learners* (pp. 306–14). Cambridge: Cambridge University Press.

Pawley, A., & Syder, F. H. (1983). Two puzzles for linguistic theory: Nativelike selection and nativelike fluency. In J. C. Richards & R. W. Schmidt (Eds.), *Language and communication* (pp. 191–226). New York: Longman.

Peters, A. (1983). *The units of language acquisition.* Cambridge: Cambridge University Press.

Peters, E. (2009). Learning collocations through attention-drawing techniques: A qualitative and quantitative analysis. In A. Barfield & H. Gyllstad (Eds.), *Researching collocations in another language* (pp. 194–207). New York: Palgrave Macmillan.

Prentice, M. (2010). Teacher development through personal language learning. *Studies in Language, 33*, 21–44.

Rainey, I. (2000). Action research and the English as a foreign language practioner: Time to take stock. *Educational Action Research, 8*(1), 65–91.

Read, J. (2004). Research in teaching vocabulary. *Annual Review of Applied Linguistics, 24*, 146–61.

Reason, P., & Bradbury, H. (2008). Introduction. In P. Reason & H. Bradbury (Eds.), *The Sage handbook of action research.* (pp. 1–10). London: Sage.

Reppen, R. (2009). Exploring L1 and L2 writing development through collocations: A corpus-based look. In A. Barfield & H. Gyllstad (Eds.), *Researching collocations in another language multiple interpretations* (pp. 49–59). New York: Palgrave Macmillan.

Reppen, R. (2010). *Using corpora in the language classroom.* New York: Cambridge University Press.

Revier, R. L. (2009). Evaluating a new test of whole English collocations. In A. Barfield & H. Gyllstad (Eds.), *Researching collocations in another language* (pp. 125–38). New York: Palgrave Macmillan.

Riggenbach, H. (1991). Toward an understanding of fluency: A microanalysis of nonnative speaker conversations. *Discourse Processes, 14*, 423–41.

Ross, J., & Bruce, C. (2012). Evaluating the impact of collaborative action research on teachers: A quantitative approach. *Teacher Development, 16*(4), 537–61.

Rundell, M. (1999). Dictionary use in production. *International Journal of Lexicography, 12*(1), 35–53.

Ryan, S. (2009). Self and identity in L2 motivation in Japan: The ideal L2 self and Japanese Learners of English. In Z. Dornyei & E. Ushioda (Eds.), *Motivation language identity and the L2 self* (pp. 120–43). Bristol: Multilingual Matters.

Sacks, H., Schegloff, E. A., & Jefferson, G. (1974). A simplest systematics for the organisation of turn-taking for conversation. *Language, 50*(4), 696–735.

Schmidt, R. (1992). Psychological mechanisms underlying second language fluency. *Studies in Second Language Acquisition, 14*, 357–85.

Schmitt, N. (2008). *Vocabulary in language teaching.* New York: Cambridge University Press.

Schmitt, N., & Carter, R. (2004). Formulaic sequences in action. In N. Schmitt (Ed.), *Formulaic sequences: Acquision, processing and use* (pp. 1–22). Amsterdam: John Benjamins.

Schmitt, N., & Underwood, G. (2004). Exploring the processing of formulaic sequences through a self-paced reading task. In N. Schmitt (Ed.), *Formulaic sequences: Acquisition, processing and use* (pp. 173–90). Amsterdam: John Benjamins.

Scholefield, W. F. (1996) What do JTEs really want? *JALT Journal, 18*(1), 7–25.

Sechrest, L., & Sidana, S. (1995). Quantitative and qualitative methods: Is there an alternative? *Evaluation and Program Planning, 18*, 77–87.

Sewell, A. (2013). English as a lingua franca: Ontology and ideology. *ELT Journal,* *67*(1), 3–10.

Shih, R. H.-H. (2000). Collocation deficiency in a learner corpus of English: From an overuse perspective. In A. Ikeya (Ed.). *Proceedings of the 14th Pacific Asia conference on language, information, and computation* (pp. 281–8). Tokyo: PACLIC 14 Organizing Committee.

Shin, D., & Nation, P. (2008). Beyond single words: The most frequent collocations in spoken English. *ELT Journal, 62*(4), 339–48.

Sholdt, G., Konomoto, B., Mineshima, M., & Stillwell, C. (2012). Sharing experiences with quantitative research. In A. Stewart & N. Sonada (Eds.), *JALT 2011 conference proceedings.* Tokyo: JALT.

Sinclair, J. M. (1987). Collocation: A progress report. In R. Steele & T. Threadgold (Eds.) *Language Topics. Essays in honour of Michael Halliday. Volume II* (pp. 313–31). Amsterdam: John Benjamins.

Sinclair, J. M. (1991). *Corpus, concordance, collocation.* Oxford: Oxford University Press.

Sinclair, J., & Renouf, A. (1988). A lexical syllabus for language learning. In R. Carter & M. McCarthy (Eds.), *Vocabulary and language teaching.* New York: Longman.

Skehan, P. (1998). *A cognitive approach to language learning.* Oxford: Oxford University Press.

Smadja, F., & McKeown, K. (1991). Using collocations for language generation. *Computational Intelligence, 7,* 229–39.

Somekh, B. (1993). Quality in educational research – The contribution of classroom teachers. In J. Edge & K. Richards (Eds.), *Teachers develop teachers research.* Oxford: Heinemann.

Somekh, B. (2006). *Action research: A methodology for change and development.* New York: Open University Press.

Spada, N. (1997). Form-focused instruction and second language acquisition: A review of classroom and laboratory research. *Language Teaching, 30*(2), 73–87.

Stanley, C. (1998). A framework for teacher reflectivity. *TESOL Quarterly, 32*(3), 584–91.

Stanley, L., & Wise, S. (2010). The ESRC's 2010 framework for research ethics: Fit for research purpose? *Sociological Research Online, 15*(4). Retrieved from www.socresonline.org.uk/15/4/12.html

Stephens, J., Barton, J., & Haslett, T. (2009). Action research: Its history and relationship to scientific methodology. *Systemic Practice and Action Research, 22*(6), 463–74.

Stubbs, M. (1995). Collocations and semantic profiles: On the cause of the trouble with quantitative methods. *Functions of Language, 2*(1), 1–33.

Sun, Y.-C., & Wang, L.-Y. (2003). Concordancers in the EFL classroom: Cognitive approaches and collocation difficulty. *Computer Assisted Language Learning, 16*(1), 83.

Sung, C. C. M. (2013). English as a lingua franca and English language teaching: A way forward. *ELT Journal, 67*(3), 350–53.

Tao, H. (2003). Turn initiators in spoken English: A corpus-based approach to interaction and grammar. In P. Leistyna & C. F. Meyer (Eds.), *Corpus analysis: Language structure and language use* (pp. 187–207). Amsterdam: Rodopi.

Tashakkori, A., & Teddlie, C. (2003). *Handbook of mixed methods in social and behavioural research*. London: Cassell.

Tauroza, S., & Allison, D. (1990). Speech rates in British English. *Applied Linguistics, 11*(1), 90–105.

Teubert, W. (2004). Units of meaning, parallel corpora, and their implications for language teaching. *Language and Computers, 52,* 171–89.

Tribble, C. (2008). Review of the book *From corpus to classroom: Language use and language teaching,* by A. O'Keefe, M. McCarthy, and R. Carter. *English Language Teaching Journal, 62*(2), 213–16.

Truman, C. (2003). Ethics and the ruling relations of research production. *Sociological Research Online, 8*(1). Retrieved from www.socresonline.org.uk/8/1Truman.html

Turner, J. (1993). Using Likert scales in L2 research. Another researcher comments. *TESOL Quarterly, 27*(4), 736–9.

Unlu, Z., & Wharton, S. (2015) Exploring classroom feedback interactions around EAP writing: A data based model. *Journal of English for Academic Purposes, 17*(1), 24–36.

Ur, P. (1991). *A course in language teaching: Practice and theory*. Cambridge: Cambridge University Press.

Wallace, M. J. (1998). *Action research for language teachers*. Cambridge: Cambridge University Press.

Walter, E., & Woodford, K. (2010). *Collocations extra: Multi-level activities for natural English*. Cambridge: Cambridge University Press.

Waring, R., & Takaki, M. (2003). At what rate do learners learn and retain new vocabulary from reading a graded reader? *Reading in a Foreign Language, 15,* 1–27.

Watson-Gegeo, K. A. W. (1988). Ethnography in ESL: Defining the essentials. *TESOL Quarterly, 22*(4), 575–92.

Webb, E. J., Campbell, D. T., Schwartz, R. D., & Sechrest, L. (1966). *Unobtrusive measures*. Chicago: Rand McNally.

Webb, S. (2007). The effects of repetition on vocabulary knowledge. *Applied Linguistics, 28*(1), 46–65.

Webb, S., & Kagimoto, E. (2009). The effects of vocabulary learning on collocation and meaning. *TESOL Quarterly, 43,* 55–77.

West. M. (1953). *A general service list of English words*. London: Longman.

White, C. (2008). Beliefs and good language learners. In C. Griffiths (Ed.), *Lessons from good language learners* (pp. 121–30). Cambridge: Cambridge University Press.

Wiles, R., Crow, G., Charles, V., & Heath, S. (2007). Informed consent and the research process: Following rules or striking balances? *Sociological Research Online, 12*(2). Retrieved from www.socresonline.org.uk/12/2/wiles.html

Wiles, R., Heath, S., Crow, G., & Charles, V. (2005). Informed consent in social research: A literature review. *National Centre for Research Methods Review Papers, 1,* 1–26.

Williams, J. (2005). Form-focused instruction. In E. Hinkel (Ed.), *Handbook of research in second language teaching and learning* (pp. 671–91). Mahwah: Lawrence Erlbaum Associates.

Willis, D. (1990). *The lexical syllabus*. London: Harper Collins.

Wollard, G. (2005). *Key words for fluency*. London: Thomson Heinle.

Wolter, B. (2009). Meaning-last vocabulary acquisition and collocational productivity. In T. Fitzpatrick & A. Barfield (Eds.), *Lexical processing in second language learners* (pp. 128–40). Bristol: Multilingual Matters.

Wood, D. (2006). Uses and functions of formulaic sequences in second language speech: An exploration of the foundations of fluency. *Canadian Modern Language Review, 63*(1), 13–33.

Wood, D. (2010). *Formulaic language and second language speech fluency*. London: Continuum.

Woolard, G. (2000). Collocation – Encouraging learner independence. In M. Lewis (Ed.), *Teaching collocation: Further developments in the lexical approach* (pp. 28–46). Hove: Language Teaching Publications.

Wray, A. (2000). Formulaic sequences in second language teaching: Principle and practice. *Applied Linguistics, 21*, 463–89.

Wray, A. (2002). *Formulaic language and the lexicon*. Cambridge: Cambridge University Press.

Wray, A. (2004). Here's one I prepared earlier: Formulaic language learning on television. In N. Schmitt (Ed.), *Formulaic sequences: Acquisition, processing and use* (pp. 249–68). Amsterdam: John Benjamins.

Wray, A. (2008). *Formulaic language: Pushing the boundaries*. Oxford: Oxford University Press.

Wray, A. (2009). Navigating L2 collocation research. In A. Barfield & H. Gyllstad (Eds.), *Researching collocations in another language* (pp. 232–44). New York: Palgrave Macmillan.

Wray, A., & Perkins, M. R. (2000). The functions of formulaic language: An integrated model. *Language and Communication, 20*(1), 1–28.

Wyatt, M. (2011). Teachers researching their own practice. *ELT Journal, 65*(4), 417–25.

Ying, Y., & O'Neill, M. (2009). Collocation learning through an "AWARE" approach: Learner perspectives and learning process. In A. Barfield & H. Gyllstad (Eds.), *Researching collocations in another language* (pp. 181–93). New York: Palgrave Macmillan.

Yorio, C. (1980). Conventionalized language forms and the development of communicative competence. *TESOL Quarterly, 14*, 433–42.

Index

Lightning Source UK Ltd.
Milton Keynes UK
UKHW020101301221
396376UK00004B/144